MANDATED REPORTING *of* SUSPECTED CHILD ABUSE

ETHICS, LAW, & POLICY

SETH C. KALICHMAN

American Psychological Association, Washington, DC

MANDATED REPORTING *of* SUSPECTED CHILD ABUSE

Published by
American Psychological Association
750 First Street, NE
Washington, DC 20002

Copies may be ordered from
APA Order Department
P.O. Box 2710
Hyattsville, MD 20784

In the UK and Europe, copies may be ordered from
American Psychological Association
3 Henrietta Street
Covent Garden, London
WC2E 8LU England

Typeset in Goudy by Harper Graphics, Hollywood, MD

Printer: Braun-Brumfield, Inc., Ann Arbor, MI
Cover and Jacket Designer: Anne Masters, Washington, DC
Technical/Production Editor: Paula R. Bronstein

Library of Congress Cataloging-in-Publication Data

Kalichman, Seth C.
    Mandated reporting of suspected child abuse: Ethics, law, and policy / by Seth C. Kalichman.
        p. cm.
    Includes bibliographical references and index.
    ISBN 1-55798-197-3 (acid-free paper)
    1. Child abuse—Reporting. 2. Child abuse—Case studies. 3. Child abuse—Law and legislation. I. Title.
    HV8079.C46K35 1993
    363.2′595554—dc20   93-12611
                                                                          CIP

Printed in the United States of America
First edition

To Syd and Rita B. Kalichman.
Thank you always for everything.

CONTENTS

ACKNOWLEDGMENTS

This book represents seven years of research on professional responses to mandated child abuse reporting. The ideas presented have evolved through collaborative research efforts, discussions at conventions and conferences, and numerous conversations with friends and colleagues. The following people have helped shape this book in many ways: Linda Steinman, Tony Broskowski, Diane Follingstad, and M. E. Craig contributed to the development of the first experimental studies, investigating factors that influence professional reporting decisions. Ken Pope provided valuable feedback and insights on this book when it had no covers, in addition to conducting some of the key studies related to the ethics of mandated reporting. Michael Miller reviewed portions of the manuscript and contributed substantive comments. Brian Wilcox encouraged the development of this book and provided many valuable comments on the manuscript. In addition to her own contributions to the child abuse reporting literature, Cheryl L. Brosig fueled many of the ideas presented and provided many comments throughout the development of this book. I am grateful to Tami Payne, who helped me verify the references for accuracy, and to Paula R. Bronstein of APA Books who did a remarkable job as technical/production editor. In addition to their support, encouragement, and professionalism, Julia Frank-McNeil and Ted Baroody of APA Books provided many excellent ideas for the development and structure of this book and were extremely tolerant of my impatience. I also appreciate the continuous support of my brother, Bill, and my sisters, Debbie and Phyllis. Finally, this book would not have been possible without the ideas and constant encouragement of Moira Kalichman. I have a deep appreciation for her patience with a preoccupied and often absent husband.

The following persons have also contributed to the ideas presented in many sections of this book: Jeanne Murrone, Arne Gray, Fred Cavaiani, Robert Muckenheim, Allan G. Hedberg, Nancy Townsend, Mary Ellen

Luxon, Gary R. Schoener, Jeanne E. Sokolec, Lester Lefton, Paul Jose, Art Bodin, and several clinicians and researchers who provided cases for the casebook and wish to remain anonymous. Finally, I wish to thank the more than 1,500 psychologists who took the time to respond to and return the anonymous surveys used in my studies.

I invite you to contact me regarding any comments you have in response to this book or concerning your interest in mandated child abuse reporting.

SETH C. KALICHMAN

INTRODUCTION

Debbie is a 10-year-old girl who lives with her mother, father, and younger brother. Debbie was referred to a school psychologist by her physical education teacher, who became concerned when she refused to change for swimming class. Debbie would not discuss how she was feeling or why she would not participate in swimming. Her teacher told the psychologist that Debbie was behaving differently than usual, becoming increasingly withdrawn from other students. The teacher also told the psychologist that she was concerned that Debbie might be having problems at home.

During their first session, Debbie was mostly quiet and refused to talk with the psychologist about how she was feeling. When asked specifically about how things were going at home, Debbie started to cry and left the room.

Putting yourself in the place of the school psychologist, what is the next thing that you would do? What are the psychologist's options? What actions would be in the best interest of the child? Would this case be required to be reported as a case of suspected child abuse? If so, did the physical education teacher violate the law by not reporting?

1

Child maltreatment constitutes one of the great social maladies of our time. In 1991, 2,694,000 cases of child abuse and neglect were reported in the United States, an average statewide increase of more than six percent over 1990, and more than a 40% increase nationally since 1985 (see Figure 1). The majority of reports involve neglect (48%), but physical abuse accounts for 25% of reports, sexual abuse for 15%, and emotional maltreatment for 6% of reports. Deaths resulting from child abuse also increased in 1991 to 1,282, 10% over the number of deaths in 1990 (Daro & McCurdy, 1992). Staggering as they may be, these statistics only reflect the surface of the problem. Community-based incidence studies estimate that reported maltreatment constitutes only about 40% of all cases (U.S. Department of Health and Human Services [USDHHS], 1988). The prevalence of abuse, coupled with significant budget cuts for child protection that resulted in reduced prevention and treatment programs, led the U.S. Advisory Board on Child Abuse and Neglect (1990) to declare child maltreatment a national emergency.

Human service professionals, including psychologists, social workers, counselors, teachers, nurses, and psychiatrists, are required to report known or suspected child maltreatment in all 50 states. Approximately 46% of child maltreatment reports are filed by professionals, with the majority originating from hospitals, schools, day-care centers, and mental health/social service agencies (USDHHS, 1988). Still, reported cases account for only a portion of the child maltreatment cases seen by professionals. For example,

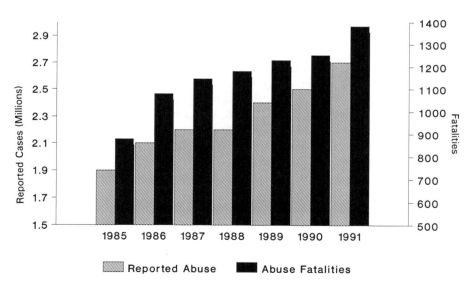

Figure 1: Number of cases of child abuse (in millions) and related fatalities reported annually since 1985. Reprinted with permission from Daro & McCurdy (1992), by permission of the National Committee for Prevention of Child Abuse, Chicago, IL.

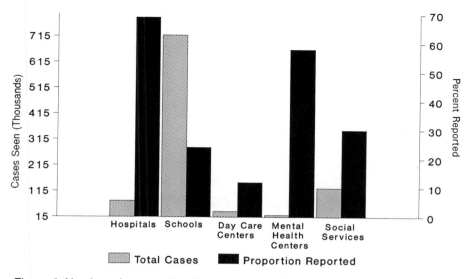

Figure 2: Number of cases of maltreatment seen (in thousands), represented along left axis, and percentage of cases reported, represented along right axis, across five professional settings. From U.S. Department of Health and Human Services (1988).

mandated reporters working within day-care centers report less than 12% of cases of suspected child maltreatment and professionals in medical hospitals report 69% of suspected cases (see Figure 2). Surveys have repeatedly shown that approximately one third of professionals have had contact with at least one case of suspected abuse in their professional work that they have declined to report (see Table 1). Similarly, the 1986 Study of National Incidence and Prevalence of Child Abuse and Neglect found that only one third of the 1,273,200 cases of abuse suspected by professionals were reported (USDHHS, 1988, pp. 6–17).

Decisions not to report suspected child maltreatment place professionals at risk for legal and professional sanctions, including fines, license suspension, jail sentences, and civil suits (Curran, 1977; Denton, 1987a, 1987b; Gray, 1987; Hedberg, 1991). Why do concerned professionals sometimes choose to break the law when it comes to reporting suspected abuse? What factors contribute to unreported suspicions of abuse? Does failure to report potentially endanger children or protect them? What can the research literature offer practitioners who face decisions to report suspected abuse? How do vague statutes result in over- and underreporting of suspected child maltreatment? These questions, among others, fuel this book with the goal of providing a comprehensive and integrative discussion of mandated child abuse reporting. The focus here is not just on the reporting requirements themselves, but also on how the reporting requirements function within professional contexts and on the issues such requirements raise.

TABLE 1
Percentages of Professionals Not Reporting Suspected Child Abuse
Based on Self-Reports of Reporting Behavior

Authors	Participants	Percent Not Reporting
Swoboda et al. (1978)	88 Mental Health Professionals	63[a]
James et al. (1978)	96 Physicians	58[a]
Finkelhor (1984)	790 Mandated Reporters	36[b]
Kim (1986)	120 Physicians	61[b]
Pope et al. (1987)	465 Psychologists	61[a]
Pope & Bajt (1988)	60 Senior Psychologists	21[a]
Kalichman et al. (1989)	279 Psychologists	37[a]
Kalichman & Brosig (1992)	527 Psychologists	35[a]
Kalichman & Craig (1991)	328 Psychologists	37[a]
Brosig & Kalichman (1992a)	297 Psychologists	39[a]

[a]Percentage of professionals not reporting at least one suspected case.
[b]Percentage of cases suspected and not reported.

This book is composed of three parts with three chapters in each part. Part 1 discusses the problems associated with mandatory reporting laws. As a logical starting point, chapter 1 presents the history and evolution of mandatory reporting laws, followed by an examination of the specific dimensions of the laws and their variability across states. Chapter 2 discusses mandated reporting as an ethical dilemma, highlighting confidentiality and informed consent, with specific references to professional settings within which maltreatment is often suspected. Next, in chapter 3, characteristic dimensions of abusive situations that affect reporting are examined in the context of report decision making. Part 2 is presented in the form of a casebook, with chapters 4 and 5 presenting cases of unreported and reported suspected maltreatment, respectively, gathered from the field. Commentary for each case is provided in the context of the reporting decision model discussed in chapter 3. Chapter 6 follows up on the casebook chapters by presenting some suggestions and guidelines for developing procedures and strategies for reporting. Part 3 includes three chapters pointing to future directions for practice, research, and policy regarding mandated reporting. Finally, four appendixes are included with specific information on referral sources for child protective services and sources for further information.

I

MANDATED CHILD ABUSE REPORTING: LEGAL, ETHICAL, AND PROFESSIONAL DIMENSIONS

INTRODUCTION

MANDATED CHILD
ABUSE REPORTING:
LEGAL, ETHICAL, AND
PROFESSIONAL DIMENSIONS

Societal reaction to the child abuse crisis has taken many forms and resulted in a number of strategies. Unfortunately, interventions have been less effective than their initial promise, and this is particularly true for mandated reporting. Within the social structures that make up the child protection system, mandated reporters assist in the identification of child maltreatment for social intervention, a role that they do not universally desire. Still, it is widely agreed that child protection depends on the process of identifying, investigating, and stopping child abuse. This first section begins with a discussion of the history of mandatory reporting statutes and their implications for the human services. Following this historical context, the process by which professionals decide to report, or not to report, is examined.

1

MANDATORY CHILD ABUSE REPORTING LAWS: ORIGINS AND EVOLUTION

While the medical profession plays a major role in the identification of the battered child and will have a primary role in the alleviation of the consequences of parental abuse and the rehabilitation of the abuser, and while welfare and social workers must play major roles in the resolution of the problem, ultimately the solution must be legal, in the form of legislation and judicial decisions, and the machinery of the state designed for the protection of the child. (McCoid, 1965, p. 3)

DEVELOPMENT OF A MANDATORY REPORTING SYSTEM

Child protection is a relatively recent social phenomenon. Until the late nineteenth century the western world showed little interest in, and had no policies for, the protection of children (for thorough reviews see Herman, 1981; M. Levine & A. Levine, 1992). Although the child welfare movement was initiated in 1875 with the advent of the New York Society for the Prevention of Cruelty to Children, it was not until the early part of the

9

century that child protective services were nationally instituted in the U.S. (M. Levine & A. Levine, 1992). The American Humane Association was developed in the late 1870s to serve as a national organization focusing on child abuse as a distinct social problem. However, child abuse was viewed as a low priority by the association, relative to infant mortality and maternal health, until well into the 1950s (M. Levine & A. Levine, 1992). Also on the federal level, the 1935 Social Security Act first funded public welfare for the protection and care of homeless, dependent, and neglected children (USDHHS, 1988). Such legislation concerning child welfare first focused on willful neglect or failure to provide adequate child care (Maryland Social Services Administration, 1988). Since the inception of the child welfare system it has been, and still is, true that any citizen may report known or suspected child abuse to child protection authorities. However, mandatory reporting of child abuse by professionals servicing children and families did not become law until the early 1960s.

Increased community awareness of child abuse as a widespread social problem and the civil libertarian social climate of the 1960s set the stage for legislative action regarding child protection (National Center on Child Abuse and Neglect [NCCAN], 1979; Newberger, 1983). The catalyst for the first wave of child abuse reporting legislation was the formalization of a medical profile of child abuse. A series of clinical reports of abuse published by pediatricians and other physicians (McCoid, 1965), as well as a symposium held by the American Academy of Pediatrics dedicated to describing battered children, formed much of the groundwork for defining child abuse as a medical problem (M. Levine & A. Levine, 1992). However, the single most influential work on child maltreatment was published by Kempe, Silverman, Steele, Droegemueller, and Silver (1962), who described the *battered child syndrome*. This new medical diagnosis was characterized by "injury to soft tissue and skeleton" (p. 17), and accompanied by "evidence of neglect including poor skin hygiene, multiple soft tissue injuries, and malnutrition" (pp. 17–18). Kempe et al. also provided specific radiologic features and clinical manifestations that were often discrepant with those available from case histories. Thus, the battered child syndrome was objectively defined with several specific features, most of which were relevant to the physical and radiological examination of children by physicians.

In addition to detailed descriptions of the trauma characterizing the battered child syndrome, Kempe et al. (1962) made specific reference to the condition being "inadequately handled by the physician because of hesitation to bring the case to the attention of the proper authorities" (p. 17). Kempe et al. speculated that physicians' reluctance to report suspicious injuries was due to their unwillingness to consider abuse as the cause. Further, Kempe et al. stated that characteristics of physician "training and personality usually makes it quite difficult for him to assume the role of policeman or district attorney, and start questioning patients as if he were investigating a crime" (p. 19). Kempe et al. noted that some physicians will ignore any suspicions of abuse despite "obvious circumstantial evidence" (p. 19). Kempe et al., therefore, set forth an agenda to establish mandatory reporting laws, and much of what they said is reflected in contemporary reporting statutes.

The battered child syndrome and Kempe et al.'s (1962) comments about physician reluctance to report brought about initiatives to develop model mandatory reporting legislation. The first of three model statutes was written in 1963 by the Children's Bureau of the National Center on Child Abuse and Neglect. This model statute was followed by two others in 1965, one proposed by the American Medical Association and the other by the Program of State Governments (Meriwether, 1986; NCCAN, 1979). By 1966 all states in the U.S., except for Hawaii which later followed, had enacted laws mandating physicians to report suspected child abuse (Paulsen, 1967), an unprecedented rate of legislative proliferation (M. Levine & A. Levine, 1992). The intent of the model statutes was to bring forward cases of the battered child syndrome that were known to physicians but that would not be recognizable to nonmedical observers (Paulsen, 1967). Specifically, the Children's Bureau statute stated:

> The purpose of this Act is to provide for the protection of children who have had physical injury inflicted upon them . . . physicians . . . should report . . . thereby causing the protective services of the state to be brought to bear in an effort to protect the health and welfare of these children and to prevent further abuses. (Paulsen, 1967, p. 15)

With respect to required reports by physicians and institutions, the model statute specified that:

> Any physician . . . having reasonable cause to suspect that a child under the age of [the maximum age of juvenile court] brought to him or coming before him for examination, care or treatment has had serious physical injury or injuries inflicted upon him other than by accidental means by a parent or other person responsible for his care, shall report or cause a report to be made in accordance with the provisions of the Act. (McCoid, 1965, p. 20)

Legislative changes subsequently broadened most aspects of these early narrow statutes, including the range of professionals and types of maltreatment meeting legal standards for required reporting. In the late 1960s and early 1970s a number of professionals were added to the list of mandated reporters. Definitions of abuse were broadened to include emotional and nutritional maltreatment (Giovannoni, 1989a), as well as sexual abuse and exploitation. Most states also dropped the term *serious* as a qualifier of injury or harm in definitions of abuse. The Child Abuse Prevention and Treatment Act of 1974 defined child abuse and neglect as follows, and set the standard for state mandatory reporting laws.

The physical or mental injury, sexual abuse, negligent treatment, or maltreatment of a child under the age of 18 by a person who is responsible for the child's welfare under circumstances which indicate the child's health or welfare is harmed or threatened thereby as determined in accordance with regulations prescribed. (Child Abuse Prevention and Treatment Act of 1974, Section 3)

States are required to closely approximate this definition in order to receive federal child protection funds. Qualifying definitions of abuse with terms such as *serious injury* resulted in Pennsylvania's ineligibility for federal funding (Daro & McCurdy, 1992; Wells, Stein, Fluke, & Downing, 1989).

Amendments to the Act further broadened the types of maltreatment encompassed by the definition. Similarly, the Child Abuse Prevention, Adoption, and Family Services Act of 1988 broadly defined maltreatment as

the physical or mental injury, sexual abuse or exploitation, negligent treatment, or maltreatment of a child by a person who is responsible for the child's welfare, under circumstances which indicate that the child's health or welfare is harmed or threatened. (Section 14. Definitions)

States continue to broaden and expand reporting laws, with California amending its statute more than 15 times since 1963 (Meriwether, 1986). The expansion of reporting statutes did not, however, consider the diversity of professionals added to the lists of mandated reporters. Because the battered child syndrome originally described cases that were most likely to be seen by emergency room physicians, radiologists, and pediatricians, the model reporting statutes targeted medical professionals. When the laws were expanded to include a range of professionals, there was a parallel expansion of definitions of abuse and conditions under which reporting was required. However, for the most part a single standard that assumed homogeneity in professional training, circumstances of practice, and conditions under which suspicions of maltreatment occur was applied across disciplines and professional settings.

Because reporting laws ignore particular aspects of various professional contexts, their uniform application is often criticized (Ansell & Ross, 1990; Berlin, Malin, & Dean, 1991; Jones & Welch, 1989; Newberger, 1983). With few exceptions, reporting statutes limit confidentiality standards and privilege rights in psychotherapy, protection of research participants' privacy, and discretion through professional judgment. Thus, laws that require reporting suspected child abuse and neglect in professional contexts often conflict with basic professional values. These conflicts in turn interfere with adherence to mandatory reporting laws.

As a central component of child protection, mandatory reporting laws hold persons responsible for alerting authorities about abuse on the premise that maltreated children are too young, too frightened, or both, to seek assistance (Besharov, 1990). There are three specific intentions on which reporting laws are grounded. First, reporting statutes are designed to expedite identification of abused children by the child protection system. Second, statutes designate specific agencies to receive, investigate, and manage cases of maltreatment. Finally, reporting statutes are intended, when appropriate, to provide protective services to prevent further abuse and to help preserve family unity and welfare (NCCAN, 1979).

AN EXAMINATION OF CURRENT STATE STATUTES

Laws that require professionals to report suspected abuse are thought to increase the number of reported cases of maltreatment. As noted by Besharov (1990), reported cases of abuse and neglect in 1987 increased to more than 14 times the number reported in 1963. This observation suggests that mandated reporting caused the increase in reports. However, this causal interpretation is not conclusive because of the numerous social changes that accompanied child protection legislation, including greater social awareness of child abuse, the elevated social consciousness of the 1960s, and means for all citizens to file anonymous reports of abuse. Still, the direct effects of the law have been observed in a naturalistic study of legislative impact. Lamond (1989) investigated increased reporting of child sexual abuse among school personnel in New South Wales, Australia, following the enactment of legislation requiring these professionals to report suspected sexual abuse. The study showed that although the overall number of reports remained constant during the study period, reports of sexual abuse filed by school personnel increased from 21% to 30%, a statistically significant difference. Schoolteachers increased their reporting of sexual abuse nearly threefold after the legislative change, which made teachers the source of almost a quarter of all reports of sexual abuse. Thus, mandatory reporting laws seemed to account for increases in reported sexual abuse among these professionals.

Mandatory reporting laws across states invariably have several core components in common. Laws define abusive situations; delineate reportable circumstances, the level of certainty that reporters must reach, the age limits of reportable children, and details of who must report; outline the sanctions for not reporting; and provide immunity from civil and criminal liability for reports filed "in good faith" (Meriwether, 1986; NCCAN, 1979). Although they share these general features, state reporting laws also vary in subtle and important ways. The greatest degree of variability between laws is in the way abuse is defined and under what conditions reporting is required. Three specific aspects of reporting laws appear to pose the most difficulty for professionals: who is required to report, what is required to be reported, and when reporting is required (see Table 2).

TABLE 2
Definitions of Abuse and Requirements to Report Excerpted
From Reporting Statutes of Fifty States

Definition	Reporting Requirement
Alabama, Code sec. 26-14-1 through 26-14-13	
Harm or threatened harm to a child's health or welfare . . . through non-accidental physical or mental injury, sexual abuse or attempted sexual abuse, or sexual exploitation.	Child is known or suspected to be a victim of child abuse or neglect.
Alaska, Stat. sec 47.17.010	
The physical injury or neglect, sexual abuse, sexual exploitation, or maltreatment of a child . . . by a person who is responsible for the child's welfare under circumstances which indicate that the child's health or welfare is harmed or threatened.	Who in the performance of the person's occupational duties has cause to believe that a child has suffered harm as the result of abuse.
Arizona, Criminal Code 13-3620	
The victim of injury, sexual molestation, death, abuse or physical neglect which appears to have been inflicted upon such a minor by other than accidental means or which is not explained by the available medical history as being accidental in nature.	Reasonable grounds to believe that a minor is or has been the victim of.
Arkansas, Stat. Ann. sec 12-12-502	
Any non-accidental physical injury, mental injury, sexual abuse, or sexual exploitation inflicted on a child by anyone legally responsible for the care and maintenance of the child, or any injury which is at variance with the history given. The term [abuse] encompasses both acts and omissions.	Reasonable cause to suspect that a child has been abused or neglected.
California, Penal Code sec. 11165	
Physical injury which is inflicted by other than accidental means on a child by another person . . . "neglect" means the negligent treatment or the maltreatment of a child by a person responsible for the child's welfare under circumstances indicating harm or threatened harm to the child's health or welfare . . . "severe neglect" includes . . . severe malnutrition, medically diagnosed nonorganic failure to thrive . . . intentional failure to provide adequate food, clothing, shelter, or medical care . . . "willful cruelty or unjustifiable punishment of a child" means a situation where any person willfully causes or permits any child to suffer, or inflicts thereon, unjustifiable physical pain or mental suffering.	Who has knowledge of or observes a child in his/her professional capacity . . . who he/she knows or reasonably suspects has been the victim of child abuse shall . . . "reasonable suspicion" means that it is objectively reasonable for a person to entertain such suspicion, based upon facts that could cause a person in a like position, drawing when appropriate on his/her training and experience, to suspect child abuse.

Definition	Reporting Requirement

Colorado, Stat. sec. 19-3-301

An act or omission in one of the following categories which threatens the health or welfare of a child . . . evidence of skin bruising, bleeding, malnutrition, failure to thrive, burns, fracture of any bone, subdural hematoma, soft tissue swelling, or death and either: the history given concerning such condition is at variance with the degree or type of such condition or death; or circumstances indicate that such a condition may not be the product of an accidental occurrence.

Known or suspected child abuse or neglect.

Connecticut, Gen. Stat. Ann. sec 17-38a(b) and 17-53

Has had physical injury or injuries inflicted upon him by a person responsible for a child's . . . health, welfare or care . . . other than by accidental means or has injuries which are at variance with the history given of them, or is in a condition which is the result of maltreatment such as . . . maltreatment, sexual abuse, sexual exploitation, deprivation of necessities, emotional maltreatment or cruel punishment, or has been neglected.

Reasonable cause to suspect or believe that any child . . . is in danger of being abused or neglected . . . or has been so abused or neglected.

Delaware, Code Ann. title 16 sec. 903

The physical injury by other than accidental means, injury resulting in a mental or emotional condition which is the result of abuse or neglect, negligent treatment, sexual abuse, maltreatment, mistreatment, non-treatment, exploitation, or abandonment, of a child.

Who knows or reasonably suspects child abuse or neglect shall make a report.

Florida, Stat. Ann. sec. 415.502

A child whose physical or mental health or welfare is harmed, or threatened with harm, by the acts or omissions of the parent . . . inflicts, or allows to be inflicted upon the child physical or mental injury . . . which includes injury sustained as a result of excessive corporal punishment . . . sexual battery . . . exploits a child . . . abandons the child . . . "physical injury" means death, permanent or temporary disfigurement, or impairment of any body part . . . "mental injury" means an injury to the intellectual or psychological capacity of a child as evidenced by a discernable and substantial impairment in his ability to function within his normal range of performance and behavior, with due regard to his culture.

Who knows, or has reasonable cause to suspect, that a child is an abused or neglected child, shall report such knowledge or suspicion.

Table 2 *(continued)*

Definition	Reporting Requirement

Georgia, Code Ann. sec. 19-7-5

Physical injury or injuries inflicted upon him/her other than by accidental means . . . or has been neglected or exploited . . . or has been sexually assaulted or exploited.

Having reasonable cause to believe.

Hawaii, Stat. sec. 350-1

Physical injury, psychological abuse and neglect, sexual abuse, negligent treatment, maltreatment of a child . . . which indicates that the minor's health or welfare has been or is harmed . . . "harmed" means . . . substantial or multiple skin bruises or any other internal bleeding, any injury to skin causing substantial bleeding, malnutrition, failure to thrive, . . . burns, poisoning, fracture of any bone, subdural hematoma, soft tissue swelling, extreme pain, extreme mental distress, gross degradation, or death, and such injury is not justifiably explained, or where the history given is at variance with the degree or type of such condition.

Who, in their professional . . . capacity, have reason to believe that child abuse or neglect has occurred or that there exists a substantial risk that child abuse or neglect may occur in the reasonable foreseeable future.

Idaho, Code sec. 16-1619

Victim of conduct or omission resulting in skin bruising, bleeding, malnutrition, burns, fracture of any bone, subdural hematoma, soft tissue swelling, failure to thrive, or death, and such condition is not justifiably explained, or where the history given concerning such condition is at variance with the degree or type of condition, or the circumstances indicate that such condition may not be the product of an accidental occurrence.

Having any reason to believe that a child . . . has been abused, abandoned, neglected, or who observes the child being subjected to conditions or circumstances which would reasonably result in abuse.

Illinois, Stat. ch. 23 sec. 2051

A child whose parent . . . inflicts, causes to be inflicted, allows to be inflicted . . . creates a substantial risk of . . . physical injury by other than accidental means, which cause death, disfigurement, impairment of physical or emotional health, or loss or impairment of any bodily function.

Having reasonable cause to believe that a child known to them in their professional capacity may be an abused or a neglected child.

Indiana, Juvenile Code—Child Abuse Ann. sec. 31-6-11

The child's physical or mental condition is seriously impaired or seriously endangered as a result of the inability, refusal, or neglect of the parent . . . to supply the child with necessary food, clothing, shelter, medical care, education, or supervision . . . is seriously endangered due to injury by act or omission of the child's parent . . . is the victim of a sexual offense.

Who has reason to believe that a child is a victim of child abuse or neglect.

Iowa, Code Ann. sec. 232-67

Definition	Reporting Requirement
Any non-accidental physical injury, or injury which is at variance with the history given of it, suffered by a child as the result of acts or omissions of a person responsible for the care of the child.	[Medical professional] who examines, attends, or treats a child and reasonably believes the child has been abused . . . (other professional) who . . . examines, attends, counsels or treats a child and reasonably believes a child has suffered abuse.

Kansas, Stat. Ann. sec. 1520

Definition	Reporting Requirement
The infliction of physical, mental, or emotional injury or the causing of deterioration of a child . . . negligent treatment or maltreatment or exploiting a child to the extent that a child's health or emotional well-being is endangered.	Has reason to suspect that a child has been injured as a result of [maltreatment].

Kentucky, Unified Juvenile Code Rev. Stat. Ann. sec. 620-030

Definition	Reporting Requirement
Child whose health or welfare is harmed or threatened with harm when his parent . . . inflicts or allows to be inflicted upon the child physical or emotional injury by other than accidental means.	Who knows or has reasonable cause to believe that a child . . . or who has attended such a child as a part of his professional duties.

Louisiana, Stat. Ann. sec. 14:403

Definition	Reporting Requirement
The infliction . . . or physical or mental injury or causing of the deterioration of a child . . . sexual abuse, sexual exploitation, or the exploitation or overwork of a child to such an extent that his health, moral or emotional well-being is endangered.	Who has cause to believe that a child's physical mental health or welfare is endangered.

Maine, Stat. Ann. title 22 sec. 4011

Definition	Reporting Requirement
A threat to a child's health or welfare by physical or emotional injury or impairment, sexual exploitation, deprivation of essential needs or lack of protection from these.	When acting in a professional capacity . . . knows or has reasonable cause to suspect that a child has been abused or neglected.

Maryland, Fam. Code Ann. sec. 5-704

Definition	Reporting Requirement
The sustaining of physical injury by a child as a result of cruel or inhumane treatment or as a result of a malicious act.	Acting in a professional capacity, who has reason to believe that a child has been subjected to [maltreatment].

Table 2 *(continued)*

Definition	Reporting Requirement
Massachusetts, Gen. Laws Ann. ch. 119 sec. 51A	
Suffering serious physical or emotional injury resulting from abuse inflicted upon him including sexual abuse, or from neglect, including malnutrition.	Who in his professional capacity shall have reasonable cause to believe that a child . . . is suffering serious physical or emotional injury resulting from abuse.
Michigan, Act No. 238, Public Acts of 1975 Comp. Laws Ann. sec. 722.621–722.636	
Harm or threatened harm to a child's health or welfare by a person responsible for the child's health or welfare which occurs through non-accidental physical or mental injury.	Who has reasonable cause to suspect child abuse or neglect.
Minnesota, Stat. Ann. sec. 626-556	
Any physical injury inflicted by a person responsible for the child's care . . . other than by accidental means, or physical injury that cannot reasonably be explained by the child's history of injuries.	A person who knows or has reason to believe that a child is being neglected or physically or sexually abused, or has been neglected or physically or sexually abused within the preceding three years.
Mississippi, Code of 1972 Ann. sec. 43-21-353	
"Battered and abused child" means a child whose parent, . . . or any person responsible for his care or support . . . has inflicted physical injury, including sexual abuse, other than by accidental means.	Any person having reasonable cause to suspect that a child brought to him or coming before him for examination, care or treatment, or of whom he has knowledge through observation is a neglected child or an abused child.
Missouri, Child Abuse and Neglect Law 210.115 RSMo 1986 Supp. 1988	
Any physical injury, sexual abuse, or emotional abuse inflicted on a child other than by accidental means . . . except that discipline including spanking, administered in a reasonable manner.	Has reasonable cause to suspect that a child has been or may be subjected to abuse or neglect or observes a child being subjected to conditions.
Montana, Code Ann. sec 41.3.101	
A child whose normal physical or mental welfare is harmed or threatened with harm by the acts or omissions of his parent . . . inflicts or allows to be inflicted . . . physical or mental injuries.	Know or have reasonable cause to suspect, as a result of information they receive in their professional capacity.

Definition	Reporting Requirement

Nebraska, Stat. sec. 28-711

Knowingly, intentionally, or negligently causing or permitting a minor child . . . to be placed in a situation that endangers his or her life or physical or mental health.

Who has reasonable cause to believe that a child . . . has been subjected to abuse or neglect, or observes such a person being subjected to conditions or circumstances which reasonably would result in abuse or neglect.

Nevada, Stat. sec. 432B.220

Physical or mental injury of a non-accidental nature . . . "mental injury" means an injury to the intellectual or psychological capacity or the emotional condition of a child as evidenced by an observable and substantial impairment of his ability to function within his normal range. . . "physical injury" means permanent or temporary disfigurement or impairment of any bodily function or organ of the body.

Who in their professional . . . capacities, know or have reason to believe that a child has been abused or neglected.

New Hampshire, Stat. Ann. sec. 169-C: 29

Who has been intentionally physically injured or been psychologically injured so that said child exhibits symptoms of emotional problems generally recognized to result from consistent mistreatment or neglect or physically injured by other than accidental means.

Having reason to suspect that a child has been abused or neglected.

New Jersey, Stat. Ann. sec. 9:6-8.10

Inflicts or allows to be inflicted upon such child physical injury by other than accidental means which causes or creates a substantial risk of death, or serious protracted disfigurement, or protracted loss or impairment of function of any bodily organ . . . creates or allows to be created a substantial or ongoing risk of physical injury.

Having reasonable cause to believe that a child has been subjected to child abuse or acts of child abuse.

New Mexico, Stat. Ann. sec. 32-1-15

Who has been physically, emotionally, or psychologically abused by his parent.

Knowing or suspecting that a child is an abused or neglected child.

New York, Social Service Laws sec. 411

Inflicts or allows to be inflicted upon such child physical injury by other than accidental means which causes or creates a substantial risk of death, serious protracted disfigurement, protracted impairment of physical or emotional health or protracted loss or impairment of the function of any organ . . . creates or allows to be created a substantial risk of physical injury.

Has reasonable cause to suspect that a child is an abused or maltreated child.

Table 2 *(continued)*

Definition	Reporting Requirement

North Carolina, Gen. Stat. sec. 7A-543

Inflicts or allows to be inflicted upon the juvenile a physical injury by other than accidental means which causes or creates a substantial risk of death, disfigurement, impairment of physical health, or the loss or impairment of the function of any bodily organ . . . creates or allows to [be] created substantial risk of physical injury to the juvenile by other than accidental means.	Who has cause to suspect that any juvenile is abused or neglected shall report.

North Dakota, Cent. Code sec. 50-25

Suffering from serious physical harm or traumatic abuse caused by other than accidental means . . . "harm" means negative changes in a child's health which occur when a person responsible for the child's health and welfare inflicts or allows to [be] inflicted . . . physical or mental injury.	Having reasonable cause to suspect that a child is abused or neglected.

Ohio, Code Ann. sec. 2151.421

Suffered any wound, injury, disability or other condition of a nature that reasonably indicates abuse or neglect of the child.	No [human service professional] . . . who is acting in his . . . professional capacity and knows or suspects that a child has suffered any wound, injury, disability, or condition of nature that reasonably . . . shall recklessly fail immediately to report or cause reports to be made of that knowledge or suspicion.

Oklahoma, Stat. Ann. title 21 sec. 846

Harm or threatened harm to a child's health or welfare . . . through non-accidental physical or mental injury, sexual abuse . . . sexual exploitation.	Having reason to believe a child . . . has had physical injury or injuries inflicted upon him/her by other than accidental means where the injury appears to have been caused as a result of physical abuse or neglect.

Oregon, Stat. sec. 418.750

Any physical injury to a child which has been caused by other than accidental means, including injury which appears to be at variance with the explanation given of the injury. Any mental injury . . . include only observable and substantial impairment of the child's mental or psychological ability to function caused by cruelty to the child.	Having reasonable cause to believe that any child with whom the official comes in contact in an official capacity has suffered abuse.

Definition	Reporting Requirement

Pennsylvania, Stat. Ann. sec. 6311

Serious physical or mental injury which is not explained by the available medical history as being accidental.	Persons who, in the course of their profession . . . come into contact with children and have reason to believe, on the basis of their professional training and experience, that a child coming before them in their professional capacity is a victim of child abuse.

Rhode Island, Gen. Laws sec. 40-11

A child whose physical or mental health or welfare is harmed or threatened with harm . . . inflicts, or allows to be inflicted upon the child physical or mental injury, including excessive corporal punishment, or creates or allows to be created a substantial risk of physical or mental injury to the child.	Any person who has reasonable cause to know or suspect that any child has been abused or neglected.

South Carolina, Code Ann. sec. 20-7-510

A child whose physical or mental health or welfare is harmed or threatened with harm . . . inflicts or allows to be inflicted upon the child physical or mental injury, including injuries sustained as a result of excessive corporal punishment.	Having reason to believe that a child's physical or mental health or welfare has been or may be adversely affected by abuse or neglect.

South Dakota, Codified Laws Ann. sec. 26-10

Has had physical injuries inflicted upon him by abuse or intentional neglect other than by accidental means.	Having reasonable cause to suspect.

Tennessee, Code Ann. sec. 37-1-403

The knowing exposure of a child to or the knowing failure to protect a child from conditions of brutality, abuse or neglect that are likely to cause great bodily harm or death and knowing use of force on a child that is likely to cause great harm or death . . . specific brutality, abuse or neglect . . . which in the opinion of experts has caused or will reasonably be expected to produce severe psychosis, severe neurotic disorder, severe depression, severe developmental delay or retardation, or severe impairment of the child's ability to function adequately in his environment.	Having knowledge of or called upon to render aid to any child who is suffering from or has sustained any wound, injury, disability, or physical or mental condition which is of such a nature as to reasonably indicate that it has been caused by brutality, abuse or neglect.

Table 2 *(continued)*

Definition	Reporting Requirement

Texas, Fam. Code Ann. sec. 34.01

Mental or emotional injury to a child that results in an observable and material impairment in the child's growth, development, or psychological functioning . . . physical injury that results in substantial harm to the child, or the genuine threat of substantial harm from physical injury to the child, including an injury at variance with the history or explanation given.

Having cause to believe a child's physical or mental health or welfare has been or may be adversely affected by abuse or neglect.

Utah, Code Ann. sec. 62-A-4-501

Damaged or threatened damage to the physical or emotional health and welfare of a child through neglect or abuse, and includes causing non-accidental physical or mental injury.

Has reason to believe that a child has been subjected to . . . or who observes a child being subjected to conditions or circumstances which would reasonably result in sexual abuse, physical abuse, or neglect.

Vermont, title 33 ch. 14 sec. 683

A child whose physical or mental health or welfare is harmed or threatened with harm by act or omissions . . . inflicts or allows to be inflicted, upon the child, physical or mental injury.

Who has reasonable cause to believe that any child has been abused or neglected.

Virginia, Code Ann. sec. 63.1-248

A physical or mental injury by other than accidental means . . . creates a substantial risk of death, disfigurement, impairment of bodily functions.

Who has reason to suspect that a child is an abused or neglected child.

Washington, Code Ann. sec. 26.44.010

Injury, sexual abuse, sexual exploitation, or negligent treatment or maltreatment of a child by any person under circumstances which indicate that the child's health, welfare, and safety is harmed thereby.

Has reasonable cause to believe that a child has suffered abuse or neglect.

West Virginia, Code sec. 49-6A-1

Infliction upon a minor of physical injury by other than accidental means.

Reasonable cause to suspect that a child has been abused or neglected . . . or observes the child being subjected to conditions or circumstances that would reasonably result in abuse or neglect.

Definition	Reporting Requirement

Wisconsin, Stat. Ann. sec. 48.981

Physical injury inflicted on a child by other than accidental means.	Having reasonable cause to suspect that a child seen in the course of professional duties has been abused or neglected . . . or that abuse or neglect of the child will occur.

Wyoming, Stat. sec. 14-3-205

"Physical injury" means death or any harm to a child including but not limited to disfigurement, impairment of any bodily organ, skin bruising, bleeding, burns, fracture of any bone, subdural hematoma or substantial malnutrition . . . "mental injury" means an injury to the psychological capacity or emotional stability of a child as evidenced by an observable or substantial impairment in his ability to function within normal range.	Any person who has reasonable cause to believe or suspect that a child has been abused or neglected or who observes any child being subjected to conditions or circumstances that would reasonably result in abuse or neglect.

Who Is Required to Report?

The first state statutes, as well as early laws outside of the U.S., exclusively targeted medical professionals as mandated reporters (Lamond, 1989; NCCAN, 1979; Small, 1992). Limiting requirements to medical professionals did not, however, last long. Part of the reason for the expansion of mandated reporters is that physicians had opposed being singled out as the sole detectors of child maltreatment. Among other things, physicians expressed concern that parents may fail to provide abused children with adequate health care out of fear of being reported. The American Medical Association stated:

> This is a social problem in which the physician plays but a part. Visiting nurses, social workers, school teachers and authorities, lawyers, marriage and guidance counselors, and others frequently learn of cases before medical care is demanded or received. To wait until the child requires medical attention is too late. To compel reporting by the physician alone may single him out unwisely. Knowing of this requirement, the parent or guardian may, for his own protection, put off seeking medical care. (American Medical Association, 1964, p. 136)

During the late 1960s and early 1970s mandatory reporting laws were expanded to include a range of health service professionals, as well as other professionals outside of health related fields, such as social service workers and teachers. Expansion has continued in recent years with respect to specific professionals required to report. For example, in 1989 some states (e.g., Colorado and Illinois) mandated commercial film developers to report suspected abuse, usually specifying suspected sexual abuse/exploitation that could be indicated by sexually explicit photographs of children (NCCAN, 1989). In addition, persons who care for or supervise children in a variety of settings have been added to the list of mandated reporters. Some states require certain professionals to report, such as pharmacists and religious healers, while other states do not. However, all states require mental health professionals, including psychologists, social workers, psychiatrists, and counselors, to report suspected abuse. Finally, in some states (e.g., Florida, Indiana, Kentucky, Minnesota, Nebraska, New Hampshire, New Jersey, New Mexico, and North Carolina), any person who suspects abuse is required by law to report (NCCAN, 1989). Across states, there are nearly 40 different professions specifically named in mandatory reporting laws (Small, 1992; Wurtele & Miller-Perrin, 1992).

There are differences among various professional groups in their adherence to reporting laws. In an early study, psychologists were shown to be less knowledgeable about reporting laws than psychiatrists, who were much less knowledgeable than social workers (Swoboda, Elwork, Sales, & Levine, 1978). Psychiatric nurses have been found to be more likely to report a hypothetical case of abuse, as compared with nonmedical mental health workers (Kalichman, Craig, & Follingstad, 1988). Similarly, Williams, Osborne, and Rappaport (1987) showed that nurses and ministers were more likely to report hypothetical abuse than family practice physicians and psychologists. These few studies suggest differences in compliance among professionals and professional settings, and caution against treating mandated reporters as a homogeneous group with respect to considerations made in their reporting decisions.

Professionals who are required to report suspected abuse are provided with civil and criminal immunity from liabilities associated with reporting, as defined and required by law. Reporters are protected when reports are filed in good faith, when there is an absence of malicious intent, regardless of whether or not abuse is substantiated on investigation. Some states specifically note that a report must be filed in good faith (e.g., Alaska, New York, Rhode Island) or without malice (e.g., Kansas, Nebraska). In contrast, other states presume that all reports are made in good faith (e.g., Alabama, New Jersey). All states, whether good faith reporting is specified or presumed, include immunity for reporters as required under the Federal Child Abuse Prevention and Treatment Act. This legislation specifically grants "immunity for persons reporting instances of child abuse and neglect from prosecution, under any state or local law, arising out of such reporting" (NCCAN, 1979, p. 10). Immunity from liability due to participation in judicial proceedings resulting from a report is also provided in almost all states (exceptions include Massachusetts and North Dakota). The intent of granting immunity is to relieve reporters of concerns about being held liable for reporting uncertain suspicions.

What Is Required to Be Reported?

A great deal of confusion exists concerning the definition of child maltreatment, much of which is a product of the vast number of different definitions serving different purposes. As a matter of classification, definitions serve a diagnostic function in medicine and other human service professions. Diagnosing child abuse points toward appropriate treatment alternatives. However, diagnostic definitions do not necessarily align with social service definitions, which function as a minimum criteria for family intervention (Giovannoni, 1989a). With respect to legal definitions of abuse, there are three different functions for which abuse is typically defined: for criminal acts, for determination of child dependency, and for identification of cases that warrant reporting. Although legal definitions for any given state will overlap across these three areas of law, there are often distinguishing characteristics. Legal definitions of abuse applied to reporting statutes determine the circumstances of required reporting, providing guidelines for persons required to report (Meriwether, 1986).

Definitions of maltreatment contained within reporting statutes vary considerably. An evaluation of these definitions of abuse shows that some forms of maltreatment are included in legal definitions but others are not. For example, 40% of state reporting laws do not include poverty-related neglect in their definitions of neglect, 22% do not include emotional maltreatment, 55% omit educational neglect, and 24% do not include medical neglect (Rycraft, 1990). Four different types of child maltreatment are most commonly included in reporting laws: physical abuse, sexual abuse, neglect, and emotional maltreatment. These different types of abuse are not mutually exclusive in that sexual abuse includes physical assault and both sexual and nonsexual abuse imply some level of emotional maltreatment. In addition, approximately 10% of reported cases of abuse fall into an *other* category, which may include abandonment and dependency (Daro & McCurdy, 1992). States do not make a distinction between reporting *abuse* and *neglect* (NCCAN, 1979). However, states do define the composition of each of the different types of maltreatment, all of which must be reported.

Legal definitions of child maltreatment focus on one of two aspects of abuse: (a) the behavior of the abusive adult or (b) the effects of abusive acts or harm suffered by the child (Meriwether, 1986). Focusing on the adult's behavior will result in a set of circumstances or general behaviors that lead to abusive conditions. On the other hand, focusing on the child's reactions or harm to the child points to presented signs and symptoms of abuse. In either case, definitions can be broad, such as the circumstances of abuse and the signs of serious injury, or narrow, such as genital fondling or subdural hematoma. Therefore, legal definitions of types of abuse represent two dimensions: circumstances versus signs, and narrow versus broad.

Laws most frequently define physical abuse as serious injury by other than accidental means. Specific signs and symptoms are the most common legal definitions offered for serious injury. (See Appendix A for a glossary of terminology used in abuse cases.) For example, Colorado includes in its definition of abuse "any case in which a child exhibits evidence of skin bruising, bleeding, malnutrition, failure to thrive, burns, fracture of any bone, subdural hematoma, soft tissue swelling, or death" (NCCAN, 1989, pp. CO-9–10). When narrowly defined, there is little ambiguity about what is required to be reported, but such narrow definitions do not represent the universe of physically abusive situations. In addition, it is impossible for professionals who do not conduct physical examinations to make such specific distinctions. On the other hand, abuse may also be broadly defined to encompass a range of unspecified injuries. For example, some states define abuse as "harm or threatened harm to a child's welfare by acts or omissions of his/her parent or other person responsible for his/her welfare" (NCCAN, 1979, p. 5). Broad definitions of abuse can be traced back to a number of the earliest statutes (NCCAN, 1979). Legislative definitions of abuse, both narrow and broad, appear to be problematic for professionals mandated to report (Jones & Welch, 1989; Smith & Meyer, 1984). Broad definitions are likely to result in high rates of reporting with many cases going unfounded, whereas narrow definitions reduce the number of false reports but at the possible expense of missed cases of abuse (Meriwether, 1986).

The complexity of defining physical abuse is further illustrated by attempts to differentiate between serious and less serious injuries. Within the context of reporting laws, some states specify *serious harm* as a part of their definition (e.g., Indiana, Massachusetts, Pennsylvania), whereas others do not make this narrow distinction (e.g., California, Florida, Kentucky). Including the word *serious* in a reporting statute leaves the reporter with a great deal of discretion as to what constitutes levels of severity but only requires reporting at the higher end of the spectrum (Meriwether, 1986). However, specifying what constitutes serious and less serious abuse often appears arbitrary. For example, in one study, Rosenthal (1988) defined serious injuries, similarly to reporting laws, as brain damage; skull fracture; bone fracture; dislocated joints; strains and twists; internal injuries; serious burns and scalds; and serious cuts, bruises, and welts. Minor injuries, on the other hand, were defined as burns, scalds, cuts, bruises, and welts not judged to be serious. Although one could argue that such injuries may be amenable to ratings based on subjective impressions or diagnostic staging, without any indication of their reliability or validity such distinctions remain arbitrary. When physical signs of abuse are visible, their cause is not necessarily apparent, and reporting laws usually specify that they must be nonaccidental.

Plausible explanations for injuries will vary with the complexity of situations and the developmental period of the child. Thus, although on the surface physical abuse would appear to be readily detectable and therefore reportable, perhaps more than any other type of abuse, suspicions of physical abuse are complicated by numerous definition problems.

Physical abuse is rarely defined as a set of acts or circumstances under reporting laws. States usually do not delineate hitting or beating as acts of abuse, primarily because to do so would be to legislate methods of parental discipline. Specifying acts as physical abuse may therefore be seen as potentially infringing on parental rights. Along these lines, parental use of corporal punishment is not prohibited in any state (NCCAN, 1979), and is specifically excluded from definitions of child abuse in some states. For example, South Carolina's statute states that abuse is excluded when conditions meet the following criteria: "force or violence of the discipline must be reasonable in manner and moderate in degree. . . . must not have brought about permanent or lasting damage to the child" (NCCAN, 1989, p. SC-8). Therefore, it would be difficult to define physical abuse by acts alone. Rather, when punishment is excessive and results in injury or harm then legal definitions of physical abuse apply because they tend to focus on symptoms and signs of abuse.

Physical signs and symptoms, on the other hand, rarely form the basis for legal definitions of sexual maltreatment. Laws also do not include as a part of their definitions behaviors, exhibited by children, that may be associated with some cases of sexual abuse. Rather, legal definitions rely on situations and abusive–exploitive behaviors that constitute sexual abuse. For example, Georgia defines sexual abuse or exploitation as child molestation, immoral or indecent acts performed in the presence of a child, enticing a child for indecent purposes, incest, and the involvement of a child in sexually explicit materials (NCCAN, 1989, p. GA-1). Georgia law goes on to specify other detailed acts and situations that constitute sexual abuse. Thus, definitions of sexual abuse, unlike physical abuse, tend to rely on circumstances, situations, and behaviors rather than signs and symptoms.

Defining sexual abuse by acts and conditions reflects the circumstances under which sexual abuse is likely to be detected (Meriwether, 1986). Experts estimate that as many as 75% of cases of sexual abuse present without any specific physical signs of maltreatment (Zielinski, 1992), and approximately 40% of substantiated cases of sexual abuse show no physical evidence (Adams, 1991; Goodwin, Sahd, & Rada, 1982). Although sexual abuse itself involves physical violation of a child, nonsexual physical abuse only co-occurs with sexual abuse in 5% of cases (Finkelhor, 1985). Unlike the relationship between bodily signs of physical abuse and corporal punishment, all acts associated with sexual abuse are readily defined as warranting criminal investigation.

Similarly, definitions of neglect tend to rely on circumstances and situations in their definitions (Dubowitz, Black, Starr, & Zuravin, 1993; Meriwether, 1986). Neglect is most typically defined as "failure to provide, by those legally responsible for the care of the child, the proper or necessary support, education as required by law, or medical, surgical, or any other care necessary for his/her well-being" (NCCAN, 1979, p. 5). For example, Minnesota defines *neglect* as:

> Failure by a person responsible for a child's care to supply a child with necessary food, clothing, shelter or medical care when reasonably able to do so or failure to protect a child from conditions or actions which imminently and seriously endanger the child's physical or mental health when reasonably able to do so. (NCCAN, 1989, p. MN-9)

Circumstances of deprivation, and failure to provide necessary care and supervision are therefore encompassed in definitions of neglect. Thus, like sexual abuse, and unlike physical abuse, definitions of neglect focus on circumstances and situations rather than signs and symptoms.

Finally, emotional or psychological maltreatment is also defined by law, although usually with great ambiguity (Melton & Davidson, 1987). Emotional maltreatment, like physical abuse, is usually defined on the basis of signs indicative of abuse, rather than conditions that result in maltreatment. Most typically, emotional maltreatment is legally defined as "an injury to the psychological capacity or emotional stability of a child as evidenced by an observable or substantial impairment in his/her ability to function within a normal range of performance and behavior with due regard to culture" (NCCAN, 1979, p. 5). As a specific example, Florida defines mental injury as "an injury to the intellectual or psychological capacity of a child as evidenced by a discernable and substantial impairment in his ability to function within his normal range of performance and behavior" (NCCAN, 1989, p. FL-10). Emotional maltreatment, as defined by law, may pose particular problems for mental health service providers, as many clinical cases will likely exhibit signs of emotional or mental impairment. Therefore, in these contexts, the source, intentions, and conditions related to the impairment are likely to play an important role in identifying a child who has been or is at risk of being abused.

Figure 3 presents a dimensional representation of legal definitions of abuse. The first dimension, represented along the vertical, involves identifying abuse as signs/symptoms or circumstances/conditions. The second dimension, along the horizontal, represents abuse as specifically/narrowly or vaguely/broadly defined. For the most part, laws usually define physical abuse in terms of specific signs, emotional maltreatment in terms of vague signs, sexual abuse as specific circumstances, and neglect as vague circumstances or conditions. Although states vary with respect to how their definitions fall along these two dimensions, this representation may be of use in conceptualizing legal definitions of abuse.

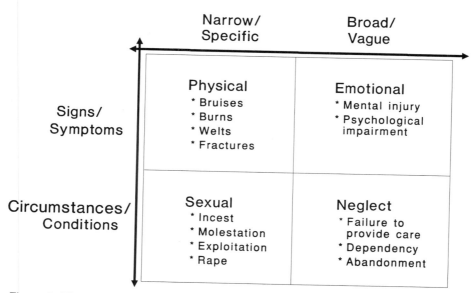

Figure 3: Dimensional representation of definitions of child maltreatment.

Both professionally and legally delineating what constitutes abuse and neglect directly affects which cases are reported. Although research has found differences in tendencies to report different types of abuse (Giovannoni, 1989a; Kalichman & Craig, 1991; USDHHS, 1988; Wilson & Gettinger, 1989; Zellman, 1990), there is little research to support the idea that signs or circumstances of different types of abuse, or narrow or broad definitions of abuse, differentially affect decisions to report. One study has, however, found a relationship between broad and narrow definitions of abuse with both reporting and substantiation rates. Rycraft (1990) evaluated legal definitions of abuse and found that states with broad and non-specific definitions (e.g., Missouri and Nevada), have the highest rates of reported and substantiated abuse. On the other hand, states with narrow and specific definitions (e.g., Maryland and Pennsylvania) have among the lowest rates. Rycraft concluded that definitions of abuse are a determining factor in reporting decisions.

When Is Reporting Required?

Professionals mandated to report child abuse are required to do so under stated conditions of the law. The circumstances that specify when reporting is required are among the more controversial aspects of reporting statutes (Jones & Welch, 1989; Kalichman, 1990, 1991; Meriwether, 1986; Wurtele & Miller-Perrin, 1992). State laws, following the model statutes, do not require reporters to have knowledge or any degree of certainty that abuse has occurred or will occur. Most often, laws use such terminology as *reason to believe* or *having reasonable cause to suspect* abuse. Few states provide any further description of conditions required to be reported. One exception, however, is California's statute, which defines *reasonable suspicion* as "it is objectively reasonable for a person to entertain such a suspicion, based upon facts that could cause a reasonable person in a like position, drawing when appropriate on his or her training and experience, to suspect abuse" (Crime Prevention Center, 1988). Still, what constitutes a reasonable suspicion, as it may be differentiated from clinical hunches, professional impressions, and intuition, remains unclear. Qualifying suspicions with the term *reasonable* seems to imply that reporters are expected to engage in a thoughtful, discretionary process when reporting. Although Kempe et al. (1962) detailed physical and radiological signs that constitute reason to believe that physical abuse has occurred, it is far more problematic to define the subjective experiences and perceptions of mental health workers as reasonable suspicions. Detecting cases of sexual abuse, neglect, and psychological–emotional maltreatment is even more problematic.

The distinction between requirements to report suspicions of abuse as opposed to reasonable suspicions of abuse may not result in many differences in actual reporting, although there has not been empirical data collected on this question. However, these language differences can be important in determining liability for failure to report (Meriwether, 1986). *Reasonable suspicion* denotes an objective standard set by a reasonable person under similar circumstances, implying reasoned discretion. In contrast, use of terms such as *reason to believe* or *suspect* by themselves denote a subjective impression under which the reporter forms an opinion (Meriwether, 1986). The more objective the language used in the statute the easier it is to enforce penalties for failure to report.

In contrast to broad requirements to report reasonable suspicions of abuse, which encompass the universe of possible circumstances, some states (e.g., Iowa, Mississippi, Pennsylvania, and Wisconsin) are similar to the Children's Bureau's model statute and limit the conditions under which reporting is required (Davidson, 1988). For example, the Wisconsin reporting statute specifies that a professional who has

> reasonable cause to suspect that a child seen in the course of professional duties has been abused or neglected, or having reason to believe that a child seen in the course of professional duties has been threatened with an injury and that abuse of the child will occur shall report. (NCCAN, 1989, p. WI-14)

Similarly, Mississippi's statute reads that a professional or other person "having cause to suspect that a child brought before him or coming before him for examination, care, or treatment, or of whom he has knowledge through observation is a neglected child or an abused child . . . shall report"

(NCCAN, 1989, p. MS-10). Thus, a number of conditions that may result in suspected child abuse fall outside of these narrow reporting laws, including a perpetrator's self-disclosure of abuse, an adult's disclosure that a child is being abused by a spouse, and virtually any other indication of abuse by any source other than the suspected child/victim (Davidson, 1988). Of course, although professionals are not required to report under these limited laws, they may voluntarily file a report concerning suspicions of maltreatment.

Unlimited and limited conditions of required reporting brought Kalichman and Brosig (1992) to investigate the effects of specific statutory wording on decisions to report suspected abuse. In this research, two studies were conducted to directly test two state statutes, one state where reasonable suspicion of abuse is required to be reported (Colorado; if one has reasonable cause to suspect that a child has been subjected to abuse or neglect or if one has observed a child being subjected to circumstances or conditions that would reasonably result in abuse or neglect) and one state where professionals are only required to report observations of a child suspected of being abused (Pennsylvania; if a child coming before them in their professional or official capacity is a victim of child abuse).

In the first study, licensed psychologists from Colorado and Pennsylvania read a case scenario depicting a child in a clinical situation who showed signs of being abused followed by one of the two state reporting laws, Colorado's or Pennsylvania's. Participants indicated their tendencies to report the case after reading it and then a second time after reading the law. In this study, the Colorado and Pennsylvania laws both resulted in a significant increase in reporting the depicted abuse. Thus, when presented with a case of a child suspected of being abused, both laws seemed to prompt professionals to report.

In the second study, Kalichman and Brosig (1992) asked an independent sample of licensed psychologists from the same two states to respond to a case scenario that depicted an adult in a clinical situation who showed signs of being abusive. This separate sample of participants also indicated their likelihood of reporting the suspected abuse after reading the adult case and then again after reading one of the two same state statutes used in the first study. The results here were dramatically different from the first study; whereas the Colorado law again resulted in an overall increase in reporting, the Pennsylvania law had the opposite effect. That is, Pennsylvania's law significantly decreased reporting tendency when the source of the suspected abuse was not the child. Kalichman and Brosig concluded that specific reporting requirements directly affected professionals' decisions to report suspected child abuse. These results were subsequently replicated by Brosig and Kalichman (1992a) in a single study that directly tested an adult case against a child case under each of these same two types of laws.

Two important points are raised by the Kalichman and Brosig (1992) and Brosig and Kalichman (1992a) studies. First, although reporting statutes are often discussed as if they were homogeneous and vague, subtle variations among statutes do appear to have specific effects on mandated reporting. As a result, it is likely that states vary in the types and severity of abuse that enter the child protection system. States such as Pennsylvania and Mississippi will be less likely to identify cases in which an adult has been suspected by a professional as being abusive. Second, in contrast to many of the characterizations of mandated reporters (Kalichman et al., 1988, 1989; Pope & Bajt, 1988; Swoboda et al., 1978), professionals do seem sensitive and responsive to legal requirements to report. Professionals may always voluntarily report reasonable suspicions of abuse, regardless of the conditions under which they are required to report. The observed decrease in reporting among professionals confronted with an adult suspected of being abusive when operating under a statute that limits requirements to report demonstrates adherence to legal standards by mandated reporters. Thus, when the law is stated in terms that fit the specific circumstances of a suspicion, professionals tend to comply. However, in the real world, unlike contrived experimental case vignettes, the complexities of conditions within which suspicions arise do not necessarily reflect legal requirements to report. Rather, cases in practice seem to interact with a number of factors that make up the context of reporting situations.

LEGAL RESPONSES TO UNREPORTED SUSPECTED CHILD ABUSE

There have been a number of cases of professionals held legally responsible for failure to report suspected child abuse. Although usually discussed in the context of "professionals beware," these cases illustrate some important elements of reporting requirements and the way suspected child abuse goes unreported. Decisions to not report can occur when professionals suspect abuse but are uncertain of its occurrence. However, most cases in which professionals are held accountable for not reporting involve mandated reporters who appear to have had some degree of knowledge of abuse, not just reasonable suspicion. It is important to note that the controversy surrounding these cases is not so much what constitutes child abuse, but rather when does the law require reporting and when are social service interventions warranted (Giovannoni, 1989a).

In most states, failure to report suspected child abuse by a mandated reporter is a misdemeanor and can carry penalties of a fine and a possible jail sentence. Professionals who fail to comply with mandatory reporting statutes may also face actions to suspend or revoke their professional licensure (Smith & Meyer, 1984). In addition to criminal charges and professional disciplinary actions, there is also the possibility for civil action against the professional as a case of malpractice (Knapp, 1983; Mazura, 1977; Paulsen, 1967). In this sense, failure to report child abuse may be viewed as a case of failure to diagnose (Bross, 1983; Smith & Meyer, 1984). Under standards of professional malpractice and negligence per se, failure to comply with a statutory mandate could result in civil liability. Indeed, several such cases of civil liability have occurred in recent years with respect to failure to report suspected child abuse (Bross, 1983; Knapp, 1983; Meriwether, 1986; Paulsen, 1967).

Landeros v. Flood (1976) represents a leading case of failure to report as malpractice. In this case, a physician failed to diagnose and report an incidence of the battered child syndrome (Besharov, 1986a). The case involved an 11-year-old girl with multiple body bruises and broken bones, most of which were consistent with Kempe et al.'s (1962) description of battered children. The hospital that treated the child released her without having conducted a full radiological examination. Subsequently, the child was taken to a second hospital within only a few weeks of the prior injuries. At the second hospital, the child presented with traumatic blows to the eye, several bites on her face, and burns on her hand. The second hospital did diagnose child abuse and filed a report. The physician who treated the girl at the first hospital was subsequently deemed negligent for failing to diagnose and report. Negligence occurred specifically because of the statutory mandate to report. In addition, subsequent injuries close in time to a failed report, as in the case of *Landeros*, may have been prevented by acting as required by law (Besharov, 1986a).

Cases of suspected child abuse unreported by mental health professionals have recently received a great deal of attention (i.e., Buie, 1989; Denton, 1987a, 1987b). These cases serve many purposes in our understanding of the role mandatory reporting laws play in mental health professions. However, the lack of appellate decisions in this area has resulted in a dearth of case law available on mandated reporting.

A widely discussed criminal case of failure to report, *People v. Cavaiani* (1988), involved a family counselor who had been treating a couple and their 15-year-old daughter. The girl's stepfather had been reported and investigated for sexually fondling her prior to starting therapy. The mother had moved out of the home with her daughter after these acts were reported. The therapist had been referred by the local child protection service agency to help resolve the family problems related to the abuse. During the course of therapy, many of the family problems subsided and the family decided to reunite and try to get their life back together. They moved to a new county; however, they remained near enough to the therapist to continue their treatment.

Shortly after moving, as therapy was nearing an end point, the mother called the therapist to confide that the girl had alleged that her husband, the girl's stepfather, had again touched her in sexual ways. The therapist responded by immediately setting up an appointment for that day to interview the girl. During the interview, the girl stated that her stepfather touched her, but was vague in describing what had occurred. When asked if she felt threatened staying in the home, the girl said that she did feel safe. The therapist felt some doubt in the girl's report because she could not provide any detail of what had happened and had been angry at her stepfather a couple of days before the allegation. The therapist also interviewed the stepfather that same day. He adamantly denied touching the girl again. He did admit the previous acts, but claimed that he had done nothing of the sort since that time.

The therapist considered the situation carefully. Knowing that the stepfather would likely be arrested because of his previous record with the department of social services, the therapist felt that this would be destructive to the family and reverse much of their progress. The therapist decided not to report. The alleged abuse became the focus of a renewed series of family therapy sessions.

Within two weeks of the therapist's interviews with the girl and the stepfather about the allegation, the child repeated her statements to a schoolteacher. The teacher, also a mandated reporter, told the girl that she should talk about the situation with her school counselor, who in turn did report the situation to the social services department in the family's new county of residence. After receiving this report, the child protection agency arrested the stepfather on the basis of his previous record in the neighboring county. The therapist was also arrested for failure to report suspected child abuse.

The therapist's attorney, however, attempted to challenge the constitutionality of the state reporting statute. The grounds for the case against the statute were that it was excessively vague and violated rights of expression. Although a lower court did find the statute unconstitutional, the state supreme court would not hear the case unless the therapist was first found guilty of failure to report. After a jury trial, the therapist was acquitted of the charges, preventing the case against the statute from proceeding further (Denton, 1987b; F. Cavaiani, personal communication, August 13, 1992; R. Mulckenheim, personal communication, August 6, 1992; *People v. Cavaiani*, 1988, 1989).

In another case, *People v. Gray* (1986), a psychologist with an established practice had been seeing a family in which the parents sought treatment for help with their 13-year-old adopted son. Although he had been a part of this family since he was three years old, he had been a difficult child throughout and had not really bonded with the family. His behavior was frequently uncontrollable, marked by aggressive actions toward other children including his siblings.

In their efforts to manage his behavior, the parents resorted to using a time-out-like procedure as both a threat of punishment and an actual practice. They were placing the boy in a furnished but secluded area of the house when his behavior was out of control as a form of time-out. The punishment had not been effective, and the parents got to a point at which the boy was spending as many as seven days at a time secluded with the exception of being allowed out to go to school, eat meals, and bathe. The parents felt that their actions had become excessive and wanted to find more effective and kind ways to deal with their child. They sought help from the psychologist, who was focusing on parent-skills training and developing an appropriate behavior management program for the child.

The psychologist was aware of the mandatory reporting requirement in his state and had reported suspected abuse on numerous other occasions. He was aware of the limited resources available to the child protective team and of the potential their investigative procedures had to be aversive to children and families. He chose not to report, believing that this was in the best interest of the child, and therefore his most ethical course of action.

Within a few months of treatment, the local department of social services received a report of suspected child neglect concerning this family from a neighbor. During the course of the investigation the psychologist was interviewed and offered his full cooperation. The social service agency substantiated child maltreatment and proceeded to place two adopted children, one of whom had not been implicated in the maltreatment, in foster care. Subsequently, a district court judge ordered the children to remain in foster care pending further investigation. This same judge issued two warrants for the arrest of the psychologist on two charges of contributing to the delinquency of a minor. Just three days later, the judge signed two more warrants for the psychologist's arrest for failure to report suspected abuse.

The psychologist was arrested in the midst of a session with a different family. The assistant district attorney in the case had been quoted in a local newspaper as saying that the arrest was intended to teach professionals a lesson. The case went to trial after the psychologist refused to settle out of court. Although the judge dropped the contributing to delinquency charges, the psychologist was found guilty on one count of failure to report suspected abuse. The judge stated, "A psychologist shouldn't be the omnipotent one who decides totally what's in the child's best interest" (Newman, 1987). The judge ruled that general misdemeanor penalties be applied, including a $200 fine, and he issued a Prayer for Continued Judgement (PCJ), meaning the case would be removed from court records. The psychologist, however, wanted to appeal the decision and it is not possible to do so without a conviction. The psychologist therefore refused to pay the fine, which in turn forced a conviction, allowing him to appeal the case. The psychologist was then sentenced to one month in jail and one year of supervised probation, although the judge suspended the jail sentence. The psychologist did appeal and his case was dismissed by a higher court (Denton, 1987a; Gray, 1987; A. Gray, personal communication, July 15, 1992).

In a third case, *People v. Hedberg* (1990), a seven-year-old girl living with her mother and stepfather was being treated for a number of behavior problems, including aggressiveness, lying, acting out oppositionally, and achieving only minimal progress in school. The girl also frequently experienced encopresis and enuresis. In addition, she had developed several health related problems that were being treated by a pediatrician, including body rashes and urinary tract infections. She also began inserting toys and other objects into her vagina.

The family constellation in this case was complex. The girl's mother had gone through a difficult divorce three years earlier, with conflicts that persisted at the time of the girl's treatment. The girl lived with her mother, who had custody of her, and her stepfather. The girl's biological father had also remarried. Both parents regularly fought over the father's visitation.

Through a court referral to assist in settling the custody dispute, the psychologist was consulted to mediate the resolution and treat the child. During this time, the child lived for brief periods with each parent in an effort to work out a visitation agreement. Treatment, which included working with the parents on appropriate child management, positive discipline procedures, and age-appropriate expectations, seemed to progress, with the child's behavior and school problems improving. During this time, the girl became somewhat more partial to living with her father, who was quick to offer his affection toward her.

Six months into treatment, the mother phoned the psychologist and said that the child had stated to her that the girl's stepfather "stuck his finger up my butt" in the middle of the night. The girl followed this statement by saying "now I can go live with Daddy." The psychologist was told by the mother that the girl made the remarks during a time that she had been playing with a neighbor boy who accused his stepfather of a similar act, which had resulted in his living with his father. The girl knew of these events and their outcome, and her mother told the psychologist that she believed they motivated her daughter's statements.

The mother brought the girl in to see the psychologist and recounted the story to him. The mother was angry and did not believe her daughter's accusation. She also explained that it was routine for her husband to check the girl's bed for wetness due to the enuresis and to assist her to the bathroom at night. In an interview with the psychologist, the child did not describe any acts of penetration. The girl said she had wet the bed the evening of the alleged abuse and did go to the bathroom to clean up. The child also said to the psychologist that she was not frightened of her stepfather. The psychologist assessed her motivations for her statements and discerned that no one had told her what to say and what not to say to him. The child could not provide any details of what had happened that night, other than general statements about touching, which presumably happened while she slept.

The father and stepmother were advised of the girl's statements and neither of them believed them to be true. They agreed to observe the girl when she was with them and watch for any new problems. The girl's pediatrician was consulted to examine her, and reported no indications of sexual abuse. The child did not mention the abuse again for two months and did not report any further indications of molestation.

Two months after the original allegation, the child made similar statements to her teacher, alleging that her stepfather had touched her in sexual ways. The girl's mother informed the psychologist of this new allegation, again denying its validity. Because the remarks were made to a person who did not have any input into the custody decision, the psychologist decided to take specific action. The psychologist called the stepfather, who categorically denied the allegation. Then the psychologist notified the parents that the incident was being reported to the state office of social services, and the psychologist proceeded to report.

Social services substantiated sexual abuse by the stepfather and the local police were so informed. The stepfather was subsequently arrested and pleaded guilty to one count of child molestation. The psychologist was also subsequently arrested for failure to report suspected abuse. Although he did in fact report, the district attorney premised the case on the earlier signs of abuse that went unreported. The case went to trial and the psychologist's defense was based on a hierarchy of abuse symptoms that a number of other psychologists stated would not have constituted reasonable cause to suspect abuse. The psychologist also used the literature on false allegations of abuse in custody disputes as a part of his defense. The psychologist was eventually acquitted (Ebert, 1992; Hedberg, 1991). However, professional sanctions were subsequently filed against the psychologist by the state's psychological association (A. Hedberg, personal communication, July 23, 1992).

Several features are shared by these three cases in which psychotherapists were charged with failure to report suspected child abuse. In each case a mandated reporter was made aware of an abusive situation through a verbal disclosure or description of the child's conditions. In all three cases the professionals were aware of the mandatory reporting law in their state. All three psychotherapists also had previous professional experience with the child protection system. In two of the three cases, Cavaiani and Hedberg, additional mandated reporters were aware of the situation but were not charged with failure to report. In all three cases the professionals were also found not guilty of failure to report. These cases serve to illustrate how legal standards of reasonable suspicion do not translate to professional settings, particularly those of psychological assessment and psychotherapy. Vague legal thresholds for reporting leave mandated reporters to define their professional standards for reporting. In each case, the professional believed that their actions were ethical and their decision making was sound. The way that mandated reporting fits within professional ethics codes and a detailed account of report decision-making processes are discussed in the next two chapters.

CONCLUSION

Mandatory reporting legislation was enacted to specifically require physicians working with children to report injuries they might otherwise not acknowledge as possible abuse. In that respect, mandated reporting has been successful. Dramatic increases in reporting rates have occurred since the first reporting laws went into effect, and this has also been seen in countries outside of the U.S. In fact, the rise in reports has exceeded the child protection system's resources available to intervene in cases of child maltreatment (Besharov, 1990; M. Levine & A. Levine, 1992; Newberger, 1983). Following the logic of the original reporting statutes, more recent and broader laws have resulted in further increases in reporting.

The greatest difficulty with mandatory reporting laws appears to be their interaction with the context of mental health services and behavioral sciences. The settings and relationships within which suspected maltreatment occurs are qualitatively different from that of emergency medicine and even pediatrics, the original targets of the legislation. Mental health professionals and other nonmedical human service professionals are unlikely to detect the battered child syndrome, although they are likely to be exposed to circumstances that raise substantive suspicions of various types of child abuse. In addition, mental health professionals often rely solely on their observations of behavior in making determinations about child maltreatment. Concerns about privacy, trust, and respect play a crucial role in mental health professionals' dissatisfaction with mandated reporting. The vague wording of the statutes overgeneralizes across many nonabusive situations seen by mental health professionals.

Despite the many difficulties posed by required reporting, few have suggested a complete reversal of the legislation, allowing professionals full discretion in reporting suspected maltreatment. Rather, many observers have called for legislative reform, such as clarifying definitions of abuse and neglect, as well as the circumstances that warrant reporting (Jones & Welch, 1989; Melton & Davidson, 1987; Meriwether, 1986). Others have suggested that professionals working with families toward stopping the abuse not be required to report (Ansell & Ross, 1990), and some have called for allowing professionals with expertise in child abuse certain degrees of flexibility in reporting (Finkelhor & Zellman, 1991). Still others claim that the current laws would function adequately if the child protection system had sufficient resources to manage the reports. Given the complexity of the issues, it is unlikely that any one answer will be found to address the child protection roles of mandated reporters. Rather, a combination of factors seems necessary, such as clarification of the laws and a greater social commitment to the child protection system (Hutchison, 1993).

Among mandated reporters, the welfare of children and families is the most important consideration in decisions to report or not to report suspected child abuse. Reporting decisions are approached carefully, with consideration given to the specific constraints of the situation, the professional's previous reporting experiences, and the family circumstances. Professionals are most likely to do what they view as being in the best interest of those they serve. Professionals who are fully aware of their legal mandate to report, however, may be unlikely to report when reporting is perceived as an ethical dilemma.

2

MANDATED REPORTING AS AN ETHICAL DILEMMA

I find it difficult to report abuse. On the one hand, I feel I must report quickly if a child is in danger. But on the other hand, reporting disrupts treatment, ruins relationships among family members, and the child protection system often acts punitively, even if the family is making therapeutic progress. I often struggle not knowing if abuse has occurred, especially when I have young children as clients. (Survey participant, Kalichman & Brosig, 1993)

The decision to report suspected abuse is a tough one. Reporting can disrupt therapy and damage rapport with clients. However, I feel protection of the child is my highest priority. In most cases I have been involved with, I have been able to work through the family's anger toward me by careful explanation of my ethical and legal responsibilities. (Survey participant, Kalichman & Brosig, 1992)

Human service professionals in general, and psychologists in particular, frequently refer to reporting suspected abuse as an ethical dilemma. A national survey of American Psychological Association (APA) members showed that issues of confidentiality were the most frequently encountered ethical dilemmas, constituting 18% of all ethically troubling situations, and that reporting suspected child abuse was among the most common confidentiality problems (Pope & Vetter, 1992). These results mirrored those reported in an earlier national survey of psychologists, in which 45% of respondents indicated that breaking confidentiality to report suspected child maltreatment was a common occurrence, and 35% stated that it was of questionable ethical behavior to do so (Pope, Tabachnick, & Keith-Spiegel, 1987). These findings have been obtained in other surveys of psychologists (Haas, Malouf, & Mayerson, 1986, 1988). In a similar study of family therapists, Green and Hansen (1989) found that reporting suspected child abuse was the most ethically significant clinical situation experienced.

Studies of professional–ethical decisions have consistently found a discrepancy between what professionals believe they should do and what they say they would do when faced with an ethical dilemma (Smith, McGuire, Abbott, & Blau, 1991; Wilkins, McGuire, Abbott, & Blau, 1990). Professionals who recognize the ethically expected course of action in ethical dilemmas tend to do less to resolve the conflict than they believe they could do (Smith et al., 1991). For the most part, professionals have indicated that internal standards and characteristics of specific situations influence their decisions to act outside of professional–ethical guidelines. However, unlike many other common ethical dilemmas, such as knowledge of an impaired colleague and dual relationships, acting outside of mandated child abuse reporting involves breaking the law. It is the legal requirement to report suspected child abuse that sets it apart from most other ethical problems.

Reporting frequently becomes an ethical dilemma as a result of complex interactions among several factors including diverse professional contexts, legal requirements, professional–ethical standards, and the circumstances of suspected abuse. The reporting dilemma also reflects the fact that breaching confidentiality and breaking the law both constitute unethical behavior (Bersoff, 1975). In addition to issues of confidentiality, mandated reporters functioning as helping professionals may perceive reporting as an unnecessary threat to professional services (Newberger, 1983). Professionals who suspect abuse may also feel that having a reasonable suspicion, although required by law, is not enough to report. Human service professionals also find themselves in the precarious situation of seeking further information to justify reporting in response to vague statutes, despite the fact that the law does not require them to do so, and that such actions may compromise their roles as helping professionals. Each of these ethical concerns—confidentiality, consequences of reporting, and diluting professional roles—are now considered.

CONFIDENTIALITY AND REPORTING SUSPECTED CHILD ABUSE

Reporting suspected child maltreatment has been most closely linked to breaching confidentiality. In professional practice, assurances of confidentiality are often regarded as necessary for the development of therapeutic relationships (Heymann, 1988; Smith & Meyer, 1984). In research contexts, guarantees that sensitive information will remain confidential are critical for participants to feel comfortable enough to reveal personal information. Procedures that assure confidentiality are therefore thought to be essential to the collection of valid research data (Turner, 1982). Thus, confidentiality is believed to allow for the revelation of the most private information, and maintaining confidentiality is well recognized as a standard of professional conduct. The APA has stated:

> Psychologists have a primary obligation to respect the confidentiality of information obtained from persons in the course of their work as psychologists. They reveal such information to others only with the consent of the person or person's legal representative, except in those unusual circumstances in which not to do so would result in clear danger to the person or to others. Where appropriate, psychologists inform their clients of the legal limits of confidentiality. (APA, 1990, pp. 392–393)

The *Ethical Principles of Psychologists and Code of Conduct* of the APA (1992) has retained this standard, stating that "psychologists have a primary obligation and take reasonable precautions to respect the confidentiality rights of those with whom they work or consult, recognizing that confidentiality may be established by law, institutional rules, or professional or scientific relationships" (APA, 1992, Standard 5.02). The Ethics Code also states that "psychologists disclose confidential information without the consent of the individual only as mandated by law, or where permitted by law for a valid purpose" (Standard 5.05a).

Confidentiality is defined as "the general standard of professional conduct that obliges a professional not to discuss information about a client with anyone" (Keith-Spiegel & Koocher, 1985, p. 57). Therefore, confidentiality is a professional–ethical concern. Confidentiality is not to be confused with privileged communication, which is "a legal term that describes the quality of certain specific types of relationships that prevent information, acquired from such relationships, from being disclosed in court or other legal proceedings" (Keith-Spiegel & Koocher, 1985, p. 58). The provision of confidentiality is common throughout human service professions and is widely held as a therapeutic necessity (Watkins, 1989), and a basic foundation in research with human participants (Turner, 1982). It is believed that only within a confidential relationship can persons freely disclose, build trust, and not be sanctioned for saying things that would otherwise be left unsaid.

In addition to holding information confidential, professional standards dictate that persons are to be informed, when appropriate, of the legal limits of confidentiality. Specifically, the Ethics Code states:

> Psychologists discuss with persons and organizations with whom they establish a scientific or professional relationship (including to the extent feasible, minors and their legal representatives) (1) the relevant limitations on confidentiality, including limitations where applicable in group, marital, and family therapy, or in organizational consulting, and (2) the foreseeable uses of the information generated through their services. (APA, 1992, Standard 5.01a)

Similar to psychologists' ethics, the *Code of Ethics* for social workers states that "the Social Worker should inform clients fully about the limits of confidentiality in a given situation, the purpose for which information is obtained, and how it may be used" (National Association of Social Workers, 1980, pp. 5–6). Informing persons about the limits of confidentiality does present some practical challenges. Professionals must avoid undermining the concept of confidentiality while also upholding the obligation of sharing information with social agents responsible for intervening when necessary, as is the case with suspected child maltreatment (Taylor & Adelman, 1989). Although informed consent is widely advocated (Butz, 1985; Keith-Spiegel & Koocher, 1985; Kelly, 1987; Koocher & Keith-Spiegel, 1990; O'Connor, 1989; Stadler, 1989), several studies have shown that informing clients of the limits of confidentiality is not a consistent practice among psychologists. For example, Baird and Rupert (1987) found that only about 50% of practicing psychologists surveyed informed clients of the limits of confidentiality, and 12% usually told clients that everything discussed in treatment was confidential.

Persons of all ages who disclose information in a confidential setting have a right to be informed of the limits of confidentiality. Informing minors about limited confidentiality, however, carries a number of additional complications, such as their willingness to discuss issues about their relationship with their parents. In a survey of practicing psychologists, Beeman and Scott (1991) found that 70% of participants obtained informed consent from adolescent clients, including an understanding of limited confidentiality. Beeman and Scott also found that limited confidentiality was rated by professionals as the single most important element of informed consent for both adolescents and adults. However, children and adolescents involved in treatment and research require parental consent. This raises the possibility that when a parent is informed of limited confidentiality for what his or her child may say, the parent may interfere with, or even discontinue the child's participation, particularly if the parent is an abusive or neglectful one who would fear possible disclosure. For example, a parent may badger a child about what is being said in therapy, or tell the child that the social service workers will take him or her away to foster care for telling family secrets. Still, professionals indicate that informed consent, including limited confidentiality, is necessary and has the potential benefit of enhancing a sense of autonomy that can help build therapeutic relationships (Beeman & Scott, 1991).

Methods used for informing clients of limited confidentiality vary widely. Psychologists who have previously experienced problems resulting from breached confidentiality are more likely to inform clients about limited confidentiality than are psychologists who have not experienced such problems (Baird & Rupert, 1987). Fifty-nine percent of practicing psychologists in one large survey believed that their clients were at least somewhat aware of professionals' requirements to report suspected abuse (Brosig, 1992), suggesting that professionals may not believe it is necessary to inform them of limited confidentiality with respect to mandated reporting. Although there is no existing standard regarding a format for informing clients of limited confidentiality, there are some noteworthy suggestions.

The APA's Ethics Code states that informing persons of confidentiality and the limits of confidentiality should occur at the outset of professional and scientific relationships. Specifically, the code states that "unless it is not foreseeable or is contraindicated, the discussion of confidentiality occurs at the outset of the relationship and thereafter as new circumstances may warrant" (APA, 1992, Standard 5.01b). Keith-Spiegel and Koocher (1985) stated this position prior to the new Ethics Code, suggesting that professionals discuss the limits of confidentiality as early in relationships as possible, such as during initial interviews. They also advise that possible breaches of confidentiality be considered carefully by professionals and discussed openly with clients.

The specific statement of limited confidentiality will vary among individual professionals and professional settings and will be influenced by the characteristics of the person to be informed. An example of a verbal explanation concerning exceptions to confidentiality that may be appropriate for children and adolescents is provided by Taylor and Adelman (1989):

> Although most of what we talk about is private, there are three kinds of problems you might tell me about that we would have to talk about with other people. If I find out that someone has been seriously hurting or abusing you, I would have to tell the police about it. If you tell me you have made a plan to seriously hurt yourself, I would have to let your parents know. If you tell me you have made a plan to seriously hurt someone else, I would have to warn that person. I would not be able to keep these problems just between you and me because the law says I can't. (p. 80)

Taylor and Adelman (1989) also suggest that the limits of confidentiality be framed to emphasize what can be discussed confidentially in order to facilitate the open sharing of information.

Keith-Spiegel and Koocher (1985) and Wilcoxon (1991) both note that clients may best be informed of limited confidentiality in writing. As an example, the Judge Baker Children's Center (1990) in Boston has constructed a pamphlet that they give out to clients entitled *Privacy and Confidentiality in Mental Health Services.* Among 11 other circumstances that involve limited confidentiality, including situations of duty to warn and child custody, the pamphlet states:

> If the clinician, in his professional capacity, has reasonable cause to believe that a child under the age of eighteen years is suffering serious physical or emotional injury resulting from abuse inflicted upon the child (including sexual abuse), or from neglect (including malnutrition), or who is determined to be dependent upon an addictive drug at birth, the clinician is required to report information to the Massachusetts Department of Social Services. (p. 3)

An alternative procedure is to provide a signed informed consent form at the outset of treatment, much like those used routinely in research settings. A form that describes all of the conditions and expectations of treatment, including limited confidentiality and appropriate releases of information, would serve to make clear all of these issues and limitations. With respect to child abuse reporting requirements, a statement can be included to the effect that:

> What is discussed in therapy is confidential unless and until you give consent to its release, with two exceptions: I will need, and am compelled by law, to inform an appropriate other person(s) if I hear that you are in danger of hurting yourself or someone else, and if there is a reasonable suspicion that a child has been abused. (California State Department of Social Services, 1991, p. 24)

Like the use of a pamphlet, an informed consent form details the conditions of treatment and can prevent later misunderstandings. Although pamphlets and forms can be of great use in structuring information and assuring that all relevant points are covered, they do not necessarily replace a discussion of confidentiality and its limits (Pope & Vasquez, 1991). Open discussions allow the professional to assess the recipient's understanding of confidentiality, as well as to invite questions and comments. Thus, persons can be informed through discussion in addition to being provided with a written explanation of confidentiality.

To the extent that reporting suspected child maltreatment involves breaking confidentiality in order to protect others, the responsibility to report suspected abuse has some things in common with the duty to warn (Besharov, 1986a; Newman, 1987). Professional obligation to warn a third party of known potential danger has been widely discussed, particularly with reference to the case of *Tarasoff v. Board of Regents of the University of California* (1976; Koocher, 1988). Responsibility to protect intended victims from harm is the characteristic that joins mandatory reporting with the duty to warn (Besharov, 1986a; Bross, 1983).

Cases of duty to warn place professional standards of confidentiality against the necessity to protect others. In this sense, reporting child maltreatment may be considered a special case of duty to warn. Reporting necessarily involves breaching confidentiality, preventing personal harm, and abiding by legal constraints on professional courses of action. Reporting suspected child abuse appears most like a case of duty to warn when the source of the information is an adult suspected of being abusive. In child maltreatment, however, a child welfare agency receives the warning and responds on behalf of the child. As can be the case in duty to warn, reports of suspected child abuse can be used as a part of criminal prosecution procedures (Leong, Eth, & Silva, 1992). However, mandatory reporting is different from most cases of duty to warn because reporting suspected abuse is, for the most part, a legal obligation with ethical implications, whereas most other situations of duty to warn are ethical obligations with legal implications.[1] Also, situations involving suspected child maltreatment appear to be more ambiguous than most cases of duty to warn, which usually result from a verbal disclosure of intent to harm. Reporting suspected abuse is also more likely to occur across a range of professional settings outside of psychotherapy.

Problems of limited confidentiality like those in clinical settings may also arise in research settings. Contrary to the common belief that researchers are not mandated reporters (Kinard, 1985), state laws do not make this exclusion. Rather, most laws provide a list of professionals who are required to report when in their professional or occupational capacities they know of or have reason to suspect child maltreatment. Thus, to the extent that research is considered a professional activity, most states include health-related researchers as mandated reporters.

The APA Ad Hoc Committee on Child Abuse Policy (Walker, Alpert, Harris, & Koocher, 1989) also noted the conflict that researchers may experience in reporting suspected child maltreatment:

> Gaps in knowledge and need for further research in the area of child abuse and neglect are considerable. Particular tensions involve efforts by investigators and institutional review boards to protect the privacy and social rights of research participants, while also remaining appropriately responsive to legal reporting requirements. (p. 12)

---

[1]Some states have enacted statutes that mandate duty to warn third parties and police of "serious threat of physical violence against a reasonably identifiable victim." For example, California enacted such a statute, Assembly Bill No. 1133, section 43.92 (1985).

Thus, not unlike clinical situations, confidentiality in the research context results in a balancing act when it comes to mandated reporting.

Abuse may be discovered in research settings if information is obtained indicating that a child may be a victim (Kinard, 1985) or an adult may be a perpetrator (Kalichman, 1991). In either case, the APA's *Ethical Principles* stated:

> Information obtained about research participants during the course of an investigation is confidential unless otherwise agreed upon in advance. When the possibility exists that others may obtain access to such information, this possibility, together with the plans for protecting confidentiality, is explained to the participant as a part of the procedure for obtaining informed consent. (APA, 1990, p. 395)

In studies in which the discovery of an abusive situation is likely, such as research in delinquency or domestic violence, or with perpetrators or victims of abuse, informed consent would most likely include limits of confidentiality regarding suspected child maltreatment. However, any situation that involves contact with children or adults can reveal circumstances indicating abuse, particularly when sensitive information is collected in a confidential setting. It is, therefore, those situations in which an unexpected discovery of abuse occurs that the researcher is faced with issues of breaching confidentiality. Thus, information gained in research, as well as practice, may pose ethical challenges.

The APA seems to recognize the complexity of standards of confidentiality in situations in which abuse is suspected. The APA's Ad Hoc Committee on Child Abuse Policy (Walker et al., 1989) wrote:

> There was unanimous agreement that the APA should have a clearer policy that strongly supports the basic principle that the social policy of protecting children from the enormous damage to a child's physical and mental well-being and subsequent development inflicted by abuse outweighs the important social policies supporting the protection of confidentiality of the therapy relationship and protection of the projected disruption of the therapy relationship that can result from such mandatory reporting. (p. 4)

Similar sentiments are found in APA's standards for confidentiality in research. The Committee for the Protection of Human Participants in Research stated:

> The protection afforded research participants by the maintenance of confidentiality may be compromised when the investigator discovers information that serious harm threatens the research participant or others. The obligation to make this information known to research participants, their associates, or legal authorities nonetheless creates an ethical dilemma in consideration of the promised maintenance of strict confidentiality. (APA, 1982, p. 72)

The experience of reporting suspected abuse as an ethical dilemma, therefore, is directly tied to two central issues related to confidentiality. First, as discussed earlier, confidentiality constitutes a core component of the value system ascribed to by human service professionals and researchers with human participants. Second, to be discussed next, is the role that professionals believe confidentiality plays in the quality of their work. Among other things, reporting decisions are affected by the degree to which breaches in confidentiality are perceived by professionals to have adverse affects on service delivery.

PERCEIVED AND ACTUAL EFFECTS OF REPORTING ON SERVICE DELIVERY

Motivated primarily to assist others, human service professionals are expected to act in the best interest of those they serve. If reporting suspected abuse is perceived by professionals as deleterious to the progress of their services, it should be expected that they will hesitate to report (Newberger, 1983). Because confidentiality is held as a necessary component of helping relationships (R. Weinstock & D. Weinstock, 1989), some have recommended that professionals err on the side of maintaining confidence as opposed to making disclosures (Watkins, 1989). Similarly, others have pointed to reporting suspected abuse as only one of many viable options available to mandated reporters (Ansell & Ross, 1990).

Contributing to the dilemma faced by professionals is the conflict between doing what is best for clients, families, and treatment, and acting in accordance with the law, almost as if these were all different things. Surveys of professional psychologists have shown that concerns about potential adverse effects on therapy are influential in reporting. Kalichman et al. (1989) found that 42% of licensed psychologists surveyed believed that reporting suspected abuse has negative consequences with respect to the progress of family therapy. Nearly one third of licensed psychologists in another study rated safeguarding the process of therapy as a relatively important report decision-making consideration (Kalichman & Craig, 1991). One participant in the Kalichman and Craig study commented, "If a family makes a commitment to treatment following a disclosure of abuse, I typically will not report unless the family drops out of treatment or fails to make use of treatment. I feel there is more to be gained therapeutically this way." These same sentiments were held by two of the three professionals discussed in chapter 1 who were arrested for failure to report.

Concerns about adverse effects on therapy, however, appear less important in reporting than other factors. Brosig and Kalichman (1992a) found that protecting children and clinical judgment were rated as more important influences than concerns about therapy in decisions to report suspected abuse, whereas lacking evidence of abuse was more important than therapy concerns in decisions not to report. Thus, although factors are weighted differently in decisions to report and decisions not to report suspected child maltreatment, concerns related to interrupting services are not the most important in either case.

Perceptions of the impact of reporting suspected child abuse may affect subsequent decisions to report. Kalichman and Craig (1991) found that psychologists who had at some point reported abuse perceived the effects of reporting as most negative for the progress of therapy, relative to its effects on the child, family, and stopping the occurrence of abuse. A full one third of participants in that study believed their reporting abuse had harmful effects on therapy (Kalichman & Craig, 1991).

The perceived relative affects of reporting, as compared with perceptions of not reporting, were investigated by Brosig and Kalichman (1992a). Eighty-one practicing psychologists who had both reported suspected child abuse and decided not to report a different case of suspected abuse rated their perceptions of the effects of both decisions on the child, family, outcome of therapy, and the maintenance of trust in therapy. Brosig and Kalichman found that there were no differences in relative perceived effects of reporting and not reporting on the child and on the outcome of therapy. However, reporting was perceived as more damaging to families and trust in therapy as compared with not reporting. Interestingly, treatment outcome and trust in therapy were viewed to be affected differently, suggesting that various dimensions of treatment may be differentially affected by reporting. It also suggests that other factors that vary in treatment settings play a role in reporting, such as whether the client is a suspected victim, a perpetrator, or a third party.

Suspected abuse may occur when the source of the suspicion is a child/victim or an adult/perpetrator. In either case, issues concerning interruption and interference with services seem to apply. The implication of informed limits of confidentiality do, however, seem slightly different under the two circumstances. A child may disclose abuse, either explicitly or through subtle signs, seeking protection and assistance. On the other hand, children may avoid making such disclosures out of fear of further abuse. With respect to adults in treatment, hiding abuse in fear of reporting and investigation is most likely, although some perpetrators may admit abuse to seek treatment. Warning clients in treatment that information they volunteer regarding previous acts of abuse that have not been reported will be required to be reported is both an ethical and a legal standard (Miller & Weinstock, 1987; R. Weinstock & D. Weinstock, 1989). Such informed consent regarding limited confidentiality may, however, induce a sense of fear and avoidance among perpetrators. On this basis, mandatory reporting laws have been discussed as discouraging abusers from seeking treatment

(Berlin et al., 1991; Miller & Weinstock, 1987; Smith & Meyer, 1984; R. Weinstock & D. Weinstock, 1989).

Two outdated state reporting statutes displayed sensitivity to these treatment issues by providing professional discretion in reporting (Heymann, 1988). Maine's law at one time permitted mandated reporters to fully use their professional discretion to not report information that emerged during the course of treatment. The statute read:

> This subsection does not require any person to report when the factual bases of knowing or suspecting child abuse or neglect came from treatment of the individual for suspected child abuse or neglect, the treatment was sought by the individual for a problem relating to child abuse or neglect, and, in the opinion of the person required to report, the child's life or health is not immediately threatened. (NCCAN, 1979, p. 10)

Similarly, Maryland's old law provided professional discretion when efforts were in progress to successfully end any potential risk of abuse or if it was believed that reporting would interfere with victims or perpetrators seeking assistance. Maryland's previous statute read:

> A person required to notify and report under the provisions of this section need not comply with the notification and reporting requirements of this section if: (1) Efforts are being made or will be made to alleviate the conditions or circumstances which may cause the child to be considered a neglected child and it is concluded by the health practitioner . . . that these efforts will alleviate these conditions or circumstances; or (2) The health practitioner . . . believes that the notification and reporting would inhibit the child, parent, guardian, or custodian from seeking assistance in the future and thereby be detrimental to the child's welfare. (NCCAN, 1979, pp. 9–10)

Maryland amended the statute to specifically exempt psychiatrists treating pedophiles from reporting:

> A health practitioner who specializes in the psychiatric treatment of pedophilia is not required to report sexual abuse if . . . reason to believe that a child has been subjected to sexual abuse is based exclusively on a report made to the health practitioner . . . providing psychiatric treatment to the individual for the purpose of curing the individual's pedophilia. (NCCAN, 1989, p. MD-13)

Thus, both Maine and Maryland's previous reporting statutes, in the spirit of child protection and abuse prevention, provided professionals with complete discretion and treated reporting decisions within the context of professional services. However, these two statutes underwent substantial reform in the late 1980s, with both laws broadened with respect to who is required to report. For example, the reformed statute in Maryland states that "all professionals and nonprofessionals are now required to report suspected neglect as well as suspected abuse" (Maryland Social Services Administration, 1988, p. 4).

After the legislative changes in Maryland, one study reported adverse effects of the new law on the treatment of perpetrators of sexual abuse. Berlin et al. (1991) found that self-disclosures of sexual abuse at their sexual offender/paraphilia treatment center changed dramatically as a result of the new reporting laws. From 1984 to 1987 Berlin et al.'s patients disclosed some 89 acts of sexual abuse during the course of treatment. However, after legislative reform in 1988 and 1989, the rate of self-disclosures dropped to an absolute zero. Berlin et al. expressed great alarm, claiming that "children at risk were not being identified by the disclosures of adult patients regardless of whether mandatory reporting was in effect. In this sense, mandatory reporting failed to achieve its desired intent of identifying and helping abused children" (p. 453). Berlin et al.'s findings support similar concerns expressed by others who have stated that laws that inhibit offender treatment put children at increased risk (Kelly, 1987; Priest & Wilcoxon, 1988; R. Weinstock & D. Weinstock, 1989).

Berlin et al.'s (1991) experience with Maryland's legislative changes was clearly not universal and may actually have been limited to their population and setting. Although self-disclosures by these repeat offenders, 55% of which were pedophiliac, ceased at this one treatment center, reports of sexual abuse increased in Maryland nearly 7% from 1988 to 1989 (see Figure 4). Also in contrast to Berlin et al.'s findings are studies that have shown that providing informed consent about the limits of confidentiality has little if any impact on a client's willingness to self-disclose (Muehleman, Pickens, & Robinson, 1985). These conflicting data point to Berlin et al.'s study as a special case, rather than a broad failure of the unlimited reporting requirements (Kalichman, 1991). However, Berlin et al.'s experience does illustrate the varied effects of a single legal standard on diverse professional settings.

Adults who are court-ordered for treatment present a number of additional complications. Because therapists tend to insist on an admission of abusive behavior as a precondition for successful treatment, court-ordered clients are often placed in a position in which their constitutional rights may be violated. Specifically, the Fifth Amendment states that "no person . . . shall be compelled in any criminal case to be witness against himself." Levine and Doherty (1991) detail the conditions under which an alleged perpetrator's rights may be placed in jeopardy. Levine and Doherty show that by refusing to admit abuse an adult may be seen as failing to comply with treatment, whereas admitting to abuse can be used as evidence against an adult in criminal and child custody cases. Thus, when a case is already progressing through the legal system, issues of confidentiality and disclosures of abuse are even more complex than cases outside the system.

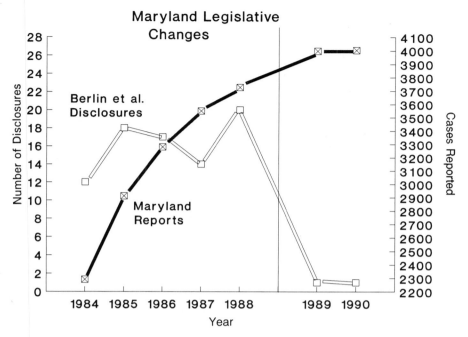

Figure 4: The relationship between data reported by Berlin et al. (1991) and cases of sexual abuse reported for the time period during Maryland's legislative change. Reprinted with permission.

Although surveys have shown that professionals perceive reporting to negatively affect therapy, and mandatory reporting laws may impede the treatment of perpetrators, little research has investigated the actual effects of reporting on human services. In a qualitative study of several clinical cases of child maltreatment, Harper and Irvin (1985) found that when cases were reported in the context of ongoing therapy, clients were unlikely to terminate treatment. Another study, which used a stronger retrospective methodology, also examined the effects of reporting suspected abuse on the progress of psychotherapy. Watson and Levine (1989) identified 65 cases of reported abuse from a child and adolescent outpatient psychiatric clinic. Reports of suspected abuse tended to occur early in the course of treatment, with more than 12% being reported at the initial interview and 50% occurring in the first three months of therapy. A careful review of the cases, including client drop out rates and quality of client–therapist relationships, as coded from clinical records, showed that most cases of mandated reporting did not have negative effects on the therapeutic alliance. Watson and Levine found that the majority of cases were unchanged as a result of the report, and nearly one third of cases showed positive outcomes from reporting. In particular, cases that were least affected were those in which the reported abuser was not the client in treatment, but rather a third party.

Watson and Levine (1989) also provided an interesting interpretation of their data. They stated that "it is possible, however, that it is trust, not absolute confidentiality, that is essential for the psychotherapeutic relationship. Trust may develop or be maintained even though confidentiality can not be guaranteed or has been breached" (p. 255). These findings and conclusions supported Harper and Irvin's (1985) suggestion that psychotherapy can benefit from reporting abusive behavior, despite breaching confidentiality. In addition, similar conclusions have been reached in a separate study that used detailed qualitative analyses of several clinical cases of reported abuse (Levine, Anderson, Terretti, Sharma, Steinberg, & Wallach, 1991; Levine, Anderson, Terretti, Steinberg, Sharma, & Wallach, 1991).

Results from Watson and Levine's (1989) study raise the issue that not reporting could have negative effects on client perceptions of trust in the therapy relationship (Van Eenwyk, 1990). Because professionals believe clients are aware of required reporting (Brosig, 1992), a professional who suspects abuse and chooses not to report may be interpreted by the client as being unwilling to get involved (Helfer, 1975). Thus, reporting suspected child abuse may have as much potential benefit as it does potential harm on therapeutic processes. Relative positive and negative effects of reporting on treatment most likely relate to the manner in which clients are informed of the limits of confidentiality, the sources of information leading to the suspicion, the quality of therapeutic alliance prior to reporting, and the degree to which the reporting process was integrated into therapy.

In summary, little evidence exists to support popular perceptions that reporting abuse has detrimental effects on the quality and efficacy of professional services. In fact, studies specifically addressing these issues in naturalistic settings find that reporting has minimal negative, and sometimes beneficial, effects on the treatment process. Still, the lack of research in this area and the known importance of confidentiality in therapeutic relationships suggests that any such conclusions remain tentative. As an ethical dilemma, reporting suspected child maltreatment may be professionally problematic for reasons outside of its effects on service delivery, such as the conflicts that may occur between the roles of helper and mandated reporter.

DILUTING PROFESSIONAL ROLES

Professionals, including psychologists, physicians, social workers, and counselors, conduct assessments and evaluations for the purposes of diagnosing a clinical problem and directing attention toward appropriate treatment options. In the case of child maltreatment, however, diagnostic decisions also carry reporting responsibilities. Thus, human service professionals often find themselves acting in the dual role of diagnostician and mandated reporter (Giovannoni, 1989a). Human service professionals are concerned foremost with the welfare of those they serve. Reporting suspected child abuse is in synch with the role of helping professional to the extent that reporting is in the best interest of the professional's client. Even when reporting is not perceived as being in the best interest of clients, the process of weighing alternatives related to client welfare is congruent with the roles of helping professionals.

Although they are not required to have knowledge of abuse, professionals tend to feel obligated to seek further information prior to reporting suspected child abuse. In one survey, 57% of responding licensed practicing psychologists indicated that they believed they had at least some ethical responsibility to find supportive information for the occurrence of abuse prior to reporting (Kalichman & Brosig, 1993). In addition, psychologists who have not reported a case of suspected child maltreatment at some point are more likely to believe they have an investigative role in determining abuse before reporting (Kalichman & Brosig, 1993). However, professionals who have reached a level of reasonable suspicion but not reported because they have not backed up their suspicion with evidence are in noncompliance with reporting laws. Thus, gathering evidence of abuse is not among the expected roles of mental health professionals.

Role conflict occurs when expectations of two or more roles are incompatible with each other (Kitchener, 1988). Professionals may experience conflicts between their perceived responsibilities as mandated reporters and their roles of helper, service provider, and keeper of sensitive information. Despite the fact that mandatory reporting laws require that reasonable suspicions of abuse be reported, and immunity is granted for reports filed, professionals are often compelled to obtain some degree of certainty before reporting abuse (Kalichman et al., 1989). Seeking further information before reporting is likely motivated by beliefs about the effects of investigations on families and professional services (Zellman, 1990), as well as wanting to make accurate reports concerning individuals professionals have committed themselves to helping.

Professionals who hold noninvestigative roles, including those employed by schools, hospitals, and mental health centers, may diffuse their professional identity and roles when they seek information about abuse to justify reporting. In addition, because most practitioners have not acquired adequate skills to investigate the occurrence of abuse, they may be overstepping their boundaries by doing so. The APA's *Ethical Principles* states that "psychologists recognize the boundaries of their competence and the limitations of their techniques. They only provide services and only use techniques for which they are qualified by training and experience" (APA, 1990, p. 390). Similarly, the new APA Ethics Code states that services are provided within competence based on "education, training, supervised experience, or appropriate professional experience" (APA, 1992, Standard

1.04a). Seeking to validate the occurrence of abuse is a specialized area of forensic evaluation, and as such requires specific skills and training (Conte, 1992). Thus, therapists who seek to investigate abuse when existing signs have surpassed a reasonable suspicion are likely to be functioning outside of their professional competence, rendering their conclusions regarding the occurrence of abuse of limited value.

Potential role conflicts in reporting suspected child maltreatment are widely recognized. For example, Kempe et al. (1962) stated that physicians would be reluctant to take on a police function by investigating abuse. They noted that the training and character of physicians would make them unwilling to question parents about possible criminal behavior. Because these observations predated reporting laws, and because of the observed effect of the Kempe et al. paper on the design of reporting laws, it is apparent that requirements to report reasonable suspicions of child maltreatment relieve professionals of pressures to seek additional information in order to be required to report. The intent of the law is to identify a maximum number of abuse cases. However, it seems that in doing so the law also allows professionals to maintain their sense of professional identity. Limiting professional roles to those defined by training and specific practices, as well as to the roles expected by clients, will result in the least amount of role conflict and confusion (Melton & Limber, 1989). The experience of diluted professional roles in dealing with cases of child abuse, however, is also a common problem for professionals working within the child protection system.

Professionals who serve an investigative function in child protection experience role conflicts similar to those found among mandated reporters. Police, who act as crime fighters, will most likely focus their attention on determining criminal intent, although reasonable suspicion is required for reporting (Willis & Wells, 1988). Child protection service workers can also experience conflict between the roles of investigator and social service provider (Cook, 1991). It is therefore important to recognize the potential for role conflicts in complex cases of child abuse encountered by a variety of professions.

Role diffusion can be minimized by first defining activities that fall within a professional's capacity and then limiting practice to those activities. In the case of practicing psychologists, for example, roles should be limited to one of evaluator, therapist, or if employed in such a capacity, as investigator (Melton & Limber, 1989). When child abuse is suspected it is within the scope of the practitioners' roles to report. Suspicions of abuse in the professional context may be quite subtle, often resembling clinical hunches or clinical intuitions (Jones & Welch, 1989). However, standards for reporting reasonable suspicions imply a degree of discretion and evaluation. It is within a practitioner's professional role to follow up suspicions with questions and queries in the context of evaluation or treatment. Probing about important life events is a regular and frequent activity of treatment. However, seeking further information outside of treatment, or delaying reporting in the hope of gathering further information at a later time, aside from being in violation of the law, goes beyond the professional roles of evaluator, therapist, or researcher.

CONFLICTS BETWEEN REPORTING LAWS AND ETHICAL STANDARDS

In the case of mandated reporting, standards of confidentiality are limited by law. The fact that a substantial number of professionals do not report child maltreatment even when they are fairly certain of its occurrence points to a conflict between standards of ethical conduct and adherence to the law. The Ethics Code of the APA (1992) notes the potential for such conflict:

> In the process of making decisions regarding their professional behavior, psychologists must consider this [APA] Ethics Code, in addition to applicable laws and psychology board regulations. If the Ethics Code establishes a higher standard of conduct than is required by law, psychologists must meet the higher ethical standard. If the Ethics Code standard appears to conflict with the requirements of law, then psychologists make known their commitment to the Ethics Code and take steps to resolve the conflict in a reasonable manner. (Introduction)

Thus, psychologists, as well as other professionals, are expected to resolve legal–ethical conflicts to the higher standard of ethical conduct, and choosing not to report suspected child abuse has been discussed as the higher standard of behavior under some circumstances. A range of positions on civil disobedience as it is related to ethical conduct have been offered. Pope and Bajt (1988) found that it is not unusual for recognized experts in ethics to violate mandatory reporting laws, including 21% refusing to report suspected child abuse. Commenting on Pope and Bajt, Ansell and Ross (1990) stated a case for failure to report as a viable option for professionals concerned with the welfare of children and ethical practice. In response to Ansell and Ross, Kalichman (1990) suggested that, although problematic, mandatory reporting laws are the law and offer no alternative to reporting. However, Kalichman failed to discuss civil disobedience in a democracy as a viable option in professional conduct (Anonymous, 1992). Stated by an anonymous commentator:

> We psychologists seek to help the individuals who seek our services. We may care deeply about the welfare of children and the world in general. In fact, we hope that in the long run our work will help others as well as the client. But at those focused, intense times when we are

working with clients, we may not be able to be effective agents of the state or help abused children in accord with recent laws that do not place what we view as a sufficiently high value on confidential psychotherapy. (p. 3)[2]

Thus, failure to report under some circumstances, in treatment as well as research settings, may be viewed as a higher ethical standard than obeying reporting laws (Wells, 1988).

Civil disobedience as a part of the democratic process, however, is a public statement of unjust policy, as opposed to private actions in the service of a profession. For failure to report to be a statement of civil disobedience, professionals would need to openly criticize reporting laws and propose legislative reform. Professionals have publicly questioned the integrity of reporting laws (e.g., Berlin et al., 1991; Denton, 1987a, 1987b; Gray, 1987; Newman, 1987), but no case has proceeded far enough to actually challenge the constitutionality of reporting laws at a state level. Thus, whereas failure to report may or may not be considered an option for professionals, taking action toward legislative reform has been advocated as a professional role (e.g., Kalichman, 1990; O'Connor, 1989; Walker et al., 1989). In this respect, a reasonable manner of resolving conflicts between ethical standards and legal requirements may be to become proactive in legislative change and perhaps public defiance.

CONCLUSION

For the most part, mandatory reporting laws limit the degree to which professionals can exercise professional judgment when facing suspected child maltreatment. Ethics codes and professional guidelines offer little to assist mandated reporters. For example, suggesting that professionals "take steps to resolve the conflict [between ethics and the law] in a reasonable manner" (APA, 1992, Introduction), leaves mandated reporters on their own. Few psychologists receive any training in managing reports of suspected child maltreatment (Kalichman & Brosig, 1993). In addition, mandated reporting rarely receives more than one or two pages of coverage in even the most authoritative ethics books. Where then do professionals turn when facing difficult cases of suspected child abuse?

As an ethical dilemma, mandated reporting can be approached like other ethically questionable situations by consulting a colleague about the situation. Discussing the circumstances of the suspected maltreatment with a colleague brings in a second and perhaps more objective perspective. More

---

[2]The author wished to remain anonymous because of controversies surrounding mandated reporting in the state in which the author practices. The paper was obtained from the anonymous author after the author learned that this book was being prepared.

than 80% of practicing psychologists discuss cases of suspected child maltreatment with colleagues (Kalichman & Brosig, 1993). In fact, professionals who discuss cases with colleagues are substantially more likely to consistently report suspected child maltreatment, suggesting that such input can help clarify difficult circumstances.

A case can be made, however, for the position that mandated reporting is not an ethical dilemma at all. When professionals uniformly discuss limited confidentiality and then report all suspected abuse, professionals have met both their legal and ethical obligations. In addition, automatically reporting suspected maltreatment also bypasses the potential diluting of professional roles that can result from continued evaluation. However, such a blanket approach to reporting is more an exception or ideal than it is a rule or reality.

Unreported suspected child abuse occurs for a variety of reasons. Mandated reporters almost invariably reflect on the perceived welfare of children, families, and privacy rights in their reporting decisions. Professionals want their reports to be accurate in order to minimize the potential adverse effects from reporting. This level of discretion may be one reason for the high rate of substantiation among maltreatment cases reported by mandated reporters (Eckenrode, Powers, Doris, Munsch, & Bolger, 1988; Giovannoni, 1989a). Despite the law, professionals tend to feel a need to reach a level of certainty that maltreatment has occurred, or perhaps surpass a reporting threshold, prior to reporting (Kalichman & Craig, 1991; Kalichman et al., 1989). Conflicts regarding reporting reasonably suspected child maltreatment, protecting children, maintaining confidentiality, protecting the integrity of professional services, and acting within one's defined professional roles are complex, involving interactions among these interrelated factors. A further explication of professionals' report decision-making processes may, therefore, be of use in understanding some of these conflicts.

3

WHEN PROFESSIONAL HUNCHES BECOME REASONABLE SUSPICIONS: A REPORT DECISION-MAKING MODEL

I feel that professionals need to be reasonably sure before reporting. A skilled professional should be able to achieve this through insights derived from interviews with the child and family, as well as by observing any marks, physical signs or psychological symptoms. (Survey participant, Kalichman & Brosig, 1992)

I have trouble with the subtleties of language of the laws, aside from the ethical issues. I tend to overreport. I feel I do not need to make the final judgement about abuse, and would rather err on the side of false positives. (Survey participant, Brosig & Kalichman, 1992a)

These perspectives reflect the variability of standards set by professionals for reporting suspected abuse. The legal standard for mandated reporting, on the other hand, is consistently stated as having a *reasonable suspicion* of child abuse, or some similar terms. In this sense, the law does not presume that mandated reporters make reporting decisions, just that they report after reaching a level of reasonable suspicion. Human service professionals, however, do engage in decision making when confronted with

61

signs of child abuse (Finkelhor & Zellman, 1991). Evidence for reporting decision processes comes from professionals' hesitations to report and the numerous factors found to influence their reporting. Professionals, particularly those in the areas of treatment and evaluation, frequently experience intuitions or hunches in the course of their usual work. The difficult distinction to make between professional or clinical impressions and reasonable suspicions of abuse has been related to professionals' failure to report (Jones & Welch, 1989). Further, unreported suspicions of abuse may result when professionals interpret the legal standard of reasonable suspicion as categorically different, or at a different end of a continuum, from subjective professional hunches (Finlayson & Koocher, 1991).

Efforts to explain professional decisions to report suspected child maltreatment have been limited to conceptual models that attempt to summarize factors that influence reporting. For example, Willis and Wells (1988) developed a model for understanding police officer compliance with mandatory child abuse reporting laws. In their model, Willis and Wells differentiated between legal and extralegal factors related to reporting. Among legal factors relevant to police work, Willis and Wells included the severity of abuse, as it is related to legal definitions and requirements, and officer knowledge of reporting laws. Among extralegal factors were characteristics of officers, such as length of service, education, attitudes, and marital and parenting status; situational factors, including victim and perpetrator social class; organizational factors, including formal reporting procedures and institutional support for reporting; and officer attitudes and experiences regarding reporting, such as experiences with child welfare and beliefs about the outcome of reporting. Willis and Wells framed their model on the premise that police frequently underreport suspected child maltreatment and confront reporting decisions from a crime fighter's perspective, focusing on severity of abuse and criminal intent.

Brosig and Kalichman (1992b) subsequently adapted Willis and Wells' (1988) model to similarly explain practicing psychologists' reporting of suspected child maltreatment. Brosig and Kalichman excluded several factors and added others in order for their model to specifically apply to clinicians. This model highlighted legal requirements, clinician characteristics, and situational factors related to reporting. Together, Willis and Wells', and Brosig and Kalichman's models encompass most of the conditions identified in reporting decisions made by human service professionals. An integration of the models proposed by Willis and Wells and Brosig and Kalichman is presented in Figure 5. The components of the model represent influences on reporting decisions, including characteristics of the suspected maltreatment, legal requirements to report, individual characteristics of the mandated reporter, and professional–organizational structures that may facilitate or inhibit reporting. In the model, double arrows represent reciprocal

SITUATION
INFLUENCES
• Victim Attributes
• Type of Abuse
• Severity of Abuse
• Available Evidence

LEGAL
FACTORS
• Knowledge of the Law
• Statutory Wording
• Legal Requirements

PROFESSIONAL
CHARACTERISTICS
• Years Experience
• Training
• Experience Reporting

ORGANIZATIONAL
FACTORS
• Ethical Guidelines
• Formal Reporting
• Institutional Policy
• Support for Reporting

DECISION TO REPORT
SUSPECTED ABUSE

Figure 5: A model of factors that influence professionals' child maltreatment reporting decisions.

relationships between components and the decision outcome. Although of descriptive value, models that detail factors influencing reporting, like the one shown in Figure 5, have provided little information regarding the report decision-making process.

Reporting suspected abuse appears similar to other types of diagnostic decision making. Although one third of mandated reporters who participate in survey studies indicate having not reported suspected child maltreatment, Muehleman and Kimmons (1981) proposed that most professionals will report immediately when the circumstances appear to warrant reporting. Muehleman and Kimmons suggested that professionals surpass a critical degree of suspicion, or a reporting threshold, prior to reporting. Others have made similar observations regarding cumulative perceptions and judgements in reporting decisions (Herzberger, 1988; Wells, 1988). Support for a reporting threshold is found in experimental vignette studies that show cumulative effects of salient indicators of abuse on reporting tendencies (Brosig & Kalichman, 1992b; Kalichman et al., 1989). Thus, as evidence of abuse increases, professionals become more inclined to report, as would be expected when surpassing a reporting threshold.

Among experimental studies, Finlayson and Koocher (1991) provide some of the strongest support for the concept of a reporting threshold. In a study of professional psychologists with extensive child–clinical backgrounds, Finlayson and Koocher showed that clinical signs specific to sexual abuse were significantly more likely to be reported than diffuse and nonspecific signs. Finlayson and Koocher demonstrated incremental increases in reporting that directly reflected signs of sexual abuse. This study suggested that clinicians view suspicions of abuse along a continuum, with a mere hunch at one end and absolute knowledge at the other end. Finlayson and Koocher concluded that reporting decisions are complicated by the need for professionals to determine what constitutes a reporting threshold, that is, the level of a reportable suspicion, because the legal standard of reasonable suspicion is vague and does not translate to clinical situations.

The role of a decision-making threshold highlights the similarity between child abuse reporting and other critical decisions made in applied contexts. A reporting threshold may be conceptualized as a criterion along a continuous dimension of abuse indicators as they are related to levels of suspicion. Thus, there are as many possible points at which a professional will report, or reporting thresholds, as there are points along a continuum of suspicion of child maltreatment. In decision theory, any single decision criterion will function optimally if it reflects the occurrence of an event given the benefits and costs, respectively, of correct and incorrect decisions to report (Swets, 1992).

A formal analysis of reporting decisions requires quantifying several parameters, including an index of abuse indicators, values for the costs of an incorrect report, specific benefits of a correct report, and the base rate of abused children in any given setting. Unfortunately, our understanding of child maltreatment is not at the point where such a formal analysis is feasible. In particular, the costs and benefits of correct and incorrect reports are difficult to determine and will vary as a function of local resources, quality of protective services, and the nature of the setting within which abuse is suspected. Although a formal analysis of reporting decisions is not yet possible, reporting accuracy may be improved to the extent that the process of report decision making is made explicit (Swets, 1992). Reporting decisions, like other diagnostic decisions, involve (a) setting a decision criteria, (b) evaluating the probability of outcomes, and (c) evaluating the costs and benefits of decision outcomes.

REPORTING THRESHOLDS AS DECISION-MAKING CRITERIA

Reporting decisions are made along a dimension of indicators of child abuse that vary across specific types of abuse and neglect. Subtle signs of abuse may be slightly suggestive, whereas more salient indicators may provide heightened suspicions or even knowledge of abuse. A continuum of maltreatment indicators is an example of a subjectively scaled probability estimate in decision theory (Swets, 1992). That is, indicators of child maltreatment are cumulatively evaluated through observation rather than formal assessment measures. In part, professionals must rely on observation to identify maltreatment because of the lack of validated assessment tools relevant to detecting child abuse. Therefore, direct and skilled observations of children and families are the best available methods of detecting child maltreatment. Experience with and specific training in child maltreatment will, therefore, most likely affect the accuracy of detection.

Several lines of evidence show that professionals are more likely to report after they have observed increased increments of child abuse indicators. For example, Kalichman et al. (1988) found that 89% of mental health professionals not reporting suspected abuse noted a lack of confidence that abuse was occurring as the most important factor in their reporting decisions. Similarly, Finlayson and Koocher (1991) found that reporting tendencies increased as a function of levels of suspicion. Other studies have also found that reporting abuse is closely associated with degrees of available evidence for the occurrence of abuse (Camblin & Prout, 1983; Watson & Levine, 1989). Overall, levels of confidence in the occurrence of abuse account for a substantial amount of the variability in tendencies to report (Kalichman & Craig, 1991; Kalichman et al., 1989; Saulsbury & Campbell, 1985). Reporting decisions are made along a dimension of indicators of abuse that translate to levels of suspicion. Decisions to report are therefore subjectively based on levels of suspicion that result from observed indicators of abuse. Figures 6 and 7 represent the relationship between indicators of abuse, levels of suspicion, and report decision criteria, or thresholds, for both physical and sexual maltreatment, respectively.[3]

Experimentally controlled case vignette studies have demonstrated several factors that influence reporting decisions. Similar to surveys asking professionals about their actual reporting experiences, studies that present hypothetical cases to mandated reporters, such as the one presented at the start of the introduction to this book, have found that approximately one

---

[3]The majority of this discussion is limited to signs of abuse presented by children suspected of being abused. Although suspicions arise from the appearance and behavior of adults thought to be perpetrators, suspicions of adults are usually less ambiguous because they tend to be based on verbal disclosures. In addition, few if any specific characteristics of abusive adults have been reliably identified (Giovannoni, 1989a).

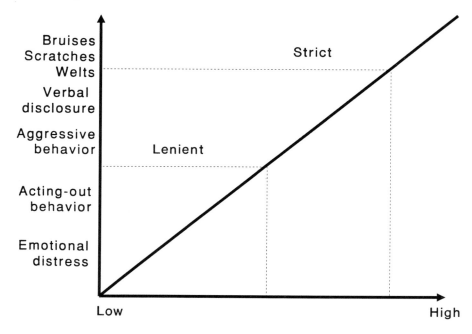

Indicators of Physical Abuse

Bruises
Scratches
Welts

Strict

Verbal
disclosure

Aggressive
behavior

Lenient

Acting-out
behavior

Emotional
distress

Low   High

Levels of Suspicion

Figure 6: Lenient and strict decision criteria for reporting suspected physical abuse as a function of levels of suspicion and indicators of abuse. Adapted from Swets (1992).

third of professionals decline to report abuse depicted in scenarios (see Table 3). It is notable that rates of reporting in these studies vary with specific manipulated factors. Although limited with respect to the validity of experimental manipulations and the lack of generalizability from hypothetical to actual cases (Brosig & Kalichman, 1992b), analogue studies that use case scenarios do show the relative salience of specific situational factors indicative of child abuse. In addition, vignette studies allow for the experimental manipulation of factors to determine their independent and interactive effects on reporting decisions.

Analogue studies, such as those that use case vignettes, have consistently shown that professionals are more inclined to report specific and salient indicators of abuse as opposed to diffuse, nonspecific clinical symptoms (Brosig & Kalichman, 1992b; Finlayson & Koocher, 1991). Signs of physical abuse, such as bruises, have been shown to increase tendencies to report over and above behavioral indicators, including unexplained behavior

Indicators
of Sexual Abuse

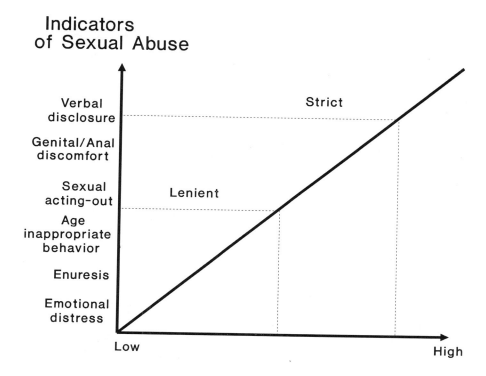

Figure 7: Lenient and strict decision criteria for reporting suspected sexual abuse as a function of levels of suspicion and indicators of abuse. Adapted from Swets (1992).

change and emotional distress (Kalichman & Brosig, 1992). In one study of practicing psychologists, 97% of participants indicated that they would be inclined to report a child with apparent bruises (Kalichman & Craig, 1991). These results were strikingly different from those obtained in previous vignette studies, which presented less specific signs of abuse. Thus, as suggested by Muehleman and Kimmons (1981), under some conditions, such as when abuse seems highly probable, almost all professionals appear likely to report. Signs of abuse that are indicative of severe abuse are also related to higher rates of reporting (Green & Hansen, 1989; Zellman, 1990). Visible signs of maltreatment, therefore, generally constitute reasonable suspicion and exceed most professionals' thresholds for reporting.

More influential than most other indicators of maltreatment, with the exception of bruises and other physical signs, are verbal disclosures of abuse (Sink, 1988). Studies have repeatedly shown that the majority of professionals will report when a child makes a specific statement alleging physical or sexual abuse (Finlayson & Koocher, 1991; Kalichman & Craig, 1991; Kalichman et al., 1988, 1989, 1992). In one study, psychologists tended to

TABLE 3
Percentages of Professionals Not Reporting Suspected Child Abuse Based on Hypothetical Case Scenarios

Authors	Participants	Percent Not Reporting
Swoboda et al. (1978)	88 Mental Health Professionals	66
Muehleman & Kimmons (1981)	39 Psychologists	49
Hass et al. (1988)	294 Psychologists	75
Kalichman et al. (1988)	101 Mental Health Professionals	18
Green & Hansen (1989)	202 Family Therapists	32
Wilson & Gettinger (1989)	132 School Psychologists	39
Kalichman & Craig (1991)	328 Psychologists	0–7[a]
Finlayson & Koocher (1991)	269 Pediatric Psychologists	0–41[a]
Kalichman & Brosig (1992)	527 Psychologists	1–48[a]
Brosig & Kalichman (1992a)	297 Psychologists	52–75[a]

[a]Range for different experimental conditions.

report when there was direct communication specifically alleging sexual abuse; 97% of participants indicated they would report a hypothetical case when there was a specific verbal statement, as compared with only 14% when indicators of sexual abuse were nonspecific and indirect (Finlayson & Koocher, 1991). Verbal statements that indicate abuse appear influential in reporting decisions because they can not be misattributed to other problems and do not allow much room for competing explanations (Finlayson & Koocher, 1991).

In a clinically derived model of sexual abuse, Sink (1988) categorically placed verbal disclosures as the most direct communication of sexual abuse, and declared disclosures as a stronger indicator than sexualized play, symptoms of posttraumatic stress, enuresis/encopresis, and other signs of generalized psychological distress. Similar to when a child speaks of abuse, reporting tendencies increase when an adult verbally discloses having been abusive toward a child (Kalichman & Brosig, 1992; Zellman, 1992). Increases are also observed when a third party, such as a nonabusive parent or a friend of the child/victim, provides information to a mandated reporter about the occurrence of abuse (Kalichman et al., 1988). Thus, when professionals are told of abuse they are likely to report the allegation.

Although verbal disclosures and direct communications of maltreatment specifically implicate abuse, verbal statements of abuse occur less frequently in professional settings than do more subtle and indirect signs of child abuse. The cognitive and emotional capacities to label and disclose abuse are complex and vary across developmental periods (Reppucci & Haugaard, 1989). In addition, children are likely to refuse to discuss abuse when questioned about it (R. Pierce & L. Pierce, 1985). Verbal disclosures of abuse in reporting decisions are further complicated by a child later recanting her or his allegation. Professionals have been shown to reduce their tendencies to report when a child withdraws a statement of being abused (Zellman, 1992; Zellman & Antler, 1990), despite the fact that it is common for abused children to do so. In one study, Attias and Goodwin (1985) showed that nearly one third of mandated reporters would not report after a child recanted a statement of being sexually abused, although recanted allegations are frequently substantiated upon investigation (Jones & McGraw, 1987). This finding demonstrates that professionals rely on some assurance that their report of abuse will be independently verified, despite their own level of suspicion raised by a self-disclosure of maltreatment. A verbal statement, recanted or not, exceeds the reporting criteria of most professionals, whereas recanted statements fall short of stricter criteria maintained by other professionals. Reporting decisions, therefore, move back and forth along a dimension of suspicion as indicators of abuse are accumulated or refuted.

Actual situations that give rise to suspected abuse are more complicated than any single factor used to suggest abuse in an experimental study. The effect of abuse indicators on reporting decisions varies with the age of the child suspected of being abused (Jackson & Nuttall, 1993; Kalichman & Brosig, 1992; Kalichman & Craig, 1991; USDHHS, 1988); younger children are more likely to be reported. Family ethnicity and social class also have been shown to influence reporting (Newberger, 1983). In a study of pediatricians, Turbett and O'Toole (Giovannoni, 1989a) found that case scenarios of African-American children with severe injuries were almost two times more likely to be seen as abuse when compared with case scenarios of White children with comparable injuries. Similar results were found for children from low income families compared with children from higher income families, suggesting that sociocultural biases may directly affect reporting decisions. Specific types of maltreatment are also differentially reported (Nightingale & Walker, 1986; USDHHS, 1988; Wilson & Gettinger, 1989; Zellman, 1990); emotional maltreatment and educational neglect are the types least likely to be reported.

Maltreatment cases are complex, with interactions occurring among many characteristics and circumstances. Professional concerns that influence reporting under low levels of suspicion are likely to be different from those that affect decisions under high levels of suspicion (Finlayson & Koocher, 1991). For example, concerns about not having enough evidence for the occurrence of abuse to warrant reporting will be more influential under low levels of suspicion, whereas concerns about the affects of reporting on the progress of treatment will exert greater influence under high levels of suspicion (Brosig & Kalichman, 1992a; Finlayson & Koocher, 1991; Kalichman & Brosig, 1992).

Knowledge, understanding, and interpretations of reporting laws can also affect reporting thresholds (Muehleman & Kimmons, 1981). After

reading a given state statute, mandated reporters fit specific case characteristics into the context of their interpretation of the law. When confronted
with a child suspected of being abused, mandatory reporting laws seem to
lower reporting thresholds, sensitizing professionals to report (Kalichman
& Brosig, 1992; Muehleman & Kimmons, 1981). On the other hand, when
an adult is suspected of being abusive, some laws lower thresholds whereas
others actually raise thresholds, making reporting less likely (Brosig &
Kalichman, 1992a; Kalichman & Brosig, 1992). Thus, the statutory wording
of mandatory reporting laws themselves may be viewed as part of the
situational context affecting report decision-making thresholds.

In summary, the continuum of abuse indicators that translates to levels
of suspicion appears to constitute the dimension along which reporting
decisions are made. The point at which indicators of child abuse are interpreted as reasonable suspicions of maltreatment is when reporting is most
likely to occur. Professionals, therefore, appear to cross a reporting threshold
when they report. The concept of a reporting threshold is useful in explaining individual differences in reporting suspected abuse. On the one hand,
a professional may report more subtle and nonspecific signs of maltreatment,
interpreting them as a reasonable suspicion of abuse. In this case, the criteria
for reporting may be seen as lenient, or as a low threshold. On the other
hand, professionals may exercise more strict criteria, or higher thresholds,
by only interpreting salient and specific signs as constituting reasonable
suspicions of maltreatment. Professionals appear likely to use, and reporting
laws provide latitude for, any number of decision criteria depending on the
circumstances of suspected maltreatment. A closer examination of report
decision criteria further illustrates individual variations in reporting.

Lenient Decision Criteria: Low Thresholds

When a professional requires only a minimal level of suspicion to
report, usually resulting from subtle signs of abuse, he or she has exercised
a lenient criterion, or low reporting threshold. Children with unexplained
changes in behavior or who appear emotionally distressed (Kalichman et
al., 1989), or who present with unexplained anxiety and somatic disturbances (Finlayson & Koocher, 1991), provide examples of such cases. As
an example of subtle signs of maltreatment, one experimental study presented practicing psychologists with the following case scenario:

> Imagine yourself as a therapist in the following situation: You have
> been working with a 7-year-old girl, Lynn, for two sessions. She was
> referred to you by her school guidance counselor who has noted that
> Lynn has been lying to her teachers, fighting with her peers, and not
> completing her homework assignments. Her counselor also indicates
> that one of Lynn's girlfriends told her that Lynn's stepfather loses his
> temper at home and hits Lynn. During the first two sessions, your focus

has been on evaluating Lynn's problems and developing goals for therapy. Lynn has been somewhat shy and withdrawn in your sessions, which has made rapport building slow. Despite this, you feel you are beginning to gain Lynn's trust.

At the start of your third session you notice that Lynn seems more tired than usual and her appearance is disheveled. When you ask her how she's feeling, she breaks down crying and refuses to talk with you further. After ending this session, you reflect back on the case and decide to phone her parents for a family session, but there is no answer at home. (Brosig & Kalichman, 1992a, pp. 487–488)

In a similar study regarding sexual abuse, Finlayson and Koocher (1991) presented the following scenario concerning a 7-year-old girl:

During the child interview, Anne appears listless, and sad. She seems disinterested in many toys in your office. Anne is polite and compliant. She offers brief responses to your questions about school, and home. You ask Anne about her stomach pain, and she responds, "It feels like someone is stabbing me." You ask her if she has any worries or concerns, and she states, "I worry about what will happen to my sister if I die." You ask Anne to tell you more about that, and she states, "I'm the only one who can take care of my sister." She becomes quiet and withdrawn and you are unable to elicit further information from her. (pp. 466–467)

Although the symptoms presented in these cases may be indicative of abuse, they may also be attributed to circumstances unrelated to abuse. This is the most likely explanation for the low rate of reporting observed among professionals responding to these cases. When signs of abuse result in a reasonable suspicion of abuse they are required to be reported. However, studies have consistently shown that professionals are unlikely to report such vague circumstances described in nonspecific cases (Brosig & Kalichman, 1992b; Finlayson & Koocher, 1991).

The mandatory reporting system, by design, accepts a high rate of false identifications in order to maximize rates of accurate detection of child abuse. The objective of the reporting system is to cast a wide net to capture as many actual cases of abuse as possible (Besharov, 1986b, 1990). That is, mandatory reporting of reasonable suspicions of maltreatment helps to ensure that within a large number of suspicions there will be a high proportion of actual cases detected. Reporting subtle signs of abuse can also be viewed as moving toward early intervention with the possibility of minimizing later abuse and limiting the potential for more intrusive state responses (Bourne & Newberger, 1977). In addition, a low reporting threshold will result in fewer false rejections, that is, cases in which abuse is actually occurring but goes unreported. Thus, lenient criteria, or low reporting thresholds, are sensitive to detecting abuse, but are not specific to cases of abuse. Therefore, low reporting thresholds can and do result in a proportion of cases being reported in which abuse is not occurring, such as those in which a child has been accidentally injured or is emotionally distressed over a nonabusive situation.

Finkelhor (1990) noted that the mandatory reporting system is similar to other social structures that weigh the benefits of correct detections against costs associated with incorrect decisions. For example, Finkelhor discusses due process in the criminal justice system as a social structure analogous to child protection. In the case of the criminal justice system, rates of reported crimes are higher than are the number of arrests, which are higher than the number of criminal convictions. This situation is similar to the ratio of reported to substantiated cases of child abuse. Finkelhor noted that the conviction rate of 55% for all violent crimes approximates the 53% substantiation rate for child maltreatment. Finkelhor points to the stringent standards of the child welfare system to explain low rates of substantiation, a situation that is also similar to that within the criminal justice system. It is unlikely that child abuse will be substantiated in a family in which maltreatment has not occurred because, unlike reporting, substantiation relies on evidence of abuse or neglect. In fact, the error rate is more likely to occur in the opposite direction, with actual maltreatment not being substantiated. High rates of reporting are at least in part attributable to lenient legal standards for reporting. This situation parallels the high rates of arrests relative to convictions in the criminal justice system. Finkelhor explains in detail the social tolerance for high rates of arrests to ensure public safety and that this same logic provides the rationale for lenient child abuse reporting criteria prescribed by law.

Correct identifications, or accurate detections of abuse, are the primary objective of mandatory reporting laws. Identification of abuse and neglect allows for social intervention, ideally resulting in child protection and preservation of the family. To the extent that social service agencies have adequate resources to assist children and families within which child abuse has occurred, there are few costs associated with the accurate detection of abuse. Of course, a case may be accurately identified through reporting but not substantiated through protective service investigation. There are potential benefits associated even with these cases in which abuse is not substantiated. For example, the investigation itself may prompt parents to change their behavior or seek treatment even if child protective action is not taken. In addition, investigations serve to send the message that society views child maltreatment as a serious problem.

Indicators of abuse are different from, although not independent of, levels of maltreatment severity. Distinctions of abuse severity are minimized in lenient criteria. Reporting thresholds are therefore reached in both serious and nonserious cases of child abuse. Few states have statutes that limit reporting to serious child maltreatment (Daro & McCurdy, 1992). The rationale for required reporting of nonserious abuse was stated by Bourne and Newberger (1977):

> The family situation in which a child suffers nonserious harm is not only not ideal, it is quite oppressive, albeit without danger to life and limb of the child. The child will consistently suffer specific, demonstrable physical or emotional harm, even though such harm does not . . . present a "substantial risk that the child will imminently suffer" such severe harm. (p. 674)

From this perspective, all child abuse, or suspicions of child abuse, can be taken as serious enough and surpass lenient reporting thresholds.

Because lenient criteria result in high rates of reporting suspicions that lack specific indicators of abuse and may appear somewhat less serious, they also result in high rates of false identifications; cases in which suspected child abuse is reported when it has not actually occurred. There are several costs associated with false identifications, including the utilization of scarce child protective service resources that may otherwise be used to serve maltreated children and their families. High rates of reporting are often thought to burden an underresourced child protection system and therefore actually reduce available services to families (Besharov, 1986b).

When reports are made in the context of treatment, professionals often believe that services may be disrupted as a result of the report (Ansell & Ross, 1990). In addition, many believe that families may experience maltreatment investigations as intrusive (Besharov, 1986b; Meriwether, 1986; Newman, 1987). There is, however, much debate concerning the extent to which treatment may actually be harmed through reporting and the actual effect investigations may have on families. Anecdotal accounts have claimed that families experience investigations as traumatic events and that social service involvement can be harmful to families (Besharov, 1990; Faller, 1985). Besharov (1978) stated this position:

> A report of known or suspected child abuse or neglect sets in motion an unavoidably stressful investigation which may lead to the removal of a child from his home and the stigmatization of a family within its community. The benign purposes and rehabilitative services of child protective agencies do not prevent them from being an unpleasant and sometimes destructive—though well meaning—coercive intrusion into family life. (p. 461)

There is, however, little evidence to support the view that reporting has adverse effects on the therapeutic process or the life of families. In fact, some evidence does exist to support just the opposite. As discussed earlier, Watson and Levine (1989) found minimal adverse affects of reporting on treatment. Similarly, a survey of family reactions to social service agency involvement following reported suspected child maltreatment suggested that investigations are not intrusive to families and can be generally positive (Fryer, Bross, Krugman, Denson, & Baird, 1990). False identifications are therefore more likely to be tolerable when the likelihood of negative effects of reporting are minimal.

In direct relation to high rates of correctly identified and falsely identified cases, lenient criteria also result in fewer overlooked, or unidentified, cases. Failure to detect abuse or neglect when it has actually occurred risks the likely continued occurrence or recurrence of abuse or neglect, further deterioration of families, and the failure to protect an unknown number of children. Under lenient reporting criteria these high costs associated with unidentified child abuse are minimized.

In summary, lenient decision criteria, or low reporting thresholds, are based on the rationale of maximizing maltreatment detection. This perspective is related to the fail-safe approach to decision making in engineering (Swets, 1992), which translates to the premise that when abuse is present the probability is very high that it will be detected. The cost of a missed case of abuse, including the possibility of continued abuse, is weighed heavily against reporting a case that is not substantiated upon investigation. Lenient decision criteria accept the costs associated with some overreporting in order to minimize the potential for underreporting child abuse. In contrast, strict reporting criteria result in a very different set of potential outcomes.

Strict Decision Criteria: High Thresholds

There is substantial evidence that when professionals underreport suspected child abuse they do so on the basis of strict decision criteria, or high reporting thresholds. Narrow interpretations of the legal standard reasonable suspicion of abuse set the stage for strict reporting criteria. As previously discussed, mandated reporters tend to report when there are specific and salient signs of child abuse. Two case examples that present salient signs of abuse that would be reportable even under strict criteria, that is, they would exceed high reporting thresholds, are provided by vignettes used in child abuse reporting research. In both cases, the majority of professionals responding indicated that they would report. The first example is provided by Kalichman and Craig (1991):

> Imagine yourself as a therapist in the following situation. You have been working with a 7-year-old girl, Kim, for two sessions. She was referred to you by her school's principal who became aware that Kim was lying to teachers, becoming socially withdrawn and getting into fights. In addition, one of Kim's friends had told a teacher that Kim was being physically abused at home.
>
> During your first two sessions with Kim, she remained somewhat shy and withdrawn, which made rapport building slow. However, during your third session you notice that Kim has a bruise on the left side of

her face and one on her left arm. When you ask her about the bruises, she breaks down crying and refuses to talk with you any further. After this session, you decide to call Kim's parents and ask them to come in for a family session. After answering the phone and listening to your explanation for the request to come in, Kim's stepfather states that he believes that the problem is with Kim and refuses to come in for the session. (p. 85)

Finlayson and Koocher (1991) used a similar scenario in their study of professionals' reporting of suspected sexual abuse. The following case was presented of a seven-year-old girl to suggest salient and specific signs of abuse:

During the child interview, Brenda is nervous and shy. You ask Brenda about what is worrying her, and she tells you, "I can't tell you." You ask her if she can show you in a drawing. She proceeds to draw a picture that appears to be two naked people. You ask Brenda to tell you about the picture and she says, "He's hurting her." You ask her to tell you more and she says, "He's peeing on her." You ask her to identify the characters in the picture and she states, "That's my daddy and that's me, and sometimes my daddy pees on me." She proceeds to cry and is unwilling to talk anymore. (p. 466)

Practicing psychologists have been found to interpret reasonable suspicions of abuse as a hierarchy of salient abuse indicators. Kalichman and Brosig (1993) showed that the most common interpretations of reasonable suspicions of abuse included verbal disclosures of maltreatment or apparent physical signs, such as bruises or other marks. Behavioral indicators were much less frequently believed to constitute reasonable suspicions, and only 14% of psychologists indicated that a suspicion alone was equivalent to a reasonable suspicion. These findings support Besharov's (1990) assertion that "behavioral indicators are not, in themselves, grounds for a report" (p. 141). Thus, professionals appear to interpret a narrow and specific range of signs, symptoms, and circumstances as reasonable suspicions of child maltreatment. These results support Finlayson and Koocher's (1991) observation that professional and legal standards for reasonable suspicion can be quite different. It appears to be the term *reasonable* that most strongly affects professionals' interpretations of legal standards for reporting.

Professionals with a history of having not reported suspected child maltreatment are less likely to believe that subjective suspicions alone constitute reasonable suspicions, and are more likely to indicate that verbal disclosures constitute reasonable suspicions (Kalichman & Brosig, 1993). This finding shows that some professionals set more stringent standards, or criteria, for defining reportable suspicions of maltreatment and that they tend to be the same professionals who have a history of not reporting suspected child maltreatment. Thus, individual differences in professionals' interpretations of what constitutes reasonable suspicions of maltreatment, at least in part, determine the degree to which they adhere to mandatory reporting laws.

Advocates of stricter reporting criteria emphasize the potential adverse consequences of overreporting. For example, high rates of unsubstantiated reports, which result from lenient criteria, are thought to overburden the child protection system, potentially interfering with child protective services (Besharov, 1986b, 1990; Eckenrode et al., 1988). In addition, potential consequences of unnecessary investigations may have negative effects on children and families (Newberger, 1983), and reporting may interfere with the treatment of perpetrators (Berlin et al., 1991; R. Weinstock & D. Weinstock, 1989). Higher thresholds for reporting minimize these potential outcomes by both lowering rates of reporting and decreasing the number of false identifications reported.

The child protection system expects high rates of reporting and compensates for overreporting by routinely screening cases prior to investigation. Case screening is based on the rationale that there are reports that do not warrant or allow for investigation. For example, 25% of child protection agencies screen out cases with incomplete information, 43% screen out cases in which the perpetrator is not named, and 50% require specific details concerning acts of maltreatment (Wells et al., 1989). Thus, the less specific the information contained in a report the less likely it will be investigated (Wells, Downing, & Fluke, 1991). Strict reporting criteria are likely to result in reports that meet screening criteria because they are more likely to include specific and detailed information regarding evidence of child abuse. In this sense, strict criteria relieve the child protection system of some of the burden. The potential cost of strict criteria, however, is a greater potential for missed cases of abuse.

Strict reporting criteria, that is, higher reporting thresholds, are primarily selected to minimize the number of falsely identified cases. That is, by only reporting cases that evidence salient signs of child abuse, fewer cases will be reported in which abuse has not actually occurred, allowing for more certainty that correct identifications will be made. Under strict criteria, or high thresholds, mandated reporters can have greater confidence that their report will be substantiated. However, strict criteria also result in higher rates of incorrect rejections, that is, cases that are not reported in which abuse has occurred. Again, unreported suspicions carry with them the high cost of the possibility for continued and further maltreatment.

In summary, strict criteria, or high thresholds, result in less incorrect identifications of maltreatment, but with increased chances of not reporting, or missing, actual maltreatment. An illustrative example of high decision thresholds is provided by the strict criteria used in research for hypothesis testing, in which more conservative criteria provide greater confidence that a result has not been obtained by chance. The relative differences between

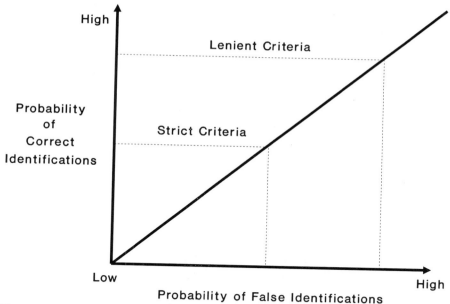

Figure 8: The relationship between decision criteria, lenient and strict thresholds, and probable outcomes. Representing the relative probabilities of correct and false identifications provides information for all possible outcomes of any given decision. Adapted from Swets (1992).

strict and lenient reporting criteria are represented in Figure 8, in which relative rates of correct identifications and false identifications vary as a function of decision criteria. Thus, lenient and strict reporting criteria have relative advantages and disadvantages to be reconciled by mandated reporters.

To illustrate the difference between lenient (low threshold) and strict (high threshold) reporting criteria, consider the report decision making of a child–clinical psychologist working in a pediatric setting. Suppose a psychologist conducts evaluations of six children per week, or approximately 300 children per year. Assume that there is a base rate of 20% of children in the particular setting where the evaluations are conducted who are victims of abuse. This means that the clinician is likely to see about 60 abused children per year. If the psychologist uses strict reporting criteria, setting a high reporting threshold and reporting only cases that involve physical signs of abuse or verbal disclosures of abuse, it may be expected that 10%, or six of the cases, will be reported. Although these six children will most likely be substantiated as being abused on investigation, 54 other abused children will go undetected. In contrast, consider a psychologist who uses lenient reporting criteria, a lower threshold in which subtle signs of abuse, such as social withdrawal or acting out behavior, are reported. Assume that this lower threshold results in reporting 75%, or 45 cases of actual abuse.

However, there may be as many cases reported in which the child involved was not being abused (see Figure 9). Thus, an optimal reporting threshold lies between these two extremes, catching a maximum number of cases while minimizing the number of incorrect reports.

Incorrect rejections in child maltreatment, that is, unreported cases in which abuse has occurred, have an increased probability under strict criteria relative to lenient criteria. The costs associated with these decisions are extremely high, including continued risk of abuse and further deterioration of the family. Given the price of a missed report, why do professionals frequently, and in opposition to the lenient criteria, select strict reporting criteria, and underreport? There appear to be a number of potential reasons for not reporting, including concerns over the quality of child protective services, maintaining professional–client confidentiality, protecting the integrity of treatment services, and protecting the child/victim against backlash abuse from angered parents. As is the case with any critical decision, the potential benefits are weighed against potential costs before a decision is made and action is taken. Thus, professionals, as decision makers, engage in a cost–benefit analysis as part of their report decision-making processes.

PERCEIVED COSTS AND BENEFITS OF REPORTING AND NOT REPORTING

An array of probable outcomes follow both reporting and not reporting suspected child abuse. The relative costs and benefits associated with reporting decisions will vary with the circumstances of the suspected abuse. For example, the relative costs associated with not reporting will increase when abuse is perceived as severe because professionals hold child protection as their greatest concern (Brosig & Kalichman, 1992b). Thus, how professionals weigh the costs and benefits of reporting suspected child maltreatment demonstrates their assumptions about the probable outcomes of reporting. Surveys of professionals have identified some of the perceived outcomes associated with reporting and not reporting, and their relative influence on reporting decisions.

Benefits that may result from not reporting suspected abuse center around issues of protecting confidentiality in both treatment and research. Professionals have widely discussed the potential effects of reporting on therapeutic relationships (e.g., Berlin et al., 1991), as well as in research settings (e.g., Kinard, 1985). In one study, 31% of practicing psychologists surveyed perceived reporting to have harmful effects on the course of treatment (Kalichman & Craig, 1991). This perception will likely motivate professionals to not report, despite evidence that reporting can have minimal adverse effects on treatment and can even be positively integrated into professional relationships (Harper & Irvin, 1985; Levine, Anderson, Terretti, Sharma, et al., 1991; Levine, Anderson, Terretti, Steinberg, et

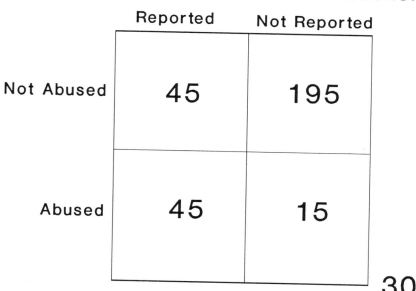

Strict Criteria / High Threshold

	Reported	Not Reported
Not Abused	0	240
Abused	10	50

300

Lenient Criteria / Low Threshold

	Reported	Not Reported
Not Abused	45	195
Abused	45	15

300

Figure 9: Relative number of cases reported and not reported for high and low thresholds in hypothetical example.

al., 1991; Watson & Levine, 1989). Professional interests revolve around what will best serve children and families. Therefore, when professionals believe unreported suspicions of abuse will result in child protection and preservation of the family their tendency will be to not report. However, unreported suspected child maltreatment is not without its costs.

One potential cost of underreporting involves legal consequences against the professional for not reporting. Failure to report suspected abuse usually carries penalties of a fine and a possible jail term, as well as potential civil suits by present and future victims. Although these outcomes have become increasingly more likely and more publicized in recent years (Buie, 1989; Denton, 1987a, 1987b), there is evidence that potential legal problems are of little concern to most professionals. For example, nearly one third of practicing psychologists in one study indicated that avoiding legal problems was not important in their decisions to report suspected maltreatment, making it among the least influential of considerations in their reporting decisions (Brosig & Kalichman, 1992a). Another survey of professionals found that fear of legal consequences for not reporting ranked lowest among factors taken into consideration when reporting or not reporting (Wilson & Gettinger, 1989). However, concerns about avoiding legal problems are viewed as more important among professionals who have consistently reported suspected abuse when compared with those who have at some time not reported (Kalichman & Brosig, 1993). Thus, some professionals may be motivated to report by concerns about breaking the law. However, Kalichman and Brosig also found concerns about legal problems for not reporting to be of little importance relative to other situational factors. The most negative potential personal consequence for professionals' failure to report is, therefore, among the least important in their decision making.

Another potential cost associated with not reporting is the possibility of continued or recurrent child abuse, which weighs heavily against all other considerations. Thus, when professionals do not report suspected child maltreatment it is most likely that they consider the risk of future abuse to be minimal. However, little is known about the accuracy and the limitations of professionals' risk estimations in this context. In addition, treatment resistance among perpetrators and their high risk for recidivism further raise the costs for unreported suspected abuse.

The benefits of reporting child maltreatment, on the other hand, represent a complementary relationship with the costs of not reporting. Reporting abuse is associated with the likely cessation of abuse. If nothing else, therefore, child protection system intervention is likely to result in reduced risk for children with regard to further abuse. The prospect of stopping maltreatment is a strong motivator for professionals to report (Finlayson & Koocher, 1991). In this respect, Kalichman and Craig (1991) found that 83% of licensed psychologists surveyed believed reporting abuse had been helpful in stopping abuse. Because the intent of mandatory reporting laws is to protect children, stopping abuse would be the expected outcome of reporting and it is clearly the most beneficial.

Reporting suspected child maltreatment also carries the additional benefit of working within the constraints of the law, eliminating the possible legal problems associated with not reporting. Professionals who report suspected abuse avoid the possible legal problems posed by not reporting and are protected against legal repercussions from reporting suspicions that are not substantiated. Reporting child abuse can also cause families to face the abusive situation head on in therapy and work towards a resolution of family conflicts. An additional and rarely discussed benefit of reporting is a potential for increases in public trust for professionals as a result of becoming involved in efforts to stop child abuse. In the case of treatment relationships, children may feel protected by the professional's involvement with the child protection system. Professionals may also be perceived as caring and willing to get involved throughout the reporting process (Watson & Levine, 1989). In a broader sense, public perceptions of professional credibility are likely to be enhanced when professionals adhere to the law (Kalichman, 1990).

There are, however, potential costs associated with reporting suspected child abuse. Human service professionals who report suspected maltreatment bring an overburdened and underresourced child welfare system into potentially abusive situations. Regardless of how efficiently a child protective investigation may proceed, it will introduce a new dimension to the ongoing process of treatment within which the suspicion occurred. The investigation process may become yet another distraction for treatment resistant families, providing a means of avoiding other family conflicts that may contribute to the abuse. The threat of removing a child from home is another very real potential cost associated with reporting. One third of physicians sampled by James et al. (1978) believed that reporting would be harmful to families or that there are better ways to handle cases of child abuse than reporting. In addition, nearly one third of practicing psychologists surveyed by Kalichman and Craig (1991) perceived reporting to be harmful to psychotherapy, and 13% believed reporting is harmful to families. Although the potential for adverse outcomes derives from social service efforts to protect children, their possible costs still exist for mandated reporters and may inhibit reporting. As noted by the U.S. Advisory Board on Child Abuse and Neglect (1990):

> In many communities, timely investigation of reports of suspected child maltreatment does not occur. Failure to conduct timely investigations and then to provide services when imminent risk is determined or a post-adjudication treatment plan is developed has serious repercussions. Professionals who serve children and families often fail to report suspected cases of child maltreatment because they have no confidence in the capacity of CPS to respond appropriately. (p. xiii)

	Cost	Benefit
Report	Disruption of treatment Reliance on CPS to handle case Family faces CPS investigation	Stopping abuse Maintain trust Uphold law
Not Report	Potential for more abuse Potential for legal problems	Maintain confidentiality Protect child from system

Figure 10: Relative relationship of costs and benefits of decisions to report and not to report.

Figure 10 summarizes the costs and benefits for outcomes of reporting and not reporting. Outcomes will vary with different circumstances of suspected abuse and will weigh differently under various conditions. The relative weight of different outcomes has a direct effect on defining decision criteria, as either strict or lenient. The benefits of reporting suspected child abuse will likely weigh heaviest when maltreatment appears most probable. On the other hand, when the occurrence of abuse is more questionable the benefits of not reporting will likely appear to be high. It is along these lines that professionals appear to subjectively define what constitutes reasonable suspicions of child maltreatment, and make determinations to report and not to report suspected child abuse and neglect.

INDICATORS OF ABUSE AS REASONABLY SUSPICIOUS SITUATIONS

Ambiguities in determining when a report is warranted is one of the key reasons for failure to report suspected child maltreatment. The question of what constitutes a reasonable suspicion of child abuse determines decisions to report. As previously discussed, salient and specific signs of abuse are rarely controversial when it comes to reporting. These indicators most usually will include bruises, cuts, burns, and other signs of physical injury. Verbal disclosures of abuse made by children and adults are also highly salient and specific. However, subtle signs and indirect communications cause confusion in determining when a report may be warranted. There are, however, common emotional and behavioral signs associated with different types of maltreatment. Unfortunately, many signs associated with maltreatment overlap with nonabusive clinical conditions (E. C. Herrenkohl & R. C. Herrenkohl, 1979). A comprehensive review of the literature on the effects of child abuse is beyond the scope of this chapter. Excellent reviews are, however, available elsewhere (e.g., Browne & Finkelhor, 1986; Faller, 1990; Finkelhor, 1986; Garbarino, Guttman, & Seeley, 1986; Gomes-Schwartz, Horowitz, & Cardarelli, 1990; Kendall-Tackett, Williams, & Finkelhor, 1993; Walker, Bonner, & Kaufman, 1988; Wurtele & Miller-Perrin, 1992). In terms of reporting suspected maltreatment, a major concern is with the initial effects, or at least the more proximal effects, rather than the long-term effects of child abuse. Following is a brief account of common initial signs of maltreatment that constitute report decision criteria.

Sexual Abuse and Exploitation

Sexual abuse of boys and girls is usually legally defined by specific circumstances, or acts, that encompass abusive situations. Clinically, sexual abuse is usually defined in a similar manner. For example, Roane (1992) found that more than one third of boys who had been sexually abused had experienced oral–genital contact, anal penetration, and/or fondling. Sexually abused children, more often than not, experience more than one type of sexually abusive act. Mental health professionals, however, can only become aware of such acts through verbal disclosures. Statements of sexual abuse by children are the single best indicator of sexual maltreatment (Adams, 1991; Herbert, 1987). Still, only about one third of cases of sexual abuse involve verbal accounts from children, and girls are more likely to disclose sexual abuse than boys (Herbert, 1987; Sebold, 1987). In fact, disclosures implicating sexual abuse of boys usually originate from a third-party source, such as a neighbor, family friend, or nonabusive family member (Reinhart, 1987). There are likely many reasons for this underdisclosing by boys, including social stigmas associated with homosexuality and social expectations for boys not to be victims (Roane, 1992).[4] Thus, for both girls and boys, suspected sexual abuse will likely result from means other than verbal disclosures.

Despite the belief that they are important in identifying sexual abuse, physical signs in these cases are even less common than verbal statements (Conte, Sorenson, Fogarty, & Rosa, 1991). Most sexually abused children, including those who experience vaginal or anal penetration, are asymptomatic on physical examination (Adams, Harper, & Knudson, 1992; Ellerstein & Canavan, 1980; Reinhart, 1987). Even in the case of medical examinations using such techniques as the colposcope, a procedure that affords

---

[4]More than 90% of boys who are sexually abused are victimized by men (Finkelhor, 1984; Reinhart, 1987; Roane, 1992).

binocular magnification of the vaginal canal, physical signs are not definitive when they are present because there are no established standards for anatomical findings (Adams, Phillips, & Ahmad, 1990). But even when visible signs of sexual abuse are present they are concealed and of little value to mental health professionals. However, there are common complaints of discomfort that are associated with physical trauma of sexual abuse that should raise suspicions. Complaints of pain or irritation of the anal or genital region, painful urination, or bleeding are signs of sexual abuse, although these symptoms may be caused by nonsexual conditions (Adams, 1991). Medical examination is necessary to determine the nature of such physical symptoms.

Because verbal disclosures of sexual abuse occur in a minority of cases and bodily signs are rarely identified by mental health professionals, suspicions often occur as a result of child behaviors and emotional reactions. Sexualized acting out behaviors can be specific and salient indicators of sexual abuse and are among the frequent symptoms exhibited by sexually abused children (Kendall-Tackett et al., 1993). Such behaviors, in both boys and girls, include excessive masturbation, masturbating in front of others, and touching other children or adults in sexual ways (Adams, 1991; Browne & Finkelhor, 1986; Herbert, 1987; Roane, 1992). In a large empirical study, Friedrich et al. (1992) found behaviors related to sexual self-stimulation, sexual aggression, gender-role behaviors (e.g., cross-dressing), and behaviors that involve personal boundaries (e.g., touching and rubbing against others) occur with greater frequency among sexually abused children relative to normative samples. Goldston, Turnquist, and Knutson (1989) found that 24% of sexually abused girls excessively masturbated, 17% masturbated in public, and 11% had sexually experimented with peers. These rates were substantially higher than those of a nonsexually abused clinical sample. Sexual acting out is more likely to occur after longer periods of abuse and therefore may not be apparent in cases involving few episodes of abuse (Roane, 1992). Acting out sexually is not, however, specific to sexually abused children (Herbert, 1987), and sexually abused children are also likely to act out in nonsexual ways (Browne & Finkelhor, 1986; Kendall-Tackett et al., 1993). Behavioral signs have not, therefore, in any combination, been shown to be reliable indicators of child sexual abuse (Levine & Battistoni, 1991).

There have been a number of attempts to identify emotional responses to sexual abuse. One of the more common findings is the high rate of depressive symptoms in sexual abuse victims (Adams, 1991; Browne & Finkelhor, 1986; Goldston et al., 1989; Kendall-Tackett et al., 1993). In addition, various symptoms of anxiety, withdrawal, shyness, and sleep disturbance are frequently discussed in victims of sexual abuse (Adams, 1991; Browne & Finkelhor, 1986; Herbert, 1987). Signs of extreme fearfulness are also common in sexually abused children, with as many as 83% of victims presenting fearful responses across a variety of situations (Browne & Finkelhor, 1986), as well as nightmares and diffuse symptoms of anxiety (Krugman, 1990; Mannarino & Cohen, 1986). The affective–emotional responsiveness of sexual abuse victims tends to be restricted in range or flat in tone as a result of traumatization, posttraumatic stress-like symptoms (Kendall-Tackett et al., 1993), and repeated assessment interviews (Jones & McGraw, 1987). Sexually abused children are also often described as having a low sense of self-esteem, although not necessarily to a greater degree than nonabused children (Browne & Finkelhor, 1986; Kendall-Tackett et al., 1993). Again, nonsexually abused clinically distressed children present similar patterns of emotional symptomatology.

Suspicions of sexual abuse that result from symptoms of general distress are difficult to interpret because of their overlap with symptoms of living in stressful nonabusive family situations. Children's reactions to parental conflict, separation, and divorce resemble many of the signs of distress described among sexually abused children. This is particularly true of children in families involved in custody disputes (Eastman & Moran, 1991; Ebert, 1992; Paradise, Rostain, & Nathanson, 1988; Wakefield & Underwager, 1988, 1991; Weissman, 1991). Finkelhor (1987) discussed a number of characteristics of family constellations that are common, although not unique to, families with child sexual abuse. Identified factors included families with one biological parent in the home, parents who use punitive discipline or are physically abusive, and children who perceive their parents as being unhappy with each other. In addition, more than 40% of sexually abusive families also have violent conflicts between the parents themselves. Thus, most of the vague signs of anxiety and depression, in the absence of corroborating indicators, are unlikely to lead to strong suspicions of sexual maltreatment. Finally, the large number of children who have been sexually abused but do not present any signs of abuse means that an absence of indicators cannot be used to rule out the occurrence of sexual abuse (Gomes-Schwartz et al., 1990).

Physical Abuse and Neglect

In contrast to sexual maltreatment, physical abuse is likely to involve apparent physical signs specific to abuse. The most common physical sign is soft-tissue damage, or bruises or welts. Burns and scalds are less common, occurring in less than 10% of cases (Haughton, 1977). Bone fractures and internal injuries are common in physical maltreatment of younger children, but these injuries are more likely to be seen in emergency rooms than observed by mental health professionals. Because bodily injuries may not always be apparent, verbal disclosures also play an important role in suspected physical abuse.

As was the case with sexual abuse, acting out behaviors can also be indicators of physical abuse. However, the behaviors acted out are more likely to involve acts of physical aggression. Common aggressive behaviors include hitting other children, including peers, younger children, or siblings (Ammerman, Cassisi, Hersen, & Van Hasselt, 1986; Hoffman-Plotkin & Twentyman, 1984). Physically abused children also tend to display more disruptive behaviors than children from nonproblem families, although not necessarily more so than children from nonabused but distressed families (Gelardo & Sanford, 1987). Longer-term signs of physical abuse also point toward aggressive behavior. Engfer and Schneewind (1982) found a modest but significant predictive pattern of physical abuse in the development of conduct disorder. Similarly, the rate of physical abuse in histories of juvenile delinquents is substantially higher than that among nondelinquent children (Lewis, Shanok, Pincus, & Glaser, 1979). Thus, as was the case in sexual abuse, acting out behaviors may also be indicative of physical abuse. However, aggressive acts are not specifically associated with physical abuse victims.

Emotional responses associated with physical abuse can also raise suspicions of maltreatment. For example, physically abused children tend to present signs of social maladjustment across developmental periods. Maltreated infants appear minimally attached to their parents, and abused children are generally less prosocial than nonabused children (Ammerman et al., 1986). Physically abused children have also been shown to have negative self-perceptions and low self-regard, although not necessarily lower than other clinically distressed children (Oates, Forrest, & Peacock, 1985). It is also common for these children to experience somatic symptoms of anxiety and in some cases symptoms that resemble posttraumatic stress disorder (PTSD) (Green, 1983). Intellectual impairment and academic deficits are also frequently characteristic of physically maltreated children and are often thought to be the result of damage to the central nervous system caused by the abuse. However, no study has established the direction of this relationship, so it is possible that such deficits exist before the occurrence of abuse (Ammerman et al., 1986; Gelardo & Sanford, 1987).

There is, unfortunately, little information available regarding the identifiable signs of physical neglect independent of physical abuse (Crouch & Milner, 1993). Neglect in infancy may result in nonorganic failure to thrive, which has several readily identifiable features (Gelardo & Sanford, 1987). However, the characteristics of neglect in childhood are less well defined. Malnutrition, lack of adequate clothing, poor hygiene, inadequate health care, unsafe living conditions, and periods of being left without supervision are all circumstances regarded as child neglect (Walker et al., 1988). Still, these circumstances must be viewed in the context of cultural expectations and values, and the inextricable relationship between social neglect and poverty.

Social withdrawal is one of the few identified signs that characterize the behavior of neglected children (Hoffman-Plotkin & Twentyman, 1984). In addition, children who suffer neglect are likely to present internalized symptoms, such as anxiety and depression (Gelardo & Sanford, 1987). Again, these symptoms are common among non-neglected children with clinical problems. Thus, suspicions of neglect that will surpass most professionals' reporting thresholds result from knowledge of the child's life circumstances and parental behaviors, usually through observation, a home visit, or the child's description of his or her living situation (Meriwether, 1986).

Psychological–Emotional Maltreatment

Among the different types of maltreatment, psychological maltreatment is the vaguest and most poorly defined (Garbarino et al., 1986; Melton & Corson, 1987). Much of the confusion and ambiguity surrounding psychological maltreatment results from its definitional unreliability and variability of signs across different circumstances (Melton & Corson, 1987; Melton & Davidson, 1987). Brassard and Gelardo (1987) noted seven different conditions of psychological maltreatment, five of which were also discussed by Garbarino (1987): *Rejecting*, treating a child as second to others or refusing to act on a child's needs; *degrading*, name calling and public humiliation; *terrorizing*, threats of harm, forcing the witness of violent acts; *isolating*, locking away in closets or rooms alone, denying access to relationships; *corrupting*, teaching or encouraging antisocial acts or beliefs; *exploiting*, using for self-gain at the child's expense; and *denying emotional responsiveness*, ignoring initiatives and needs for affection and emotional contact. Similarly, Melton and Davidson suggested the following factors as contributing to psychological maltreatment: rejecting, intimidation, humiliation, hostile or violent acts that produce fear or guilt, lack of nurturance, lack of acceptance, and damage to psychological and intellectual capacity.

T. Baily and W. Baily (1986) empirically defined circumstances of psychological maltreatment on the basis of expert responses to a series of brief vignettes depicting a spectrum of potentially abusive situations. The resulting list of 17 conditions ranged in ratings of severity. Examples of emotional maltreatment defined by T. Baily and W. Baily include:

> The parent shows no attachment to the child and fails to provide nurturance; the parent exposes the child to maladaptive and harmful influences; the parent confuses the child's sexual identity; the parent does not permit the child autonomy or independent learning; the parent regularly denigrates and ridicules the child, stating, without foundation, that he or she reminds everyone of a person who is totally offensive and unacceptable to the family. (p. 8)

These descriptions move us closer toward operational definitions of emotional maltreatment.

Although the circumstances of psychological–emotional maltreatment have begun to be described, there is little information concerning the signs of psychological maltreatment exhibited by children. Behaviors that are self-destructive, aggressive, or incorrigible may be taken as signs of psychological maltreatment (Melton & Davidson, 1987). Thus, similar to physical neglect, when suspicions of psychological maltreatment occur that surpass reporting thresholds they have likely resulted from verbal disclosures of the child's circumstances or from direct observations of abusive conditions.

In summary, physical signs and direct verbal disclosures of maltreatment, although not specified by law, would invariably constitute reasonable suspicions of child maltreatment and surpass the reporting thresholds of most mandated reporters. Behavioral signs, on the other hand, overlap substantially with other nonabuse-related clinical problems commonly seen in children. Although sexual and aggressive acting out may be indicative of child maltreatment, children exhibiting these problems are not always maltreated. However, child behavior problems that form the basis for a report of suspected child maltreatment do lead to substantiated cases. For example, Giovannoni (1989b) found that 20% of substantiated cases of child sexual abuse had been reported as a result of behavior problems. Generalized and diffuse symptoms of depression and anxiety are least specific to child maltreatment and would therefore result in the highest rates of false identification in the absence of other signs of abuse. Figure 11 presents a dimensional representation of maltreatment indicators as they may be related to each other in the context of reporting criteria.

Given the chronic psychological sequelae of child maltreatment, it is likely that child victims respond to abuse and neglect with some degree of traumatic reaction (Gelinas, 1983; Green, 1983). In this sense, symptoms of PTSD may provide a unifying dimension for symptoms of abuse, such as nightmares, somatic anxiety, fearfulness, and withdrawal. Although abused children may not be diagnosed with PTSD, symptoms of the disorder may suggest abuse when alternative explanations are absent and other signs of abuse are present. Nonspecific signs of maltreatment can also be viewed as being additive, in that several suggestive symptoms may lead to suspected abuse. The family history and context will also contribute to the interpretation of nonspecific signs of maltreatment. For example, children in the midst of custody battles should be expected to present signs of emotional traumatization. Thus, identifying a complex network of signs of abuse, possibly linked together by a traumatic reaction, will most likely lead to heightened suspicions of abuse and reported cases when physical signs and verbal disclosures are unavailable.

	Low specificity	Moderate specificity	Specific	High specificity
Sexual abuse	Anxiety Depression Low Self-Esteem Social Maladjustment	Sexual Acting Out	Complaints of Genital or Anal Discomfort	Detailed Verbal Account
Physical abuse	Anxiety Depression Low Self-Esteem Social Maladjustment	Aggressive Acting Out	Verbal Account of Maltreatment	Bruises Welts Burns Marks
Physical neglect	Anxiety Depression Low Self-Esteem Social Maladjustment	Social Withdrawal	Inadequate Clothing Poor Hygiene Unsupervised	Malnutrition Impaired Health
Emotional maltreatment	Anxiety Depression Low Self-Esteem Social Maladjustment	Verbal Account of Humiliation Rejection Degradation Terrorizing		Observe Humiliation Rejection Degradation Terrorizing

Lenient Criteria Threshold — High False Identification Rate

Strict Criteria Threshold — High Correct Identification Rate

Figure 11: Probable signs of maltreatment, their specificity, and their relationship to reporting criteria.

CONCLUSION

To date, no study has evaluated the process of child abuse report decision making engaged in by human service professionals. Therefore, at this point any conclusion must rely on studies that survey professionals regarding the factors that are weighed in reporting suspected maltreatment. Researchers have selected a number of possible outcomes from all of those that seem apparent and asked professionals to rate them along some dimension of reporting tendency. When surveyed, professionals can only respond to a limited number of possibilities. Of course, the circumstances under which professionals respond are also quite different from those within which suspicions really occur. Despite their ecological invalidity, their reliance on retrospective accounts, and their susceptibility to response bias, surveys provide the only available information regarding the considerations made by professionals when they contemplate reporting suspected child maltreatment. This limitation of the literature should be kept in mind when considering the results of studies discussed in this chapter.

Much more needs to be studied and learned regarding professional report decision making. For example, another factor that directly affects decision criteria, or in this case reporting thresholds, is the base rate of maltreated children or perpetrators in a given context (Swets, 1992). Settings in which many cases of abused children are seen will benefit more from a lenient criteria for reporting because lenient criteria result in a higher rate of correctly identified cases. On the other hand, settings that service fewer abused children or perpetrators may use stricter criteria. Again, it is difficult to determine the impact of base rates on professionals' decisions because little is known about the relative base rates of child maltreatment across service settings. The roles that professional experience, training, and beliefs regarding the child protection system play in reporting decisions are also mostly unknown. As a result of further study in this area, as well as an increase in awareness among professionals, reporting accuracy can be expected to increase because the report decision-making process should become more explicit (Swets, 1992).

An examination of the relative costs and benefits of reporting suspected abuse shows that the costs of reporting can be minimized and the benefits can be maximized. Among the potential costs of reporting, professionals have consistently pointed to breaches in confidentiality as their greatest concern (Berlin et al., 1991; Brosig & Kalichman, 1992b). This potential cost can be reduced through sensitive procedures informing persons of the limits of confidentiality early in the professional relationship. After informed consent has been obtained, breaches in confidentiality are consistent with understood professional roles and responsibilities. Costs of reporting can also be minimized by openly discussing the report up front with children and parents. The aftereffects of breached confidentiality are minimized when explanations are tied back to previously discussed limits, making clear the way in which the present circumstances fall within understood constraints (Taylor & Adelman, 1989). In order to maintain trust and bring reporting into the content of an ongoing relationship, it is important to tell families why the report is necessary and what they can expect from an investigation, as well as to assure them that they will receive the reporter's support throughout the investigation process (Racusin & Felsman, 1986; Watson & Levine, 1989). Reporting can therefore send a message of care, concern, and support to families. Professionals can also encourage families to cooperate with the investigation. Treating suspected abuse seriously communicates the importance of stopping abuse. Thus, professionals can build a context within which potential costs of reporting are minimized.

Interpreted in its broadest sense, the legal standard of reasonable suspicion poses a lenient decision criteria, or low reporting threshold. Behavioral signs of abuse, emotional indications of maltreatment, nonspecific forms of somatic distress, and indirect communication may be considered reportable by professionals using lenient criteria for reporting and not reportable by professionals using stricter criteria. In contrast, a narrow interpretation of reasonable suspicion sets a strict criteria, or high reporting threshold, under which only salient and specific signs of abuse and direct communications are considered reportable. Indicators of child abuse that exceed strict reporting criteria would likely be reported by most professionals. How, then, a professional interprets the legal standard of reasonable suspicion is the hinge on which reporting decisions rest. What is reported depends on what signs of abuse are observed, the family context within which they occur, and how they are interpreted in reference to reportable suspicions. When abuse indicators are salient and specific, resulting in high levels of suspicion, some professionals still choose not to report. These decisions usually reflect the perception of greater costs associated with reporting than with not reporting. Specific cases of both reporting and not reporting illustrate many of the concepts involved in the report decision-making process.

II

CASES OF SUSPECTED CHILD ABUSE: REPORTED AND NOT REPORTED

INTRODUCTION

CASES OF SUSPECTED CHILD ABUSE: REPORTED AND NOT REPORTED

Despite the unique challenges posed by individual cases of child abuse, common themes are found across abusive situations that are relevant to mandated reporting. For example, all cases involve determining a threshold for reporting, managing breaches of confidentiality if reported, and acting in the best interest of children. Chapters 4 and 5 present cases from the field that were not reported and cases that were reported, respectively. A casebook illustrating the conflicts surrounding reporting suspected child abuse was called for by APA's Ad Hoc Committee on Child Abuse Policy (Walker et al., 1989). The committee suggested that a casebook would be useful as a part of a broader agenda for addressing policy issues in child maltreatment. The next two chapters are a response to this need, presenting a range of cases gathered from a variety of professional settings. These cases are based on cases collected nationally from clinicians in the field. Following each case, the issues surrounding the circumstances of reporting or not reporting are discussed, with specific reference to the report decision-making model presented in chapter 3. Following the case presentations, chapter 6 proposes guidelines for reporting suspected child abuse.

4

UNREPORTED CASES OF SUSPECTED CHILD ABUSE

The following cases present situations within which child maltreatment was suspected and not reported to child protective services. The cases provide a sense of the complexity of situations that constitute unreported suspected maltreatment.

CASE 4.1: UNREPORTED INDICATORS OF ABUSE AND NEGLECT

A mental health counselor was treating a four-year-old girl for sexual abuse perpetrated by a teenage male cousin. The abuse had occurred when the girl was two years old and had been reported to authorities who conducted an investigation of the allegation. The family was of low income and limited in social supportive resources. During the course of therapy with the child and family, several incidents came to the counselor's attention that raised a suspicion of current physical abuse. The parents were both living under a great deal of stress and had repeatedly demonstrated low frustration tolerance with respect to caring for their child. The parents often spoke of "losing it" when the children misbehaved. The father once stated that he had "whopped" his daughter on the head with his hand. On another occasion, he stated that he "accidentally" hit her in the head with a bathroom door. The counselor never actually saw any physical injuries to the child, and the girl did not verbally report having injuries.

The mother also described several incidents in which her daughter had been in dangerous situations that could have been prevented had there been closer supervision. For example, there was a time when a kitchen cabinet had fallen on top of the girl after she tried climbing up on it. At another time, the girl had swallowed the contents of a bottle of the mother's makeup. On yet another occasion, the girl had stuffed a pencil eraser into her nose, which was discovered only after her nose became infected. On each of these occasions the parents had taken their daughter to the hospital for medical care. The counselor believed that the physician was in a better position to ascertain any injuries and that the treating physician could report the abuse if necessary. However, to the best knowledge of the counselor, reports of suspected maltreatment were not filed by any other professionals.

During the course of the counselor's work with the family, however, a neighbor reported the family for child maltreatment. This report was followed by an investigation in which abuse was not substantiated. Although the counselor had a great deal of concern about the children in this family, a report was never made by the counselor, who reasoned that because the family was participating in treatment and making gains, a report could have interfered with this process by damaging the therapeutic relationship and potentially driving the family out of treatment. The counselor also did not report because physical signs of maltreatment were not directly observed, and when the child had been injured she was immediately taken for medical treatment during which a physician had the opportunity to evaluate the child and report, but failed to do so. Finally, because the family had a history of involvement with social service agencies, yet another report was believed by the professional to be unlikely to have any benefit, unless it was for a fairly severe incident.

Case 4.1 Commentary

Although the signs of maltreatment that led to the suspicion of child maltreatment in this case were somewhat salient, the counselor might have further inquired about what the parent meant by "whopping" the child and how the child could have been "accidentally" hit with a door. Rather than verbal descriptions of abusive acts, the counselor was looking for signs of physical injury or a verbal description of injury from the four-year-old child. Also seen is a search for injuries as a basis for suspicion of neglect. Because the parents sought medical care for the child after she was exposed to potential harm, the counselor did not report.

The medical professionals' failure to report served to verify the counselor's decision-making criteria. The counselor believed that the child's physicians would be in a better position to report because they would be more likely to observe injuries to the child. Here again, the counselor's emphasis is on injuries as criteria for reporting. In addition, a neighbor's report was not substantiated. These events further supported the counselor's reporting criteria.

The counselor believed that another report of suspected abuse would not mean much to child protective services given this family's history of social service involvement. However, repeatedly filed reports accumulate and may result in higher levels of priority and greater assessed risk with each subsequent report. In addition, because the parents did seek immediate medical care for the child and were in treatment themselves to improve their child management skills, the counselor was hesitant to disrupt their progress. Finally, because the case does not provide information on the other children in this family, one is left wondering about their living conditions.

CASE 4.2: SUSPECTED PAST SEXUAL ABUSE OF AN ADOLESCENT GIRL

A psychologist in private practice was seeing a 15-year-old girl concerning self-dissatisfaction and problems achieving in school. She asked the psychologist at the first session of treatment whether her parents have to be told if she were to tell the psychologist "a secret." The psychologist told her that what they talked about would be confidential, except if she disclosed thinking about harming herself or someone else, in which case her parents would have to be told for her own safety. The girl proceeded to tell the psychologist that she had been sexually abused by an adult cousin when she was 12 years old. The cousin was currently living out of state and the girl did not feel he could harm her again. The girl also told the psychologist that if her parents were told about this, she would never come back to therapy. The psychologist tried to get the girl to inform her parents herself but she refused. After several sessions, some of which addressed the incident of sexual abuse, the girl started acting out. She got involved with drugs, became increasingly truant from school, and behaved belligerently toward her parents. The psychologist held a conference with the girl's parents and hinted about the sexual abuse, hoping that the parents would pick up on it without the child's confidentiality actually being broken. The psychologist did not, however, disclose the abuse to the parents. The psychologist felt that the girl would benefit if she stayed in therapy, and believed that breaking confidentiality would cause the girl to stop coming for treatment.

Subsequently, however, the girl did stop coming for therapy anyway. Weeks later, the mother called the psychologist stating that the girl had told her about the sexual abuse. In that conversation, the psychologist informed the mother that the girl had disclosed the abuse and explained why it was not discussed in their conference. Therapy with the girl did not resume and the abuse was not reported.

Case 4.2 Commentary

The specific indicators of abuse in this case, namely the verbal disclosure of sexual abuse, would likely surpass even strict report decision-making criteria. However, the professional's reporting was inhibited by concerns about confidentiality and the child's immediate welfare. The psychologist could have avoided much of the dilemma by having accurately stated the limits of confidentiality early in the therapeutic relationship. Although the professional did indicate that disclosures of potential self-harm would require breaking confidentiality, suspected maltreatment was not included as a condition of limited confidentiality. The psychologist failed to tell the parents about the disclosure because of concern that the girl would discontinue treatment if confidentiality was breached. However, the girl dropped out of treatment even though there was no break in confidentiality. In addition, although the psychologist experienced a dilemma about telling the girl's parents about the abuse, there is no indication that reporting to the child protection agency was even considered.

An additional concern in relation to this case is the potential for future sexual abuse perpetrated against other children. Although the unreported incident could have been an isolated event, it is just as likely, perhaps even more likely, that it was not. Although the child in this case was not at any present risk of further harm, it is not possible to know whether or not she or other children would be at risk in the future.

CASE 4.3: SUSPECTED EMOTIONAL MALTREATMENT

The mother of an 11-year-old boy was being treated for moderate depression, parenting issues, and low self-esteem. The woman was divorced but on occasion still saw her ex-husband, who continued to emotionally abuse her. The woman's son also continued to spend time with his father on a regular basis.

The incident that led the psychologist to suspect maltreatment and consider reporting occurred in a session with the mother. She described to the psychologist the following incident: During a parent–teacher conference at the son's school, the father stood up in the middle of a discussion with his son's teacher and decided that it was time to go. The father told the boy to get up and leave and then proceeded to go out to his car. However, the son stayed and talked with some friends. After a period of time passed, the father returned to the classroom, angry to find his son still there. In front of other children, parents, and teachers, the father grabbed the boy by the shoulders, shook and ridiculed him, and pushed him out the door. Concerned about the incident, the teacher called in both the mother and father for another parent–teacher conference. However, the father did not come to the second conference. The teacher did not report the incident to the child protective agency. The mother's account of the incident led the psychologist to become concerned about physical and emotional abuse of the boy. Although the state reporting law did not mandate seeing the child for reporting to be required, the psychologist did not report because the account was given secondhand from the mother, and the father lived apart from the child. The psychologist continued to work with the mother on setting limits with the father and opening up further communication with her son regarding his relationship with his father.

Case 4.3 Commentary

This case demonstrates that suspected maltreatment may occur without direct contact with the child/victim or perpetrator. In a few states (e.g., Mississippi, Pennsylvania, Wisconsin), situations in which the child is not seen by the professional are not legally required to be reported. However, professionals are always permitted to voluntarily report suspected child abuse. Based on the humiliation and degradation involved, the situation described in this case is characterized by specific indicators of psychological–emotional maltreatment. However, the suspicion was based on a verbal report from the mother, who was separated from the father. The professional in the case could have had the child come in for an interview but did not because this action may not have been appropriate, given the role of the professional as the mother's therapist. The seriousness of the description and the fact that the father would continue to have contact with the child would have formed the basis for reporting. However, reporting may have been inhibited by the confusion that revolves around defining acts of emotional maltreatment.

CASE 4.4: SUSPECTED INSTITUTIONAL ABUSE OF AN ADOLESCENT BOY

During an interview with a staff psychologist, a male patient on an adolescent residential unit alleged that a female staff member was pursuing him sexually. When the psychologist questioned him about the situation, the patient described various "looks" the staff person had given him and his interpretation of things he claimed she had said. The boy's major allegation was that the staff person had entered the shower room while he was naked. He said that she made some suggestive remarks and then grabbed him. Examination of the patient's chart found that the incident was described in detail, and the staff person had recorded that the patient had lured her into the shower room by asking her for help, and then dropped his towel and exposed himself. The staff person wrote that the patient actually approached her and she pushed him away, told him to get dressed, and left the room. The patient also had a history of similar acts with other female staff that were documented in his chart. The psychologist chose not to report the incident but did develop a component of the patient's treatment plan to address the problem.

Case 4.4 Commentary

Although this case presented a verbal disclosure of sexual abuse, the allegation appeared to be part of a patient's emotional–behavioral problems. On the other hand, the occurrence of institutional abuse is becoming increasingly more recognized. Although an investigation by a child protection agency determines the occurrence of abuse, the psychologist in this case chose not to report on the basis of the situation and the patient's past behavior. To have reported the incident, even if it was not substantiated, may have harmed the staff person's career, a factor obviously weighed in the decision. The situation was viewed by the psychologist as part of the patient's behavior problems and incorporated into his treatment plan. Thus, although the case was not reported, the allegation was also not completely dismissed.

CASE 4.5: SIBLING ABUSE AND SUSPECTED CHILD NEGLECT

A 13-year-old girl being counseled by a school psychologist for a number of school related problems stated that her older brother had been rough with her and that during some fighting between them he had bruised her. The girl did have bruises that the psychologist saw, but the psychologist did not believe that they constituted serious injuries. The girl's mother was aware of her daughter's bruises but did not feel the need to break up the fighting. After consulting with a colleague the psychologist decided that the incident was not abuse because it was not perpetrated by an adult. The psychologist did, however, recognize that the mother may be neglectful because she was potentially leaving her daughter open to injury by not intervening. Still, the psychologist did not feel that the incident constituted a pattern of neglect and, therefore, did not report. The psychologist did focus on getting the mother to realize the seriousness of the situation and tried to motivate her to intervene when her daughter could be at risk of getting hurt. The psychologist told the mother that if she did not intervene, eventually the problem would be reported as a case of child neglect.

Case 4.5 Commentary

This school psychologist was sensitive to the requirements of the law in his or her state and seemed to follow them to the letter. The girl did have bruises, but they were not inflicted by an adult. The mother did leave her daughter vulnerable to injury, but there was no pattern of neglect. The professional, therefore, seems to represent the approach to reporting only as required by law. These strict criteria make it unlikely that a false identification will occur, but in doing so leave open the risk of further abuse. In this case, the logic used by the professional was to only report when the state definitions of abuse and neglect were met. The psychologist also used reporting as a threat to motivate the mother to change her behavior. Although potentially effective, this tact could inhibit future disclosures of abusive acts and frames reporting as punishment rather than a potential source for help.

CASE 4.6: A VERBAL DISCLOSURE IN A RESEARCH SETTING

An experimental psychologist was conducting a research project related to stressful life events and coping among grade-school children. The study involved a standard scale of self-reported stressful life events that included the items "I was touched in a way that I did not like" and "My parents have been mean to me." The researchers saw these items as important indices of childhood stress, but also realized that they could be indicators of abuse. The study was approved by the University Institutional Review Board and the school administration where the study was being conducted. Parents were informed that the study concerned stressful events experienced by children and the measures were available for them to inspect.

The researchers were aware of their requirement to report suspected child maltreatment if it should occur during the course of their study and had decided to collect the data anonymously from children in order to encourage honest and forthcoming responses. The researchers thought it would be of questionable ethical practice to assure the children that their responses were anonymous and confidential and then ask any child indicating abuse to come forward. The researchers wanted to maintain confidentiality and remain sensitive to their reporting requirements, but at the same time they recognized that their measures could potentially stir up memories of difficult experiences that the children may want to talk with someone about. The researchers discussed their methods with colleagues, reviewed the APA Ethics Code, and consulted the university legal department in order to develop a procedure for handling any situations of suspected abuse. A short list was constructed of area hotlines that children could call if they wished to talk with someone further about the sorts of things mentioned in the questionnaires. The children were also told that they should talk with their parents, teacher, or school social worker about anything that might be troubling them. Finally, the researchers informed the children that if they told them anything in person that was seriously bothering them, the researchers would have to tell the school administration about it.

One day after a child completed the measures for the study, she told a research assistant that the question about having been touched in a way that she did not like made her think about something bad that had happened to her. When questioned further about this, the girl said "never mind" and walked away. The research assistant discussed the situation with her faculty advisor on the project and they decided to inform the school principal about the incident. After telling the principal, the researchers took no further action and were not aware of any action taken by the school.

Case 4.6 Commentary

Suspected child abuse may be a common experience of developmental, experimental–child, educational, and school psychologists, as well as others who work with children and families outside of traditional clinical settings. The researchers in this case were sensitive to their measures and the emotional response they might have evoked from children. In addition, they considered the possibility that items on the measures could prompt a disclosure of an abusive experience. Although their data collection procedure was anonymous, the researchers made an effort to communicate the need to discuss difficulties related to stressful events with parents or teachers. They also included in the informed consent procedure the necessity of telling school personnel about any identifiable information regarding things that might be seriously bothering a child. Unfortunately, informing school personnel of suspected abuse does not constitute filing a mandated report. Although some states include "cause a report to be filed" as one option in making a mandated report, the researchers in this case did not follow up on action taken by the school and did not verify that a report had been filed. Because the researchers were mandated reporters, a more general statement as to who would have to be notified in cases of suspected maltreatment could have been included in the informed consent procedure. For example, the researchers could have said that they would be required to tell "people whose job it is to protect children from harm." Such a statement would accurately describe child protective services. A similar statement could also be included in parental consent provided for minor participation.

CASE 4.7: CHILD SEXUAL ABUSE PERPETRATED BY A NEIGHBORHOOD BOY

A marital therapist was treating a couple experiencing continual conflicts and communication problems. During a therapy session, the wife told the therapist that their three-year-old daughter and the child's friend of the same age had been fondled and coerced into sexual play by a teenage boy in the neighborhood. The couple told the therapist that they had informed the boy's parents about what he had been doing and had taken several steps to ensure that he would not have access to their daughter. The marital therapist asked specific questions regarding the action the parents took to protect their daughter from further harm. The therapist learned that the girl and her friend were not presenting signs of trauma and the therapist felt confident that they were out of future danger. The therapist also intended to follow up on the girl's status during later sessions. The therapist did not report the case to the child protection system because the parents appeared to have done an adequate job protecting their daughter, as well as her friend.

Case 4.7 Commentary

This verbal account of two cases of sexual abuse was not reported because the victims appeared to be well protected from future abuse. The therapist carefully evaluated the situation and found that steps had been taken to protect the children. However, looking beyond the two known victims, the safety of other children in the neighborhood as well as attempts at early intervention for the perpetrator could not be addressed by the marital therapist without reporting. In addition, because the boy and his parents were outside of the family being seen by the therapist, there were no apparent costs that would have been associated with the therapist's reporting.

CASE 4.8: SUSPECTED SEXUAL ABUSE IN THE MIDST OF A FAMILY CRISIS

A psychologist was treating an 11-year-old girl for acting out aggressively against her peers, showing symptoms of depression, and using unacceptable language at home and school. During a session of therapy, the girl told the psychologist that her father, now divorced from her mother, had fondled her before her parents were separated and continued to fondle her when she visited him. However, since the last time she had seen her father, both of the parents' lawyers had agreed that the father would not have further contact with his daughter. The therapist decided not to report the child's disclosure because of concerns that the girl and her mother could not manage the additional stress that might have resulted from a child protection investigation and actions that would have been taken by the state. The therapist did address the abuse in a number of later sessions with the girl. The therapist also involved the mother in therapy to further address these issues. Although the father no longer had contact with his daughter, he was not in treatment and it was not possible to know whether or not he had contact with other children.

Case 4.8 Commentary

Because of concern for the mother and daughter, particularly regarding their ability to manage the potential stress of a child protection investigation, the psychologist did not report this case. The girl was no longer permitted to have contact with her father and, therefore, was perceived as safe from further harm. There is still, however, the issue of necessary social service involvement with cases of child sexual abuse. The father, as a perpetrator, was at continued risk for sexually abusing other children. Without social sanctions for the abuse, it is not possible to bring external pressure on the father to receive treatment or to keep him from harming other children.

CASE 4.9: DIFFERENTIATING PUNISHMENT FROM CHILD ABUSE IN REPORTING DECISIONS

A 10-year-old boy attending an alternative school for emotionally disturbed children told his school counselor that he was thinking about killing himself. The counselor explored in great detail his feelings and thoughts of suicide. During their discussion, the boy revealed that his father had hit him across the back with a dog leash the previous night. The counselor looked at the boy's back and saw no signs of welts or bruises. The boy said that the beatings were frequent and occurred when his father was angry with him. The boy also said that the beatings occurred when his mother was not home, although he had told her about his being hit. The counselor contracted with the child not to hurt himself and told him that his mother would be called to discuss the beatings and his safety.

The counselor had had close contact with the boy's mother in the past and called her regarding what was discussed in the session. The mother told the counselor that she knew that her husband hit their son, but it was his way of punishing the boy, and she never knew it to get out of hand. The mother said that she was not aware of anything that she would call a "beating." The counselor told the mother that her son said he was thinking of doing harm to himself on account of the alleged beatings. The mother was surprised and concerned about this. The counselor proceeded to tell the mother that she should talk to her son about his father's discipline, but that he should not be reprimanded in any way for talking openly in the counseling sessions. The counselor also told her that if her son reported any future beatings or if there were ever any marks on him the school would have to report the incident. The counselor also discussed with the mother the importance of acknowledging her son's difficulties and asked her to observe him for any signs of depression and contact the school if she saw anything that concerned her.

Case 4.9 Commentary

The counselor elected not to report this case, although the child's verbal disclosure led the counselor to inquire about possible abuse. The boy described a situation that sounded like abuse, and the counselor gathered additional information by inspecting for marks or physical injury and discussing the situation with the boy's mother. The counselor also placed a great deal of trust in the boy's mother's ability to judge the limits of her husband's use of punishment and her ability to monitor situations over which she may have had little control. The counselor also used reporting as a last resort in dealing with this situation. Thus, although the professional in the case did not report, some steps were taken toward child protection.

This case is also complicated because the boy expressed suicidal thoughts related to the abuse he described. By not reporting, the counselor might have been risking the boy's reacting with suicidal behavior to any further hitting, whether it be labeled abuse or punishment. Although the counselor took actions to contract with the child and monitored him for any further problems, the amount of child protection that could be offered by the counselor alone seems limited.

With respect to report decision making, this case illustrates the difficulties in distinguishing corporal punishment from acts of abuse (Straus & Gelles, 1990). For the mandated reporter in this case, consistent with most legal definitions, the distinction between punishment and abuse seems to have been related to the occurrence of physical injuries. Although the debate between parental rights and child protection is often cast in philosophical dilemmas, professionals are charged with making clear determinations based on their observations. This is particularly problematic when nonmedical professionals suspect physical and sexual abuse and are not qualified to examine a child for physical signs of abuse. Thus, an appropriate reporting criteria again seems to be a child's verbal disclosure of circum-stances that describe acts of abuse.

CASE 4.10: A RESEARCH CONTEXT IN WHICH THE DATA INDICATE CHILD ABUSE

A research team was conducting a study of children's memory for recent and distant past life events in an elementary school setting. The study used questionnaires and interviews. The parents of participants pro-vided informed consent that included defining the terms of limited confi-dentiality. An eight-year-old girl who was a study participant described a recent memory of an incident that involved being hit by her mother when she had misbehaved. The girl stated that her mother hit her "very hard and that it hurt bad for a long time." The researcher who interviewed the girl discussed the situation with the research team and decided to call the parents to ask about the situation. The parents acknowledged the incident and openly discussed their use of corporal punishment without being at all defensive. They said that they had established limits to situations in which they hit their child and only did so under certain circumstances. The parents stated that they did not feel that they were ever extreme in their use of punishment. The research team then discussed the conversation the re-searcher had with the parents and decided that the situation did not con-stitute child abuse and, therefore, did not report the case. The researchers did, however, have another conversation with the child the next day. They told the girl that if she ever felt in the future that someone, including her parents, was hurting her or touching her in ways that she did not like, she should tell her teacher, principal, and other adults about what was happening.

Case 4.10 Commentary

This case illustrates how professionals might blur their professional roles in order to further explore suspected child abuse before reporting. The researchers sought further information from parents to find out more about a situation that a child had disclosed, although such inquiries were outside of usual professional roles. The researchers acted to explore their suspicions before making a decision about reporting, although the parents had been properly informed of the necessity to report suspected child abuse before data was collected from the child. The researchers also took additional action outside of their professional roles to discuss abuse prevention with the child. Thus, the case illustrates how professionals might do more than they should just to avoid making a report to the child protection system.

CASE 4.11: A CASE OF UNINTENDED, UNREPORTED, SUSPECTED CHILD MALTREATMENT

A psychologist working as a consultant for a child abuse prevention program was conducting information and education presentations for children in a public school setting. After a presentation, an eight-year-old girl approached the psychologist and said "My aunt hits me in ways like you said." The psychologist probed the girl for more information, but the child only stated that she lived with her aunt and that her aunt "beats" her. As a consultant to the program, the psychologist believed that it would be best to discuss the disclosure with the project supervisor and the program director. After informing the program director of the incident, the psychologist was told that the situation would be reported. In discussing the situation with the supervisor, the psychologist stated that as a mandated reporter it seemed like a report should be filed directly as well as through the program. The supervisor, however, stated that consulting psychologists in the program really had no need to report because that decision was made by the staff social workers. Given that this was the first situation of suspected child maltreatment that the psychologist had ever experienced as a consultant for this agency, the supervisor's advice was taken and the psychologist did not file a report to the child protection system. Several weeks later, the psychologist learned that the program director did not report the case.

Case 4.11 Commentary

Professionals employed by interdisciplinary agencies may have to work under particular policy and procedure structures when reporting suspected child abuse. Consultants also will have to work within these structures, but could find themselves with more poorly defined roles than regular staff persons, as appears to have occurred in this case. As a mandated reporter, the psychologist recognized the necessity to report the suspected abuse. However, the agency involved had a policy for reporting through the staff social workers. Although the psychologist did report the suspected abuse to the program director, an official report was never filed. In many states mandated reporters can cause a report in response to mandated reporting, although they are ultimately responsible for following up on the case to ensure that a report was in fact eventually filed. In this case, the psychologist was under the impression that the agency would report and took the supervisor's word without following up.

CASE 4.12: DIFFERENTIATING PARENTAL DISCIPLINE FROM PHYSICAL ABUSE

An outpatient therapist at a mental health center was referred a case involving a 14-year-old girl who exhibited poor school performance and acted "disrespectful toward her mother." The girl lived with her twin brother and their mother, who had been divorced from their father since the children were five years old. As a matter of first-session routine, the therapist interviewed the girl and her mother, both separately and together. The therapist found that both mother and daughter described very similar accounts of the girl's behavior. They both stated in separate interviews that the girl lacked motivation to succeed in school and had become friends with other children who had encouraged her to smoke cigarettes, skip out of classes, and stay out past the time her mother set for her to be home. The girl's mother described herself as feeling out of control with respect to managing her daughter's behavior and feeling as though she needed help.

Also as a matter of routine, the therapist asked the mother and daughter separately about how the mother had been disciplining the children. The mother stated that when her attempts to set curfews and ground her daughter as a form of discipline failed because the girl completely disregarded any rules, she started using "physical discipline" with the girl. Questioned further, the mother said that she had been punishing her daughter by "hitting her on the backside with a heavy cloth belt." The therapist very directly asked the mother if the hitting ever left any marks on her daughter. The mother denied that any marks were ever left and claimed that the belt was too lightweight to leave any marks. The mother did, however, admit that her hitting her daughter did not help matters and that she continued doing it mainly because it helped her get her anger out. The mother also stated that she had not been hitting her son, who was much better behaved.

Wanting to verify the mother's account of what was happening, the therapist asked the girl about the discipline in a separate interview. Her description was strikingly similar to her mother's. Although she hesitated at first, the girl said that her mother hit her with a cloth belt and that she never had visible marks afterward. The therapist, whose entire practice involved child and family therapy, had established a working threshold for reporting physical child maltreatment only when there were marks. Therefore, the therapist did not report this case.

Case 4.12 Commentary

This case illustrates the problem professionals face when they are left to determine a working definition of reasonable suspicion of child abuse as a criterion for reporting. The therapist in this case had set a standard for reporting physical abuse based on marks being left on the child, a criterion consistent with most legal definitions of abuse. Based on the verbal reports of the mother and daughter, the therapist was convinced that the mother's punishment, although extreme, did not constitute reportable maltreatment. The therapist's response falls within a certain interpretation of the law emphasizing that the suspicion must fit legal definitions of abuse in order to warrant reporting, because the child did not sustain harm or injuries. On the other hand, an interpretation of the law focusing on the potential for harm or injuries would suggest that this case did surpass legal standards for reporting. Thus, the case clearly illustrates the role of professional judgement and discretion when suspicions of child maltreatment are subthreshold and based on subjective interpretations of legal standards.

CONCLUSION

These cases, as limited as they are in detail, show the complex interactions among factors that raise suspicions of child abuse, along with the complexities of reporting decisions. Although some cases involve vague and nonspecific indicators of maltreatment, others are characterized by highly specific and salient signs, such as marks on a child and verbal descriptions of abusive situations. However, these indicators are frequently buffered by a number of counterconditions. Disclosures of abuse in which the perpetrator no longer has access to the child demonstrate a minimal degree of potential for future harm to that same child. Although concern for the child known to have been abused was the focus of the professional's attention, a broader view of the problem might have prompted reporting. Another frequent inhibitor of reporting included concern about confidentiality and shielding victims and families from involvement with the child protection system. Thus, even when indicators of abuse surpassed strict reporting criteria, reporting was often inhibited.

Suspected child abuse occurs across a wide range of professional settings and circumstances, and more than one mandated reporter may fail to report a single case. However, in the cases discussed, when more than one professional had seen the same case, it is noteworthy that there was limited, if any, communication among the different professionals. Researchers could have discussed situations of suspected abuse with school administrators, therapists with physicians, and social workers with teachers. Decisions to report, as well as not to report, would have been more sound with input from different professionals with diverse sources and degrees of information. Consultation with other professionals involved in a case would have provided for a more objective decision-making process and a more confident sense of actions taken.

Problems observed in educational and mental health service settings often involve the inability to detect the battered child syndrome under nonmedical circumstances. The overlap between emotional signs of child maltreatment and nonabusive situations was observed in several of the cases presented. In addition, such subtle suspicions often occur within the context of an ongoing therapeutic relationship in which concerns about privacy, trust, and respect play a crucial role in intervention. Reporting laws also seem to overgeneralize and function indiscriminantly in many situations. These factors have led to the dissatisfaction mental health professionals have often expressed regarding mandatory reporting laws. However, mandated reporters widely recognize the necessity of reporting and the need for mandatory reporting legislation.

In chapter 5, a series of cases of reported suspected abuse are presented. The relative circumstances of these different cases provide further evidence of the range of indicators leading to suspicions of maltreatment and demonstrate the manner in which suspected child abuse is managed.

5

REPORTED CASES
OF SUSPECTED
CHILD ABUSE

The following cases were collected in the same manner as those presented in chapter 4. However, these cases of suspected child abuse were reported to the child protection system. As in the previous chapter, these situations are not intended to be exhaustive or representative, but rather a selection of suspected maltreatment.

CASE 5.1: SUSPECTED SEXUAL ABUSE REPORTED
BY A STUDENT INTERN

A predoctoral psychology intern at a medical hospital was working on a substance abuse treatment ward. During a routine screening of a client for the substance abuse program, the intern completed a standard assessment protocol. During a clinical interview, the client complained of depression and a number of family problems that he said were contributing to his drinking. He also claimed that many of his problems stemmed from his relationship with his wife and stepchildren. Because the client's wife was waiting for him in the lobby, the intern asked to speak with her in order to obtain a comprehensive assessment of the problems contributing to the client's substance abuse. At first reluctant, the client eventually agreed to allow his wife to join the interview.

During the interview with the couple, the man's wife spontaneously cried and in an outburst said to the intern "Did he tell you what he did to my baby?" She then proceeded to tell the intern, in front of the client, that the client had fondled her 10-year-old daughter, his stepdaughter. The man admitted to the acts, cried, and said that he was sorry for what he had done. He also said that he wanted help for all of his problems, including what he had done to his stepdaughter.

Exposed to mandated reporting laws in graduate school, the intern was certain that he was required to report the case. The intern informed the client and his wife that a report would be filed, although limited confidentiality had not previously been discussed. Before reporting, however, the intern discussed the case with the rotation supervisor. Much to the intern's surprise, the supervisor stated that the hospital policy was not to release any adult patient information without a signed release. In addition, the intern was told that the state reporting statute, unlike the law in his home state, specified that a child needs to be seen firsthand by the mandated reporter for a report to be required. The hospital policy was, therefore, consistent with the state reporting law. Thus, the intern was instructed by the rotation supervisor not to report.

Troubled by the situation, the intern went to the internship clinical training director. After explaining the incident and the supervisor's response, the intern was informed by the director that the supervisor understood the law correctly and the intern was not required to report. However, the director believed that there was an ethical–moral obligation to report the case, including protecting children and getting the patient into treatment. The director instructed the intern to report and to inform the family that a report had been filed.

Case 5.1 Commentary

This case represents an instance of suspected abuse that was reported although it was not mandated by law. The case illustrates two different perspectives displayed by the two supervisors: The first responded in accord with the letter of the law, whereas the second responded from the position of reporting as a means of child protection. The rotation supervisor was likely concerned with hospital policy, patient rights, and the fact that the man was seeking treatment for substance abuse. On the other hand, the clinical training director expressed concern for ensuring protection for the alleged victim as well as other children. The case also demonstrates the necessity of informing persons at the start of professional relationships, including short-term screening assessments, of limited confidentiality.

CASE 5.2: REPORTED PHYSICAL ABUSE OF AN ADOLESCENT GIRL

A therapist had been seeing a 14-year-old girl brought in for treatment after a disclosure of sexual abuse perpetrated by a neighborhood boy eight years earlier. The girl discussed the incident with her parents, who in turn reported it to the child protection agency. The girl presented many characteristics common among adolescents with a history of sexual abuse, including tendencies to do harm to herself, depression, and erratic changes in mood. She attended only two sessions with the therapist and then she stopped coming to therapy, either canceling sessions or not showing up for appointments.

Three weeks after the girl's last session, the therapist received a phone call from the girl's father. He described a "family emergency" that had resulted from a family argument. The father said that an argument he had with his daughter had gotten out of hand and he ended up "smacking her." The family came in for a session the following day and the therapist noticed a sizable bruise on the side of the girl's face. When the psychologist questioned the girl about the bruise, she stated that her father had slapped her the previous day in an argument. Although it seemed that such acts of violence were infrequent in the home, the therapist believed that the father's striking the girl and leaving a bruise warranted an investigation by child protective services. The therapist proceeded to inform the family that it would be necessary for the therapist to file a report with the authorities. The therapist was motivated to report because it seemed that the external pressures on the family to get into treatment would force them to begin working on their problems.

Case 5.2 Commentary

In addition to following legal requirements to report, the professional in this case was motivated to report in order to structure a more consistent pattern of intervention among family members. The message sent to the family was that the situation was serious and deserving of close attention. The professional did, however, delay reporting the father's account of the situation in order to schedule an appointment the next day to see the child and further discuss the situation. Although a report could have been filed immediately, the professional exercised discretion based on previous experiences with the family, as well as the father's disclosure of the situation to the professional. The therapist in this case, therefore, acted in the best interest of the child and family as well as adhering to the mandatory reporting law.

CASE 5.3: SUSPECTED POTENTIAL FOR SEXUAL ABUSE INFLICTED BY A FELLOW PROFESSIONAL

A woman was in therapy for help adjusting to her recent divorce. The woman had a 14-year-old daughter who lived with her. She told her therapist that her daughter was in mandated treatment at a local sex therapy clinic because she had been sexually abused by her father, and the abuse had been substantiated. Because the mother and father were now divorced there was no longer a threat of continued abuse. The mother told the therapist that her daughter also admitted that when she was about seven years old she did some sexual exploration with her younger brother, who was only about three years old at the time. The professional treating the daughter was a woman. She decided that the girl was a perpetrator as well as a victim and wanted to do some testing, including the use of a vaginal plethysmagraph, a vaginally inserted instrument that measures changes in blood flow. The girl would be shown sexual pictures to which her responses would be monitored and interpreted as levels of arousal. The mother was resistant to allowing this procedure, but was being pressured by the treatment center to allow it. The mother told her therapist about these events and her concerns. The therapist was of the opinion that this examination would be sexually abusive to the daughter, given the girl's history of sexual maltreatment. Concerned about the potential for further harm to the child, the mother's therapist felt responsible to report this information to the local child protection agency.

Case 5.3 Commentary

The professional who reported this case was concerned about the potential harm that could result from another professional's use of an invasive assessment procedure. Reporting would therefore be consistent with protecting the child and within the scope of mandatory reporting laws. This case helps demonstrate the breadth of circumstances that could reasonably be considered suspected child maltreatment. The therapist, however, could have first notified the girl's therapist, as suggested whenever a professional questions another professional's ethical conduct (APA, 1992). This contact would not have necessarily replaced the report to the child protection system. In addition, informing the therapist of these concerns directly might have opened a channel for discussion that could have been beneficial to all involved.

CASE 5.4: REPORTED PSYCHOLOGICAL–EMOTIONAL MALTREATMENT

During a psychoeducational evaluation, a psychologist interviewed an eight-year-old boy who appeared depressed and withdrawn, but who denied any serious problems at home. During the beginning of the evaluation, as a means of developing rapport, the boy was asked to answer "the animal question": "If you could be an animal, what kind of animal would you like to be?" The boy responded, "A horse." When asked why, he said, "Well, they mostly work and people ride on them." The psychologist then said, "That does not sound like fun. What wouldn't you want to be?" The boy then said, "A cow . . . because you'd be butchered and eaten." The psychologist proceeded to talk with the boy at greater length, asking him many abuse-related questions. In doing so, the psychologist learned that the boy's parents left him alone for long periods of time and criticized him endlessly, leaving him feeling verbally attacked on many occasions. Although he did not state that he had been hit or beaten, the boy acted very fearful of adults. As a part of the evaluation, the parents were interviewed by the psychologist. The parents confirmed what their son had claimed about the home situation. It became clear that the parents were verbally abusive and had been failing to protect their son from possible harm for at least the past year. The psychologist informed the parents that this kind of behavior constituted a type of maltreatment that could be as harmful as physical abuse and that it would be necessary to change this pattern of events at home. The parents were also informed that it was necessary that the professional report the situation to the child protection system.

Case 5.4 Commentary

The child's disclosure of his parent's actions, and confirmation by the parents themselves, constituted the basis for reporting this case. The psychologist also informed the parents of the report beforehand. There were no factors presented that would have inhibited reporting in this case, including the fact that the professional relationship was evaluative in nature rather than therapeutic. Detecting abuse could be seen as one product of the evaluation process in this case. The professional also perceived psychological–emotional maltreatment as a serious threat to the child and intervened accordingly.

CASE 5.5: REPORTED SUSPECTED CHILD NEGLECT IN A SCHOOL SETTING

A counselor employed in an inner-city therapeutic school managed the treatment program of a 13-year-old girl for more than two years. Having had regular and frequent contact with the girl and her family, the counselor was familiar with her living situation. The girl came from a disadvantaged background that included a low income family living under minimal standards. For example, the family had an apartment that was often occupied by as many as 16 people at any given time. Thus, the girl's environment was often impoverished and chaotic. The child protection system had had previous contact with the family as a result of the application process for welfare and other social support services.

Although the counselor was aware of the child's living conditions, concerns related to poverty and neglect were kept distinct. However, in the most recent school year, the child began to present a number of problems not previously seen by the counselor, including frequent school absences without any contact from the child's parents and frequent complaints of illness but no apparent responsive medical treatment. The girl was also acting out when she was in school by showing pictures of herself in her underwear, openly discussing drinking alcohol, having sex with several boys in the school, and bragging about stealing from local convenience stores. Despite numerous attempts, the counselor was unable to reach the girl's parents. The counselor subsequently reported to child protective services at two different times: when the child was repeatedly truant and when she was sexually acting out. The child protection worker assigned to the case stated that neglect was difficult to substantiate in poverty stricken families and they were doing all that they could to protect the child.

Case 5.5 Commentary

The distinction between impoverished living conditions and child neglect is apparent in this case. The professional seemed to define neglect based on the omission of actions by the child's caregivers. As signs of maltreatment accumulated, it appeared that the child's welfare was not being attended to and the professional became increasingly inclined to report. The professional also suspected neglect when the girl exhibited behaviors that could put her at risk for injury. Because the professional was not able to get a response to messages left for the parents, it seemed that a pattern of neglect had emerged and warranted reporting.

That the child protection system was unable to take action in this case was likely to result in a sense of frustration by the professional as well as other school staff involved in the case. Neglect and psychological–emotional maltreatment are the more difficult types of child maltreatment for mandated reporters to identify and define and are also the more difficult types of maltreatment for the child protection system to investigate and substantiate. Thus, not only will mandated reporters find it more difficult to define reporting thresholds for neglect, but child protection workers could also be limited by the same factors that cause problems for mandated reporters.

CASE 5.6: SUSPECTED SEXUAL ABUSE
OF A CHILD IN FOSTER CARE

A psychologist was acting as a consultant for a foster care agency by conducting evaluations and providing crisis intervention. On one occasion, a biological mother called the psychologist to talk about her concerns regarding her three-year-old daughter who had been placed in foster care. The psychologist, who had evaluated this case, was familiar with the child as well as her biological and foster parents. The girl's mother told the psychologist that she had visited her daughter the past weekend only to discover that she had been left alone with two teenage boys who were living in the foster home. The mother was surprised and upset that the girl was left alone with the boys. One of the boys had told her that he was in charge and took care of the girl. He also said that he cared for her at night and they slept in one bed. The mother took her daughter aside and asked if "anyone had been touching her down there" (pointing to her lower pelvic area). The mother told the psychologist that the girl responded yes. The psychologist told the mother that a report would be filed with child protection services. Subsequently, the child was placed in a new foster home based on her having been left unattended, although sexual abuse was not substantiated.

Case 5.6 Commentary

The psychologist in this case reported a disclosure of suspected sexual abuse without acting to verify the allegations, interview the child, or in any other way support the suspicion of abuse. This case illustrates many of the legal reporting standards for professionals in most states. However, in some states, such as Pennsylvania, Mississippi, and Wisconsin, the case would not be required to be reported because the child was not directly observed by the mandated reporter. Although professionals can report any suspicion in any state, specific requirements for reporting vary from state to state. Still, the immediate action of the professional in this case provides an example of directly responding without hesitation to an allegation.

CASE 5.7: A CASE OF ANGER TURNED TO PHYSICAL ABUSE

A therapist working in an outpatient alcohol and drug treatment center had been treating a woman recovering from alcohol abuse. Their therapeutic relationship had developed over the course of three months following the woman's completion of an inpatient treatment program. The woman, the mother of a 14-year-old boy and a 10-year-old girl, had been divorced from her children's father for seven years and was separated from her second husband. During a session, the mother told the therapist that she had been having a difficult time coping with the stress of raising her two children alone. She said that she was becoming increasingly frustrated and felt that she could not manage her children's behavior, particularly her son's.

The therapist questioned the woman about how she was coping. The woman said that she found herself unable to do anything that worked with her son and that she ended up getting very angry at him for not listening. When asked how she vented her anger, the woman said that she sometimes ended up hitting him. Although she did not believe that hitting her son affected his behavior, she said that it made her feel less angry and more in control. The therapist asked her to describe the way that she hit her son. The woman was very forthcoming and told the therapist that she had hit her son on the lower back with the rubber end of a toilet plunger. The woman said that she had used the plunger because it was the most readily available object.

The therapist believed that the woman's behavior constituted child abuse and required reporting. This decision to report was based solely on the mother's use of an object to hit her child out of anger. The therapist, during that same session, discussed the potential harm that could occur when the woman's anger got out of control. The therapist told the woman that she seemed to be experiencing some really tough times, and the problems she was having should become the immediate focus of their therapy. The therapist also told the woman that it was necessary to report the incident of abuse to social services. The therapist said that social services would evaluate the situation to assure that the woman's children were safe, and then therapy could focus on her anger.

Case 5.7 Commentary

This case represents two simultaneous factors that appear to have influenced reporting. First, the act described by the mother, hitting her adolescent son with a rubber plunger, surpassed the professional's reporting threshold. In this case, the therapist's criteria for reporting did not require information about any injuries sustained. Second, the decision to report was likely influenced by the potential for future harm because the mother's anger had been escalating, increasing the chances of further abuse. Thus, the therapist reported in response to the law, but was also motivated to protect the woman's children from potential harm.

The therapist's manner of reporting is also worth noting. The context of the report was within an established therapeutic relationship in which the mother had made substantial progress in terms of her alcohol abuse. The therapist was very up front with the woman about reporting and the need to break confidentiality. The therapist did, however, place reporting in the context of their ongoing therapy and framed the report as a necessary part of dealing with the woman's difficulties as well as protecting her children. The report was, therefore, filed in the context of the therapeutic relationship.

CONCLUSION

Mandatory child abuse reporting legislation was enacted specifically to require physicians to report injuries they might otherwise not acknowledge as possible child abuse. The laws were broadened with the intent that all human service professionals should be able to identify cases of child maltreatment. In this respect, mandated reporting has been successful at increasing the number of reports filed by professionals; dramatic increases in reporting have occurred since the first reporting laws were enacted. However, these increases have often exceeded the resources available to manage them (Besharov, 1990; M. Levine & A. Levine, 1992; Newberger, 1983).

Despite the difficulties posed by required reporting, few commentators have suggested a complete reversal of mandatory reporting legislation. Rarely are policies instituted that would allow professionals full discretion in reporting suspected child abuse. Rather, many observers have called for legislative reform, such as clarifying definitions of abuse and neglect (Jones & Welch, 1989; Melton & Davidson, 1987) or allowing for the delay of reporting by professionals addressing the abusive situation in therapy (Berlin et al., 1991). Others have suggested that there are no problems with the laws themselves, but rather that the child protection system is insufficiently resourced to deal with the magnitude of the child maltreatment crisis.

Mandated reporters are most likely to be concerned with the welfare of children and families. In this respect, mandated reporters share common goals with the child protection system. As can be seen in the cases presented in this chapter, reporting decisions take into consideration the specific constraints of situations, the professional's reporting experiences, and the circumstances of the family. Professionals who are fully aware of their legal mandate to report and decide to report usually do so with little instruction in or structural guidelines for making a report. Chapter 6 provides some suggested guidelines to consider when reporting.

6

REPORTING SUSPECTED
CHILD ABUSE:
SUGGESTED GUIDELINES

The enactment of a reporting statute is a foolish business unless reported children are, in fact, protected from further injury and offered a brighter life either within the family or with others, should remaining at home prove impossible. (Paulsen, 1967, p.3)

I have difficulty reporting suspected abuse to overburdened, underpaid, and often inexperienced social service workers. Too often reports are made, social services come into a family, make charges, write a report and proceed to do nothing for children. The therapy process is disrupted due to reporting and this can be damaging to families. Reporting abuse does not seem to always be the best solution to abuse—but it is the law in my state. (Survey participant, Kalichman & Brosig, 1992)

As a result of their own reporting experiences, professionals may develop individualized procedures and protocols for making reports of suspected child maltreatment. Experiences with the child protection system, including learning how cases are managed and how investigations are conducted, could affect subsequent reporting decisions. Reported suspicions of child abuse, therefore, have the potential to increase in accuracy and efficacy with repeated reporting experiences. However, because professional experience is often unrelated to improved clinical judgement (Dawes, 1989; Garb, 1989), and because cases of child abuse are unique and child protection policies vary across local agencies, general guidelines should be applied to the reporting process. Rules of thumb to assist professionals in reporting and to improve the reporting process for all persons involved, including children and families, have not been available. Although they play an important role in the child protection system, mandated reporters have received very limited training in the child protection process (Howe, Bonner, Parker, & Sausen, 1992; Kalichman & Brosig, 1993; Pope & Feldman-Summers, 1992).

Professionals making reports to child protection agencies will need to communicate specific information to workers who receive reports. Reports set in motion a series of activities within the child protection system, including a screening process, investigative procedures, risk assessments, and the potential for intervention by the child protection system. Mandated reporters can track the progress of cases through the child protection system, and it is often possible for professionals to maintain communication with caseworkers. Follow-up information can then be fed back into the mandated reporter's professional relationship with the family. Thus, mandated reporting may start with a phone call, but professional roles usually extend into the child protection process, which invariably involves multiple levels of intervention (Besharov, 1988). Unfortunately, few mandated reporters have acquired a working knowledge of the child protection system. Figure 12 represents the typical flow of events that occur when reports are made to child protection agencies.

After reaching a decision to report suspected child abuse, professionals will necessarily make further decisions including the way to inform parents or guardians and children about the report, the appropriate information to release in the report, and the correct procedures for following up on the report. Professionals will also have expectations about the reporting process that can be verified by asking questions of the child protection agency. Procedures that take these factors into account will likely assist the professional in reporting suspected child abuse.

INFORMING PARENTS OR GUARDIANS AND CHILDREN OF THE REPORT

Professionals who initiate a report of suspected child abuse will need to decide to what extent parents or guardians and children will be involved in the reporting process. At minimum, parents or guardians will usually need to be informed of the professional's decision to make a report (Racusin & Felsman, 1986). Parents should not be informed only under circumstances

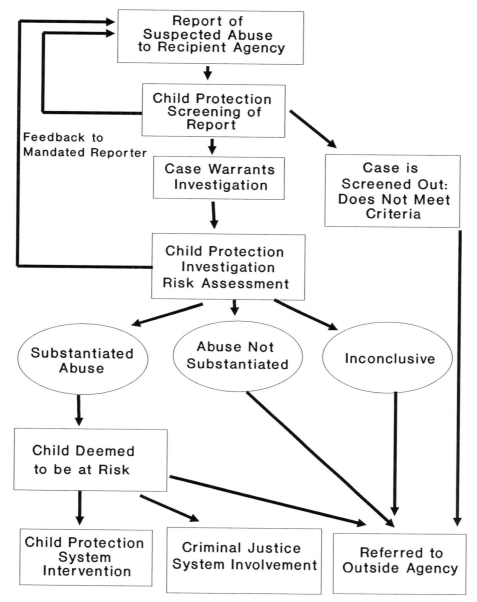

Figure 12: Flow of events following a report of suspected child maltreatment.

in which doing so would likely result in increased potential harm to the child (Besharov, 1990). Failing to inform parents and children about the decision to report creates a "secret," possibly implying that reporting, and therefore the professional's behavior, is harmful. There is, of course, the possibility that angry parents will react to the report by lashing out at the professional or by abusing the child, particularly when the source of the suspicion is contact with the child rather than the parent. Professionals who inform parents of the report before, as opposed to after, contacting the child protection system can assess the situation and take any action necessary to reduce parental anger.

There is also an ethical obligation to inform the parents regarding the breached confidentiality, as discussions of confidentiality are renewed "as new circumstances may warrant" (APA, 1992, Standard 5.01). Telling parents and children that confidentiality must be breached will be easier if they were adequately informed of the limits of confidentiality at the outset of the professional relationship. Persons who have been informed of limited confidentiality will usually expect a report when indicators of child abuse surface. When proper informed consent has been provided, professionals only need to remind parents and children of the professional, ethical, and legal obligations to report. In this context, persons can be encouraged to openly discuss their feelings about the report, and attempts can be made to resolve anger or misunderstandings.

When the suspected perpetrator of abuse is also the person who is being informed of the decision to report, as is often the case when the source of the suspicion is an abusive parent, this person may be encouraged to report himself or herself to the child protection system (Stadler, 1989). Although a self-report does not replace the professional's mandated report, self-reported maltreatment could demonstrate the perpetrator's recognition of the problem and the seriousness of the situation, and could serve as a personal request for assistance to the child protection staff. Self-reporting also affords the individual an opportunity to assume responsibility for his or her own actions and allows for at least some control in what might otherwise be a powerless situation. The parent's self-report can be made from the professional's office, where the professional can support the parent/perpetrator before, during, and after he or she reports. Again, the benefits of self-reporting can be explained to suspected perpetrators who then may be encouraged to report, but a self-report does not replace the professional's mandated report. Professionals should follow up on the self-report by contacting the assigned child protection worker.

The reactions of parents and children who are informed of an impending report are primarily determined by the context within which the information is delivered. Professionals can communicate that the report is being made out of care and concern for the child and family, as well as the professional's ethical responsibility and legal mandate to act. Discussing the circumstances with the family can help bring the report into the context of the professional setting. Expressing concern and a willingness to get involved by reporting helps to focus attention on child protection and can even increase trust in professional relationships (Levine, Anderson, Terretti, Sharma, et al., 1991; Levine, Anderson, Terretti, Steinberg, et al., 1991;

Watson & Levine, 1989). In a treatment setting, reporting can be related to ongoing efforts to resolve family conflicts and child emotional–behavioral problems.

In a research setting, reporting can be an act of concern for the welfare of study participants. The parents and child can also be reassured that they will not be abandoned by the professional during the child protection investigation. The reporter can make the family aware of what to expect from the investigative process and can act as a resource. Thus, issues of confidentiality can be openly dealt with and trust can be enhanced when informing those concerned that the situation requires reporting.

REPORTING SUSPECTED CHILD ABUSE

Although it may seem that the first action in reporting is to telephone a child protection agency, there are some prereporting actions that the professional should first consider. Collecting and organizing the information needed to file a report is often a first step (Finlayson & Koocher, 1991). Although local agencies differ with respect to details required for reporting, there is specific information that will assist child protection workers. Details such as the child's name, age, sex, address, and current whereabouts; information about any other children known to be in the home; the names and addresses of the child's parents; and information regarding the circumstances of abuse and identity of the suspected perpetrator are almost invariably required for reporting.

Mandated reporters are also required to provide their names to the intake worker at the time of filing a report. Although in most cases the reporter's identity will remain confidential, the limits of this confidentiality should be discussed with the intake worker as states vary in the degree to which confidentiality of reports is limited (Meriwether, 1986). Under most circumstances, however, the confidentiality of the professional who reported is of minimal concern to mandated reporters because they will have informed parents themselves that they will be reporting or have reported. When parents have not been informed because doing so might have posed a threat to the child, this potential threat should also be communicated to the intake worker as a part of the report.

The mandated reporter should also consider taking some information from the worker receiving the report, such as the worker's name and any impression of the status of the report he or she can provide. One means for organizing all of the information involved in reporting is through the use of a written record retained by the professional, an example of which is shown in Figure 13. An internal form that records the information contained in a report provides a record for the mandated reporter, making it unnecessary for the reporter to remember exactly what was said in the report.

Report Information Sheet

Report Date: _____ Time: _____ Received by: _____

Child's Name: _____ Sex _____ Ethnicity _____

    Address: _____ Telephone: _____

    Child's present whereabouts: _____

    Primary language: _____

    Name of child's school: _____

Names and ages of other children in home: _____

    _____   _____

    _____   _____

Parent/Guardian name: _____

    Address: _____ Telephone: _____

Narrative of events leading to suspicion/report:_____

    _____

    _____

    _____

    _____

Information relevant to present risk (include any known abuse history)_____

    _____

Suspected perpetrator name:_____

    Address:_____

Worker's indication of screening status:_____

Time line for agency action _____

Figure 13: Information potentially needed to make a report and information to collect when reporting.

Once the information is collected and organized, the next step is to contact the social service agency responsible for taking reports. (See appendix B for a listing of state reporting agencies.) The level of detail released in the report should be limited to the amount that minimizes breaches in confidentiality and maximizes child protection (Melton & Limber, 1989). Information does not need to be released unless it would assist the social service agency in making determinations of maltreatment and taking action on behalf of the child suspected of being abused. As stated in the APA Ethics Code, "In order to minimize intrusions on privacy, psychologists include in written and oral reports, consultations, and the like, only information germane to the purpose for which the communication is made" (1992, Standard 5.03a). In reporting suspected child maltreatment, information is released specifically for the purpose of child protection and should therefore be limited as such.

State statutes usually detail the minimum amount of information required in a report. For example, Minnesota's state law specifies:

> Any report should be of sufficient length to identify the child, any person believed to be responsible for the abuse or neglect of the child if the person is known, the nature of the child's injuries, and the name and address of the reporter. (NCCAN, 1989, p. MN-6)

Similarly, Oregon's statute reads:

> If known, such reports shall contain the names and addresses of the child and his parents or other persons responsible for his care, the child's age, the nature and extent of the abuse (including any evidence of previous abuse), the explanation given for the abuse and any other information the person making the report believes will be helpful in establishing the cause of the abuse and the identity of the perpetrator. (NCCAN, 1989, p. OR-3)

Professionals should also be aware, however, that including more information than is necessary in a mandated report, as well as providing additional information after the report, can violate a person's rights to privacy and could raise issues of liability (Pope & Vasquez, 1991). Circumstances unrelated to the suspicion of abuse, such as details of family life and family relationships that are peripheral to the abuse, need not be included in the report. For example, information about the parents' marital relationship or a parent's history of being abused as a child might be of clinical importance but would not necessarily be relevant to the purposes of reporting. The narrative section of the report, in which the circumstances of suspected abuse are discussed, should be limited to the signs, symptoms, acts, omissions, and verbal disclosures accounting for the suspicion that led to and exceeded the professional's reporting threshold. Mandated reporters are encouraged to cooperate with the child protection system, but should also think carefully before divulging any information after the initial report (Pope & Vasquez, 1991).

Intake workers will probably request from mandated reporters information that is necessary to conduct the investigation and risk assessments. For example, workers might need to know whether or not the child requires medical attention or if medical services have been sought. Workers might also want reasons for any lag between the reporter's awareness of the situation and the actual reporting, knowledge of any witnesses to the abuse, information about parental substance abuse that may be related to child maltreatment, and the reporter's impressions of danger to the child (Wisconsin Department of Health and Social Services, 1985). If they are unsure of the ethics of divulging certain information, professionals should communicate their concerns to the worker and take steps toward providing information necessary for child protection while maintaining confidentiality to the greatest degree possible (Melton & Limber, 1989). Thus, balancing disclosure and confidentiality remains a critical task for mandated reporters.

Ultimately, with information organized and ethical concerns addressed, reports of suspected child maltreatment are made by telephoning the state or local child protection agency. In many states, verbal reports are required to be followed by a written report. A written record of the information included in the verbal report, if organized ahead of time, will be useful in preparing the written report. Many states provide forms for written reports that limit the amount of detailed information required. Figure 14 presents two examples of written report forms. In states that use such forms, they are available to reporters from child protection agencies. If obtained in advance, these forms could serve as a basis for organizing information for the verbal report as well, completing both steps of reporting at once.

The explicit purpose of information contained in the verbal report, as well as that in the written report, is to inform the child protection system that a child may have been maltreated or may be at risk for maltreatment. After receiving the report, the first step taken by the child protection agency is to screen the report and conduct an assessment of the child's potential risk for maltreatment.

REPORT SCREENING AND INITIAL RISK ASSESSMENTS

High rates of reported child maltreatment have made it necessary for child protection agencies to develop procedures for initial screening of reports, prioritizing reports, and preliminary assessing of child risk (Besharov, 1987a, 1990; Wells et al., 1989). Verbal reports received by child protection workers are screened along a number of dimensions for minimal criteria to determine their status in the child protection system. Table 4 summarizes the common activities that could take place throughout child protection system involvement, including screening and initial risk assessments. Cases only move past the initial report after surpassing a second decision threshold set by the child protection system. The screening of cases includes an initial risk assessment that allows the intake agency to use

TABLE 4
Child Protective Service Actions Following Reported Suspected Abuse

I Intake	II Meets Screening Criteria: Initial Assessment	III Substantiated Case: Provision of Services
Report received Family is checked for current and previous recorded reports Report is screened Risk assessment conducted Appropriate referrals are considered Investigation status determined	Investigative contacts and visits conducted Child risk assessment continued Emergency services provided Court involvement determined Case management assigned	Risk assessment continued Thorough family assessment conducted Intervention strategy developed and executed Appropriate services provided and progress evaluated

discretion in determining whether or not to accept a report for investigation (Wells et al., 1989).

The criteria for screening reports varies considerably across local agencies (Wells et al., 1989). One set of minimal criteria for screening requires only that enough information be provided to enable agencies to locate the child and parents who are the subjects of the report. Screening might also include a determination of whether or not the indicators of abuse included in the report fit the state definition of child abuse or neglect. For example, the Illinois Department of Child and Family Services (1992) retains reports under the condition that "if the allegation presented were true, the situation would constitute abuse or neglect as defined" (p. 300-6). Thus, reports in that state must meet state definitions of maltreatment in order to proceed further into the Illinois child protection system.

Because the person who takes the report is most often a social service worker, screening decisions are often made during the initial report. Mandated reporters, therefore, can request information regarding the status of their report at this first contact. The worker can often tell the reporter whether or not enough information has been provided to warrant an investigation. Reports that are screened out of the system could be terminated from further action, or referred to an agency outside of the child protection system for intervention. Reports deemed inappropriate for action because they do not meet the minimum criteria for investigation might still warrant services, and child protection agencies will frequently make outside referrals (Wells et al., 1989). Cases that are found to be appropriate for child protective system involvement are investigated and undergo a more thorough and comprehensive process of risk assessment. If the report is not investigated, professionals can request that the report remain on file with

SUSPECTED CHILD ABUSE REPORT

To Be Completed by Reporting Party
Pursuant to Penal Code Section 11166

B. REPORTING PARTY

NAME/TITLE

ADDRESS

PHONE ( )   DATE OF REPORT   SIGNATURE OF REPORTING PARTY

C. REPORT SENT TO

☐ POLICE DEPARTMENT   ☐ SHERIFF'S OFFICE   ☐ COUNTY WELFARE   ☐ COUNTY PROBATION

AGENCY   ADDRESS

OFFICIAL CONTACTED   PHONE ( )   DATE/TIME

D. INVOLVED PARTIES

VICTIM

NAME (LAST, FIRST, MIDDLE)   ADDRESS   BIRTHDATE   SEX   RACE

PRESENT LOCATION OF CHILD   PHONE ( )

SIBLINGS

NAME	BIRTHDATE	SEX	RACE	NAME	BIRTHDATE	SEX	RACE
1.				4.			
2.				5.			
3.				6.			

PARENTS

NAME (LAST, FIRST, MIDDLE)   BIRTHDATE SEX RACE   NAME (LAST, FIRST, MIDDLE)   BIRTHDATE SEX RACE

ADDRESS   ADDRESS

HOME PHONE ( )   BUSINESS PHONE ( )   HOME PHONE ( )   BUSINESS PHONE ( )

E. INCIDENT INFORMATION

IF NECESSARY, ATTACH EXTRA SHEET OR OTHER FORM AND CHECK THIS BOX. ☐

1. DATE/TIME OF INCIDENT   PLACE OF INCIDENT   (CHECK ONE) ☐ OCCURRED   ☐ OBSERVED

IF CHILD WAS IN OUT-OF-HOME CARE AT TIME OF INCIDENT, CHECK TYPE OF CARE:

☐ FAMILY DAY CARE   ☐ CHILD CARE CENTER   ☐ FOSTER FAMILY HOME   ☐ SMALL FAMILY HOME   ☐ GROUP HOME OR INSTITUTION

2. TYPE OF ABUSE: (CHECK ONE OR MORE)   ☐ PHYSICAL   ☐ MENTAL   ☐ SEXUAL ASSAULT   ☐ NEGLECT   ☐ OTHER

3. NARRATIVE DESCRIPTION:

4. SUMMARIZE WHAT THE ABUSED CHILD OR PERSON ACCOMPANYING THE CHILD SAID HAPPENED:

5. EXPLAIN KNOWN HISTORY OF SIMILAR INCIDENT(S) FOR THIS CHILD:

SS 8572 (REV. 7/87)   *INSTRUCTIONS AND DISTRIBUTION ON REVERSE*

DO NOT submit a copy of this form to the Department of Justice (DOJ). A CPA is required under Penal Code Section 11169 to submit to DOJ a Child Abuse Investigation Report Form SS-8583 if (1) an active investigation has been conducted and (2) the incident is **not** unfounded.

Police or Sheriff–WHITE Copy; County Welfare or Probation–BLUE Copy; District Attorney–GREEN Copy; Reporting Party–YELLOW Copy

Figure 14: Two examples of typical child maltreatment report forms. From State of California and State of Connecticut Departments of Social Services.

their agency for use by workers should the same family be reported again in the future. Reports kept on file also provide an official record of the mandated report.

Beyond screening for investigation, reports are usually arranged according to their priority for protective services action. Criteria for prioritizing reports can include the type of abuse, the child's age, and the apparent risk

REPORT OF SUSPECTED CHILD ABUSE/NEGLECT

CYS-136　　(Rev. 2/90)

STATE OF CONNECTICUT
DEPARTMENT OF CHILDREN AND YOUTH SERVICES
Division of Children and Protective Services
170 SIGOURNEY ST., HARTFORD, CONNECTICUT 06105

See reverse side of yellow copy for Summary of Connecticut law concerning the protection of children. In cases of suspected child abuse, an ORAL REPORT SHOULD BE MADE IMMEDIATELY TO PROTECTIVE SERVICES in the Department of Children and Youth Services Regional Office having authority over the area in which the child resides. (See list of Regional Offices below). This written report should be prepared WITHIN 72 HOURS and submitted to the same agency.

REPORTER: Keep YELLOW copy. Send the WHITE COPY to PROTECTIVE SERVICES of the Department of Children and Youth Services Regional Office.

REGIONAL OFFICE: Enter name of agency and social worker to whom case is assigned on the WHITE copy for your records.

Please print or type.

CHILD'S NAME	CHILD'S ADDRESS	AGE OR BIRTHDATE

Parents or other person responsible for child's care:	NAME	ADDRESS

WHERE IS THE CHILD AT PRESENT?	DATE CHILD EXAMINED

ORAL REPORT WAS MADE TO	DATE OF ORAL REPORT	DATE OF SUSPECTED CHILD ABUSE *(If known)*

Suspected perpetrator, if known:	NAME	ADDRESS

NATURE, EXTENT AND EXPLANATION OF THE SUSPECTED ABUSE

LIST NAMES AND AGES OF SIBLINGS, IF SUSPECTED ABUSE

REPORTER'S NAME AND AGENCY	ADDRESS	TELEPHONE NO.

REPORTER'S SIGNATURE	POSITION	DATE

DCYS USE ONLY

REGIONAL OFFICE LOCATION	NAME OF ASSIGNED SOCIAL WORKER	NAME OF AGENCY ASSIGNED, IF NOT PROTECTIVE SERVICES

DCYS REGIONAL OFFICE LOCATIONS

CITY	STREET ADDRESS		PHONE NO	CITY	STREET ADDRESS		PHONE NO
BRIDGEPORT	1115 Main St	06604	579-6150	HAMDEN	2105 State St.	06514	786-0500
DANBURY	131 West St	06810	797-4040	NORWICH	331 Main Street	06360	886-2641
HARTFORD	1049 Asylum Ave	06105	566-4184	ROCKVILLE	1 Court Street	06066	872-6222
MERIDEN	Bldg #2 Undercliff Rd	06450	238-6185	STAMFORD	1642 Bedford St	06905	348-5865
MIDDLETOWN	121 Main Street Ext	06457	344-2120	TORRINGTON	352 Main St	06790	482-0669
NEW BRITAIN	149 Main St	06051	827-7137	WATERBURY	414 Meadow St	06702	753-9541
				WILLIMANTIC	1320 Main St	06226	450-2000

Figure 14 (continued).

of harm or injury to the child (Kentucky Department of Social Services, 1989). Cases might also be prioritized according to the case load demands of the agency and available agency resources. Some states do not proceed with cases that do not meet a minimum level of risk or in which there is insufficient information to identify or locate the child and parents (Wells et al., 1989). On the other hand, some states prioritize reports, but do eventually investigate all reports received (Kentucky Department of Social Services, 1989).

A report might be classified by the receiving agency as an emergency requiring immediate action, often within one hour of the report. Emergencies are usually defined as a child being in imminent danger, and response may involve notification of a law enforcement agency. Nonemergency cases are assigned to a caseworker who is required to contact the child or family within 24, 48, or 72 hours, depending on the state. Reports might also be prioritized according to the type of maltreatment described by the reporter. For example, reports are prioritized by some agencies into three different levels. The highest level of priority is given to reports that involve death, brain damage, subdural hematoma, internal injuries, wounds, torture, sexually transmitted diseases, sexual molestation, failure to thrive, and malnutrition. A second level of priority is assigned to reports that include none of the characteristics of the first level but do include burns, scalds, poisoning, bone fractures, cuts, bruises, welts, human bites, tying or closed confinement, or substantial risk of physical injury or abandonment. The third level of priority is assigned to reports of consistently inadequate food, shelter, or clothing, and other forms of environmental neglect (Illinois Department of Child and Family Services, 1992). Thus, agencies respond to reports according to the designated level of priority, with the most severe reports assigned for immediate investigation.

CHILD PROTECTION SYSTEM INVESTIGATIONS

Cases that are accepted by the child protection agency proceed into the system through a series of actions required by state law. Specific interventions vary across local agencies. For example, North Carolina law requires that

> the Department of Social Services shall make a prompt and thorough investigation in order to ascertain the facts of the case, the extent of the abuse or neglect and risk of harm to the juvenile, in order to determine whether protective services should be provided or the complaint filed as a petition. When the report alleges abuse, the Director shall immediately, but no later than 24 hours after receipt of the report, initiate the investigation. (NCCAN, 1989, p. NC-7)

Illustrating a different set of requirements in mandated agency action, Arizona's statute requires that

> after receipt and initial screening . . . of any report or information . . . immediately: (a) notify the municipal or county law enforcement agency; and (b) make a prompt and thorough investigation of the nature, extent, and cause of any condition which would tend to support

or refute the allegation that the child should be adjudicated dependant. (NCCAN, 1989, p. AZ-8)

As reflected in these two statutes, the role of law enforcement agencies in child maltreatment investigations also varies across communities. Some states require law enforcement officers to be notified on receipt of the report, others require law enforcement involvement only with substantiated reports, and still others immediately involve police with some types or conditions of abuse but not others. For example, some states require immediate law enforcement notification and a joint investigation with child protection workers only for reports of sexual abuse. When law enforcement officers are required to be involved it is the child protection agency's responsibility to make these additional or collateral contacts.

Child protection investigations involve, at minimum, home visits by an assigned worker who interviews the parents, child, and alleged perpetrator. Individuals included in the report, such as children, parents, and siblings, must be interviewed for the investigation to proceed. Not interviewing persons included in the report is officially acceptable to agencies after repeated attempts to contact these persons have failed. In addition, teachers, school administrators, family members, neighbors, and others might be interviewed as a part of an investigation. Interviews usually solicit information and answer specific questions regarding the alleged maltreatment. Investigation procedures are typically idiosyncratic to the circumstances of the report, the local agency procedures, and the individual style of the assigned worker. Investigations are conducted to determine the conditions the child is living under and the potential risk for harm and injury to the child. Thus, the purpose of the investigation is fact finding for evidence of maltreatment to determine the level of risk for the child.

Whereas investigations evaluate the extent of any present harm to a child, risk assessments are primarily conducted to predict whether or not a child will be maltreated in the future. Risk assessments involve a comprehensive examination of the child's well-being, family resources, and living conditions (Pecora, 1991). Although a brief assessment of risk for abuse is conducted during the initial intake, risk assessments are an ongoing process and involve more elaborate methods during the course of the investigation. One method commonly used by investigation agencies involves rating a number of child and family characteristics along a number of dimensions of potential risk. Factors that could be assessed include parenting skills, frequency and severity of maltreatment, the perpetrator's accessibility to the child, the child's ability for self-protection, and the recency of maltreatment. Each factor would then be rated as low, moderate, or high level of risk (Pecora, 1991; Wisconsin Department of Health and Social Services, 1985). A matrix is then constructed to comprehensively represent levels of risk for each factor. Figure 15 presents an example of a few of the typical components

Risk Factor	Positive Indicator	Low Risk	Moderate Risk	High Risk
Protection of child	Caretaker willing and able to protect child, using good judgment	Caretaker willing but occasionally unable to protect child	Caretaker vacillates or inconsistently protects child	Caretaker refuses or is unable to protect child
Extent of emotional harm	No emotional harm or behavioral disturbance	Minor distress or impairment in role functioning	Behavioral problems that impair social relationships or role functioning	Extensive emotional or behavioral impairment
Extent of physical injury or harm	No injury, no medical treatment required	Superficial injury, no medical attention required	Significant injury, unlikely to require medical attention	Major injury, substantial effect on development requiring medical treatment

Figure 15: An example of a risk assessment matrix. Adapted with permission from Caldwell et al. (1992).

in some risk assessment matrixes. Risk factors rated in the assessment usually consist of a group of commonly associated factors or empirically defined predictors of child maltreatment (Pecora, 1991).

In addition to assessments that tabulate risk factors, matrixes have been developed to assess family strengths and resources, which are often overlooked in risk assessments. Assets and strengths provide valuable information for long-term predictions of maltreatment that might not be readily apparent to field workers, particularly when working with families from unfamiliar cultural backgrounds (Caldwell et al., 1992). Family strengths can be used as a context within which risk factors are embedded, allowing for more comprehensive maltreatment determinations. It could, therefore, be useful to note family strengths and assets in reports of abuse.

Among the more objective risk assessment instruments used by child protection agencies is the Child at Risk Field (CARF) (Holder & Corey, 1986). This system allows the worker to define risk levels on the basis of a comprehensive evaluation of five factors, or force fields: the child, parent(s), family/home, maltreatment, and intervention (Pecora, 1991). The worker identifies the potential threats within each factor for each maltreatment situation using a set of standard definitions for each level of potential risk. For example, parenting behavior is scored along a continuum from appropriate parenting to destructive parenting, in which appropriate parenting is defined by CARF as:

> [The parent] generally exhibits parenting behavior which takes into account the child's age capacity; possesses reasonable expectations for the child; understands and acts on the child's strengths/limitations/ needs; uses varied and acceptable disciplinary approaches; provides basic care, nurturing and support; demonstrates self-control. (DePanfilis, Holder, Corey, & Oelson, 1986, p. 273)

In contrast, destructive parenting is defined as:

> [The parent] exhibits parenting behavior which is based on the parent's needs; demonstrates expectations which are impossible for the child to meet; ignores the child's strengths/limitations/needs; aversion to parenting; employs extreme/harsh disciplinary approaches, including violence, threats and verbal assaults; generally does not provide basic care and/or support; deliberately takes frustrations out on the child; self-righteous. (DePanfilis et al., 1986, p. 273)

Thus, CARF provides a framework for the worker's observations, impressions, and judgements, resulting in a comprehensive estimate of child risk. The system also assesses the urgency of maltreatment, again using the factors related to the child, family, home, and so forth. Factors are aggregated and summarized to determine relative levels of risk. For example, a child under the age of six years who requires medical attention, with a parent who is impaired or excessively agitated, would constitute an urgent case of maltreatment (DePanfilis et al., 1986).

There is little data available to support the reliability and validity of risk assessment instruments that use matrixes and comprehensive rating systems for structuring maltreatment evaluations (Pecora, 1991). Studies that have investigated the accuracy of these instruments in detecting risk levels have been varied, with correct classification rates as low as 15%, and false negative rates as high as 50% (Pecora, 1991). In addition, studies have only been conducted on the association between risk assessments and past occurrence of maltreatment. There have been few studies of predictive validity and virtually no studies have been prospective in design (Pecora, 1991). Finally, little data have been collected on the reliability, including indexes of interrater and internal consistencies, of even the more established and widely used risk assessment instruments (Pecora, 1991).

CHILD MALTREATMENT INVESTIGATION FINDINGS

The goal of the child protection investigation is a determination of the occurrence or nonoccurrence of child abuse. Local agencies vary in definitions and criteria for substantiation of maltreatment. Typically, however, there are three potential outcomes from a child protection investigation:

> *Substantiated.* Maltreatment has been found to occur and protective services for the child may be appropriate. The family problems might also be complex and require specific intervention. The objectives from the point after substantiation are to protect the child and assist the family.
>
> *Unsubstantiated.* Insufficient information exists to pursue charges of child maltreatment (Weissman, 1991). Maltreatment is not found and the family is not in need of protective services. However, the family might be experiencing problems and, therefore, might be referred to an outside agency for services.
>
> *Not able to substantiate/inconclusive.* Maltreatment is indeterminable due to an unavailability of factual information, as is the case when the child or parents cannot be located for an investigative interview.

Approximately half of all reports of child maltreatment are substantiated on investigation (U.S. Department of Health and Human Services, 1988). Substantiation rates for reports filed by mandated reporters are as much as 23% higher for physical abuse and 13% higher for sexual abuse compared with reports filed by nonmandated reporters (Eckenrode, Munsch, Powers, & Doris, 1988; Eckenrode, Powers, et al., 1988). Unsubstantiated reports filed by professionals could reflect the discrepancy between professional reporting criteria and child protection system substantiation criteria, including definitions of serious maltreatment that might be stricter for substantiation criteria (Giovannoni, 1989a). The intent of reporting laws, namely detecting a maximum number of cases of child maltreatment, sets discrepancies in the direction of reports not being substantiated because mandated reporters are required to report reasonable suspicions of child abuse, whereas substantiation is determined by collecting evidence to support the occurrence of maltreatment. Thus, the existence of two different operating standards, reasonable suspicion and preponderance of evidence, may explain why many reports cannot be substantiated.

Unsubstantiated reports tend to be characterized by incomplete information and vague descriptions of situations. Reports with less detailed information are less likely to proceed through each step of child protection (Wells et al., 1989). Unsubstantiated cases do not necessarily mean that abuse has not occurred, but rather that the preponderance of information resulting from the investigation does not warrant child protection intervention. Thus, the criteria set by the protection system results in a high threshold for intervention and accepts a high rate of false negatives. The logic behind the system as a whole, therefore, is that mandated reporting accepts high rates of reported false positives (reported cases in which abuse may not be occurring), balanced by high rates of unsubstantiated false negatives (cases in which abuse is occurring but not substantiated). The result is that there are necessarily more reports by professionals than there are investigations and more investigations than there are substantiated cases of maltreatment.

Another reason for higher substantiation rates among reports filed by mandated reporters is that they are more likely to obtain detailed and specific information regarding child maltreatment than nonmandated reporters. For example, medical professionals are likely to observe injuries consistent with nonaccidental harm that are expected to raise suspicions of child abuse. Likewise, mental health professionals frequently observe emotional and behavioral changes that raise suspicions of child abuse. Mental health practitioners, guidance counselors, schoolteachers, and other professionals who develop trusting relationships with children are also likely to be told of stressful life events, including abusive experiences. However, every instance of suspected child abuse does not necessarily constitute a reasonable suspicion, and therefore might not warrant reporting. Mandated reporters who consult colleagues about difficult cases can get an objective perspective on challenging cases. Professionals could also contact a child protection worker and informally ask about a case to get his or her impression of whether or not the circumstances warrant reporting. Professionals, therefore, can take steps to increase levels of confidence in their reporting decisions.

CONCLUSION

Child protection workers are known to be overburdened and poorly resourced. Agency standards for not assigning more than 25 to 30 new cases per month to a single worker are often exceeded as a result of the national crisis in child protection. Given this potential for heavy work loads, it is likely that child protection workers will need to turn cases over as rapidly and efficiently as possible. Thus, providing workers with well-organized and complete information will assist them in the process of investigating reports. Mandated reporters can also request information from workers regarding the status of their reports. Information regarding the screening and prioritizing of reports at the initial intake, as well as the time line for an investigation, provides useful feedback to the mandated reporter. Reporting laws specify that mandated reporters be informed of the final status of their reports, but more information could be useful to reporters throughout the process. Thus, interorganizational relationships between mandated reporters and investigative agencies can be mutually beneficial (Wells, 1988).

Assuming that a cooperative relationship between mandated reporters and the child protection system will result in greater child protection (Wells, 1988), professionals can take action toward building such relationships. For example, contacting the worker assigned to a case can facilitate an ongoing relationship among reporters and child protection workers. Another mechanism for building a relationship with the child protection system is to request a discussion group or presentation from the child protection agency. Small groups of mandated reporters could interact with and ask questions of workers about the child protection system and procedures related to reporting. Direct contact with workers can foster a liaison-like relationship and provide a channel for asking questions about future cases. Open communication and cooperation between mandated reporters and child protection workers throughout the reporting and investigation processes could benefit all involved, including children and families.

III

DIRECTIONS FOR PRACTICE, RESEARCH, AND POLICY

INTRODUCTION

DIRECTIONS FOR PRACTICE, RESEARCH, AND POLICY

Mandatory child abuse reporting laws are not the solution to the child maltreatment problem, but they act as the mechanism that links human service professionals to the child protection system. Because child maltreatment is one of the most pressing contemporary social problems, mandated reporting of suspected child abuse promises to be a persistent professional issue. Previous chapters discussed many of the complex professional dilemmas associated with mandated child abuse reporting. The research and commentary reviewed have resulted in greater understanding of the issues raised when professionals believe a child may be at risk for maltreatment. The information gathered and synthesized can be used to form a basis for initiatives and strategies directed at improving professional responses to child abuse and social policies. This section examines the most promising avenues to pursue in responding to and studying mandated reporting. Suggestions drawn from the literature are offered for developing professional standards and practices for mandated reporting, objectively identifying and defining problem areas through directed research, and effecting legislative change.

7

FUTURE DIRECTIONS FOR PROFESSIONAL PRACTICE AND TRAINING

It is critical that psychologists know what constitutes an appropriate psychological assessment of suspected child abuse so that they know how and when to respond to the legal requirements of mandatory reporting laws. This includes knowing how to recognize reportable situations and what steps to take in specific jurisdictions where they practice. (Walker et al., 1989, p. 8)

My primary concern is always for the child. At times I have worked with "questionable" abuse, such as when a child is hit more than I would like but no bruises are left, or when abuse has occurred in the past and the perpetrator is no longer involved with the child. I do not report many of these cases and it concerns me. (Survey participant, Kalichman & Brosig, 1993)

Historically, professionals have received little training in recognizing and dealing with child maltreatment and have had few resources for managing cases of child abuse and neglect. In fact, child maltreatment is a relatively recent area of mental health practice and a new area of objective research (M. Levine & A. Levine, 1992). As recently as 1978, 32% of psychologists were unfamiliar with mandatory reporting laws (Swoboda et al., 1978). Thus, professionals have often been at a loss for proper guidance and appropriate action when faced with mandated reporting. Steps, however, can be taken by professionals to effectively address many of the current problems associated with mandated reporting of suspected child abuse. In this chapter, suggestions are drawn from the child maltreatment and mandated reporting literature relevant to professional service delivery and research conducted with human participants. Specific recommendations are offered for developing professional standards for reporting as well as for training professionals to better manage cases of suspected child maltreatment. Proactive efforts to resolve ethical and professional conflicts related to mandated reporting can be implemented by individual professionals, professional organizations, and interorganizational structures. The suggestions that follow can be implemented at any of these levels of intervention.

ETHICAL STANDARDS AND MANDATED REPORTING

Mandatory reporting as an ethical dilemma is closely related to the perceived conflict between professional standards of confidentiality and legal requirements to report. Disclosing information obtained in confidence goes against the value systems of many human service professionals, particularly among therapists, counselors, and researchers. Many professionals view breaches in confidentiality as a serious threat to professional relationships (Keith-Spiegel & Koocher, 1985; Watson & Levine, 1989), but at the same time, breaking the law is itself unethical. Conflicts between professionals' values and legal requirements to report define the horns of the reporting dilemma (Bersoff, 1975).

As previously discussed, when it comes to mandated reporting, ethics codes are not particularly helpful in resolving conflicts between professional practice and legal standards. Professionals are advised to "make known their commitment to the Ethics Code and take steps to resolve the conflict in a reasonable manner" (APA, 1992, Introduction). Ethics committees, of course, do not advocate breaking the law and ethics codes do not establish standards for professional behavior outside of the law. It is understandable that standards for managing suspected child abuse and reporting are not outlined in ethics codes because ethical principles are written for a broad spectrum of circumstances rather than for specific situations.

Legal standards for defining child maltreatment and determining when to report are also of little help to professionals because they are either too vague or too narrow to apply to cases in practice and therefore provide inadequate criteria for professional decision making (Jones & Welch, 1989). It is widely known that legal standards for reporting do not translate to standards of professional practice (Finlayson & Koocher, 1991). As a result, professionals are left to define their own personal standards for what constitutes reasonable suspicions of child abuse. In recognition of the lack of standards, there have been several suggestions for professionals to use lenient reporting criteria, taking the perspective that it is better to err on the side of reporting than nonreporting (i.e., Finlayson & Koocher, 1991; Walker et al., 1988). The philosophy behind this position is that it is more sound to accept the probability of false identifications in order to minimize the potential for missing cases of child maltreatment. On the other hand, stricter reporting criteria have also been advocated, stressing the negative aspects of breaking confidentiality and cautioning against the overwhelming effects of overreporting on the child protection system (e.g., Ansell & Ross, 1990; Besharov, 1990). The latter position emphasizes the value of professional judgement in clinical decision making as well as focusing on parental and family rights to privacy. Although an argument can be made for either position, the ultimate decision remains with individual professionals who are left to interpret the meaning of *reasonable suspicion* on their own and establish personal reporting thresholds.

Reporting standards often define reasonable suspicions of child maltreatment as situations in which a reasonable person would suspect maltreatment. For example, the California Code defines reasonable suspicion as when it is "objectively reasonable for a person to entertain such a suspicion, based upon facts that could cause a reasonable person in a like position, drawing when appropriate on his or her training and experience, to suspect child abuse" (California Crime Prevention Center, 1988, p. 48). Under this standard, professionals are to consider the range of potential abuse indicators that originally raised their suspicion of child abuse and determine a working definition of child maltreatment suitable to their professional practice and setting. It is difficult for professionals who set their own standards for reporting ambiguous cases to respond to the law and to be held accountable for their reporting decisions. As an alternative approach, experts in child abuse and neglect could formulate a set of parameters, based on indicators of maltreatment, to define reasonable suspicions of child abuse. Professional standards could therefore be derived from empirical studies of child maltreatment with direct input from clinicians and researchers. An objective standard for determining suspected child maltreatment would clarify expectations for actions taken by mandated reporters. Even if such an agreement were reached, however, and standards were set for defining suspected child abuse and reporting, ethical implications related to mandatory reporting laws would remain.

Ethical–legal conflicts that surround mandated reporting have been addressed in the development of professional standards of confidentiality (APA, 1992). Prompted by growing concerns over duty to warn, standards of confidentiality now acknowledge the importance of informing persons of the limits of confidentiality as an essential step to minimizing the confi-dentiality–disclosure dilemma. In practice, discussions of limited confiden-tiality can be framed within a context consistent with professional roles. When professionals inform persons of the need to disclose information regarding suspected child abuse, professional roles of family advocate and concerned helper can be stressed. Reporting suspected child maltreatment requires actions that include breaking confidentiality, as is the case when professionals take steps to stop persons from causing self-inflicted harm or harming someone else. Mandated reporters can convey that they are mo-tivated by concern for the persons involved in the report, as well as by their legal–ethical requirements to protect persons from harm. Limited confiden-tiality can, therefore, be framed in a context that stresses strict confi-dentiality for things discussed in the professional relationship, with a few exceptions: if the client signs an information release; if information is disclosed regarding potential harm to self or others; if there is reason to suspect that a child, elderly person, or a person with a disability is at risk for abuse; or if a court order is issued. Framing limited confidentiality in the context of an otherwise confidential relationship helps put the focus on the overall degree of privacy in the professional relationship and may facilitate an environment of trust and open disclosure (Taylor & Adelman, 1989).

Although professions and professional organizations have not yet es-tablished ethical guidelines specifically directed at child abuse reporting, several conclusions can be drawn from previous chapters and could be sum-marized as points of ethical consideration in mandated reporting. Although the following points could be useful to professionals who are considering the ethical implications of their reporting decisions, these recommendations cannot be considered an ethics code for managing cases of child maltreat-ment. Ethical guidelines always develop from professional consensus or some other means of convention. However, if a governing body should undertake the development of standards or guidelines for reporting, the following could serve as a starting point.

POINTS OF ETHICAL CONSIDERATION
IN MANDATED REPORTING

The 11 ethical signposts summarized on the next few pages are not standards of practice. Rather, they are presented for consideration by man-dated reporters. These ideas were developed in the hope of fueling future discussions and research of mandated reporting as a legal issue with ethical implications.

- Knowledge of state mandatory reporting law
- Informed consent with details of limited confidentiality pro-vided

- Disclosures of abuse that surpass reporting thresholds
- Suspicions based on subtle signs not immediately dismissed
- Boundaries of professional competence and roles maintained
- Parents or guardians informed of reports unless doing so would endanger children
- Keeping detailed records of reports
- Following up reports with child protective service workers
- Verifying cases believed to have been reported by supervisors, colleagues, or others
- Discussing ambiguous cases with colleagues
- Training in recognizing signs of abuse that parallels potential contact with abuse cases

Knowledge of state laws regarding requirements to report suspected child maltreatment is necessary for all mandated reporters. Over the past two decades, professionals have become increasingly aware of mandated reporting. Professionals still, however, need to increase their familiarity with specific state definitions of child abuse and neglect, the conditions under which reporting is required, and the mandatory procedures for reporting (e.g., time constraints and filing written versus verbal reports). It is also important for professionals to be familiar with the legal requirements of responding child protection agencies, as well as the operations of the child protection system. Familiarity with reporting laws and the child protection system provides professionals with accurate expectations and allows them to be effective resources for families.

Treatment and research professionals need standard informed consent procedures that clearly detail the conditions under which confidentiality is limited. Persons should be provided with informed consent, including the limits of confidentiality, at the onset of professional relationships. Procedures for informing persons of limited confidentiality may be written or verbal, but in either case it is important that all limitations be comprehended by persons who provide consent. When a written informed consent is used, limitations of confidentiality and other important points should be discussed and clarified. Thus, the optimal procedures would involve a discussion of limited confidentiality and a written statement that persons can take with them.

Disclosures of child abuse can be interpreted as evidence of maltreatment and should surpass reporting thresholds. Disclosures of abuse or neglect by a child or perpetrator invariably warrant investigation. It is beyond the role of human service professionals to discern the credibility of a disclosure when the costs of undetected maltreatment are so high. Disclosures by persons other than the victim or perpetrator are more complex given the potential motives for accusations of child abuse. However, all disclosures or allegations of abuse warrant child protective system investigation to verify the occurrence of alleged abuse.

Suspicions of child maltreatment based on behavioral or physical indicators that do not appear to warrant reporting require close evaluation before reporting can be completely dismissed. Suspicions of child maltreatment rarely occur without identifiable indicators and signs. When the signs do not meet reporting criteria, professionals could probe their sources for further information by using specific and pointed questions (Pruitt & Kappius, 1992). Professionals could consult with colleagues or make preliminary contact with the child protection system in order to further evaluate their concerns over reporting specific cases.

Professionals operate within their areas of competence and defined professional roles and should not overstep their limitations to verify the occurrence of child abuse. When dealing with suspected child abuse, mandated reporters should avoid taking actions that they would not otherwise take in fulfilling thier typical and regular professional duties. When professionals feel compelled to go beyond their skills and roles, they should recognize the need for investigation and should therefore report.

It is necessary to inform parents or guardians of a report before it is filed unless doing so would endanger the welfare of the child or children. The negative effects that reporting might have on professional relationships can be minimized by dealing with the report in the context of professional relationships. For example, informing parents or guardians about a report within a discussion of the elements of the suspicions that led to the report might minimize adverse effects. When professionals believe that informing parents of a report would endanger children, however, the child protection system should be informed of these concerns at the time the report is filed.

Professionals should keep thorough and detailed records of information released in a report. Records of oral reports as well as copies of written reports filed with the child protection system are a necessary component of reporting. If further contact with the child protection system occurs after reporting, detailed records of these exchanges should also be kept.

Professionals are expected to follow up on reports to the child protection system. Information regarding the stages of investigation, including the status of substantiation, can be requested from the child protection worker assigned to a case. Periodic contact can be made from the time the report is filed until the case is closed.

When professionals do not report suspected child maltreatment because they have caused a report to be filed by someone else, it is necessary to follow up on the case and verify that a report was filed with the child protection system. Verification of a report should be obtained directly from the child protection system rather than from the person believed to have filed the report, including situations in which a fellow mandated reporter was expected to report. The professional might also request that his or her name be filed with the original report to ensure a record of his or her compliance with the reporting statute. All reporters involved should keep a record of their own contacts with child protection workers.

Cases of suspected child abuse that do not surpass reporting criteria should be discussed with a colleague in order to achieve some degree of objective reliability in reporting decisions. Professionals who most consistently report suspected child abuse are more likely to discuss cases with colleagues (Kalichman & Brosig, 1993). Drawing on the training and experiences of a second mandated reporter results in a check on decision making and decreases the chances for errors.

Training in recognizing signs of child maltreatment should be obtained by all human service professionals to the degree to which they have potential contact with abused children or abusive adults. All human service professionals should be familiar with conditions of child maltreatment. However, training would be expected to be most extensive for professionals working with children, adolescents, and families.

Even in the best of all worlds, with specific ethical concerns regarding mandated reporting addressed, child abuse remains a complex social issue that cannot be adequately managed within the context of a single professional relationship. In this sense, professionals functioning as therapists, evaluators, educators, and consultants cannot be expected to competently function as child maltreatment investigators. Likewise, as social service agencies continue to face budget cuts and lose funding for intervention programs, they too will increasingly need to seek private referral sources to treat perpetrators, victims, and families. Pooling available interorganizational resources is necessary in order to investigate, evaluate, and intervene with child abuse and its associated problems. Mandated reporters, as part of the child protection system, can be advocates for families in the child protection process and can act as a family resource, supplying information on what may be expected in the reporting and investigation processes. Within a context that stresses cooperative efforts to resolve family problems and protect children, reporting suspected child abuse becomes an ethical course of action embedded within a legal mandate. However, before professionals can be expected to report suspected child maltreatment it is necessary to establish criteria for discerning the occurrence of child maltreatment.

STANDARD DEFINITIONS AND REPORTING THRESHOLDS

Professional associations, licensing boards, ethics codes, and reporting laws have not provided specific guidelines for the duty to report suspected child abuse. In addition, there has not yet been a review of empirical studies to help define characteristics of abused children and conditions of abuse, which could then be used to develop reporting criteria. Individual reporting thresholds that constitute strict criteria for reporting tend to rely on observations of bruises, welts, marks, and malnutrition. Descriptions of violent acts, rejection, humiliation, unsheltered living, and sexual contact also tend to surpass strict reporting thresholds (Brosig & Kalichman, 1992b; Finlayson & Koocher, 1991). When confronted with such salient signs of child maltreatment, professionals who do not report are operating outside of the law because the circumstances of these suspicions meet or exceed most legal definitions of child abuse or neglect. Under less certain conditions, such as patterns of acting out behavior, emotional distress, disturbed social relationships, or disclosures by persons other than victims and perpetrators, reporting might also be warranted, but the circumstances constitute the grayer areas for mandated reporters because they do not reflect legal definitions of abuse and neglect.

Suspected child abuse is most often characterized in the child abuse reporting literature as cases that either show highly salient and specific indicators of maltreatment, such as physical signs or verbal disclosures of abuse, or some set of nonspecific symptoms that could be taken as signs of maltreatment. Studies that have used experimental case vignettes, for example, have capitalized on these two extremes to demonstrate the effects of specific case characteristics on reporting decisions (Finlayson & Koocher, 1991; Kalichman & Craig, 1991). In practice, however, cases rarely present such circumscribed situations as to allow for the identification of specific factors indicative of child maltreatment. In most cases, suspected child abuse is more likely to result from an accumulation of signs and indicators that occur over time, as opposed to suspicions that arise from a single indicator observed on one occasion. Subtle signs, such as changes in a child's behavior or indirect discussions about home life, can lead a professional to suspect that something is wrong. These subtle and often ambiguous situations might not constitute a reasonable suspicion of child abuse, but they open the door for further exploration, if such exploration is within the professional's defined role.

Specific behaviors can also have different meanings at various periods of child development (Finkelhor, 1984; Wurtele & Miller-Perrin, 1992). For example, a preoccupation with sexual behavior, such as repeated references to sexually related topics, can be taken as sexual acting out when presented by a six-year-old but can be interpreted more normatively when presented by a 15-year-old. Although specific indicators of abuse may appear at different rates across developmental periods, the overall frequency of various symptoms and signs, at least in cases of sexual abuse, is relatively stable across developmental periods (Friedrich et al., 1992). Thus, not only will subtle signs accumulate to raise suspicions, but some salient signs of maltreatment can convey different meanings at different stages of development.

Several descriptions of abused children and abusive families are available that could be used to define and develop reporting thresholds (e.g., Besharov, 1990; Finkelhor, 1984, 1986; Sgroi, 1982; Walker et al., 1988; Wiehe, 1992). Even professionals who become familiar with empirically defined characteristics of child abuse, however, will face ambiguous cases. Mandated reporters invariably experience problems with ambiguous cases because legal requirements to report reasonable suspicions are inherently vague. Professionals can come to rely on empirically defined descriptions of victims, perpetrators, and abusive circumstances to determine whether or not suspicions constitute situations that warrant investigation. When making determinations about ambiguous cases, however, professionals can approach decisions within a hierarchical framework.

A GENERAL STRUCTURE FOR MANAGING AMBIGUOUS CASES

Professionals who have attained a level of reasonable suspicion of child abuse are not afforded professional judgement and legal flexibility in reporting. Mandated reporters who fail to report signs of child maltreatment that surpass legal definitions of abuse and neglect can be held either civilly or criminally liable, or both, for failure to report. In addition, not reporting suspected child abuse could result in disciplinary actions taken by state licensing boards and professional ethics committees. Thus, although professionals can decide not to report reasonable suspicions of child maltreatment, it is in these cases that reporting laws are violated. Professional discretion, however, can be exercised within legal limits when the suspected child abuse occurs at lower levels of the suspicion continuum. Reporting indicators of child abuse that do not surpass strict reporting criteria, such as cases in which indicators of maltreatment are nonspecific, is permitted and perhaps encouraged, but not legally required. Reporting laws are designed to free professionals from the responsibility of investigating situations of suspected child abuse. However, professionals are provided with discretion to explore vague suspicions as long as they do not take on an investigative role by acting beyond usual professional duties or seeking information outside of the professional relationship.

The range of circumstances that can result in suspicions of child abuse, along with the array of possible professional responses to suspected maltreatment, suggests that a decision tree for mandated reporting would be useful (Walker et al., 1989). The relationship between mandated reporting and duty to warn also suggests that similar decision-making processes may apply across these two situations. Southard and Gross (1982) proposed a decision tree applicable to duty-to-warn decisions. Although many of the decision points in duty-to-warn cases, such as assessing levels of dangerousness and determining whether or not the endangered person is a public official, do not translate to cases of suspected child abuse, the schema developed by Southard and Gross provides a starting place for a decision tree adaptable for use in child abuse reporting.

Under the model of report decision-making processes discussed in chapter 3, it is assumed that as professionals approach and surpass a reporting threshold they will be increasingly inclined to report suspected child abuse. When professionals observe injuries and abusive or neglectful acts, or receive verbal disclosures of maltreatment, they are likely to surpass reporting thresholds and therefore recognize their legal responsibility to report. In contrast, suspected child maltreatment resulting from less certain conditions, such as emotional distress, acting out, and social withdrawal, allow for alternative courses of action. As shown in Figure 16, when indicators of child maltreatment fall below a reporting threshold, professionals might decide not to report. This course of action is legal when the suspected maltreatment is based on indicators that are less specific than legal definitions of child abuse and neglect (e.g., there are no apparent injuries, observation of acts, verbal descriptions of abuse). However, decisions not to report even the most subtle signs of maltreatment will leave a proportion of cases of abuse and neglect undetected. The potential cost of missed cases should be weighed heavily when contemplating reporting decisions. Thus, subtle suspicions cannot be immediately dismissed and steps should be taken to minimize the probability of failing to report actual child maltreatment.

Professionals are advised not to investigate the occurrence of child abuse by engaging in activities outside of ordinary professional roles. For example, a school psychologist who has not had previous contact with a family should not delay reporting in order to first talk with family members about suspicions of maltreatment. Likewise, therapists would be taking on an investigative role if they felt it necessary to contact a child's schoolteacher before they would be willing to report suspected child abuse. Rather, reporting decisions are to be based on information gained in the course of usual professional activities, such as evaluating, teaching, providing treatment, or conducting research. It is often within professional roles to further examine areas of concern by asking probing questions and following up on important issues. Through careful examination, professionals can seek more information about the cause of the subtle signs of child maltreatment that originally gave rise to their suspicions. Making further inquiries regarding suspicions is usually within prescribed professional roles and would be less costly than prematurely dismissing subtle signs of abuse as unreportable.

Directing specific questions to children and parents about the occurrence of abuse, such as "Is someone touching you in a way that makes you feel uncomfortable?" or "Were marks left after you hit your child?" is most useful when the responses confirm the occurrence of maltreatment. However, responses that deny maltreatment are less conclusive because they

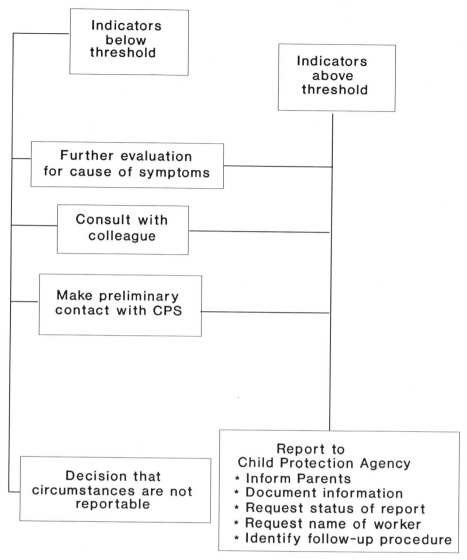

Figure 16: A report decision-making tree. Adapted from Southard and Gross (1982).

may reflect a reluctance to admit abuse or neglect on the part of both children and adults. In addition, a child or adult who responds to a direct question by becoming quiet and refusing to answer has not admitted child abuse, but this behavior may imply the occurrence of maltreatment. Verbal disclosures of child maltreatment, particularly by children and perpetrators, are highly indicative of the occurrence of maltreatment, even when statements are recanted. Asking questions for clarification and probing for descriptions of specific acts and situations might elicit information that then surpasses reporting thresholds. On the other hand, information gained from such examinations might bring professionals to decide to dismiss their suspicions as unreportable.

If an examination of the indicators leading to the suspicion is inconclusive and the reportability of the situation remains ambiguous, the professional could seek consultation with a colleague, a fellow mandated reporter who might not necessarily be of the same professional background. In anticipation of future needs, professionals could assemble a list of colleagues who would be qualified to discuss maltreatment cases (Finlayson & Koocher, 1991). Discussing difficult cases with colleagues can result in decisions based on new insights drawn from diverse experiences. Discussions with colleagues could take place in the context of case conferences and staffings, assuming that they occur regularly enough to prevent any delay of reporting. Through discussions with colleagues, indicators of child maltreatment might come to constitute a reasonable suspicion and warrant reporting. Alternatively, input from colleagues could lead to the decision not to report. If, however, the situation remains ambiguous and a reporting decision is not reached after examination and consultation, a third course of action involves making preliminary contact with a child protection worker.

Mandated reporters facing difficult reporting decisions can always contact a child protection worker and request feedback on a case before reporting to verify that particular indicators constitute a reportable situation. Professionals might discuss cases with the initial intake worker who receives reports, or with a caseworker the professional has used as a regular resource person. It is under these circumstances that establishing relationships with child protection workers can benefit mandated reporters. Even in the most difficult and ambiguous cases, input from child protection workers will most likely lead to a decision to report or not to report.

In summary, the law does not permit mandated reporters to engage in a decision-making process when there is a reasonable suspicion of child maltreatment. However, surveys of professionals and an examination of cases of unreported suspected child maltreatment show that professionals do engage in decision-making processes with regard to mandated reporting. When professionals surpass a reporting threshold and choose not to report, it is usually because they are inhibited by competing concerns, such as not disrupting professional relationships and questioning the ability of the child protection system to effectively manage reports. Likewise, lower levels of suspicion resulting from ambiguous situations can involve similar factors that inhibit reporting but provide even less impetus to report. The process of weighing options in report decision making is related to an analysis of the relative costs and benefits of potential outcomes (Fischhoff, 1992). Weighing the potential outcomes of reporting decisions can be facilitated by organizing the factors that led to the suspicion and determining the degree to which these factors approach the professional's definition of *reasonable suspicion*. When professionals believe they have surpassed a reporting threshold, the factors that might inhibit reporting can be examined and strategies for resolving these conflicts can be explored.

Decisions to report suspected child abuse are least problematic when professionals use a set of procedures that includes informing parents, organizing and documenting information, and developing communication channels for following up with child protection workers. Under some circumstances, professionals might offer persons the opportunity to self-report or to be present while the professional phones in the report (Stadler, 1989). Although standard procedures could increase the efficiency of reporting, there are currently few models for the professional management of child abuse, and most human service professionals receive little training in procedures for reporting.

PROFESSIONAL TRAINING IN CHILD ABUSE DETECTION AND MANDATED REPORTING

Training mandated reporters to recognize child abuse and understand their responsibilities to report is a common component of proposals to address issues in reporting (Besharov, 1988; Faller, 1985). Several studies have shown that human service professionals lack training in the management of child abuse cases, including mandated reporting aspects of such cases. For example, Kim (1986) found that more than half of physicians believed that they had inadequate training to detect and manage cases of child abuse. Similar findings have been reported in studies of schoolteachers (Levin, 1983) and Head Start workers (Nightingale & Walker, 1986). Among practicing psychologists, Kalichman and Brosig (1993) found that most training experiences in child maltreatment occur in postgraduate and continuing education workshops, with less than 20% of psychologists surveyed indicating that they were exposed to topics of child maltreatment in graduate school. A national survey of 290 practicing psychologists sampled from three APA divisions (clinical, psychotherapy, and independent practice) showed that psychologists most frequently perceived their graduate training in child abuse issues to be poor and viewed their internship training in this area as only slightly better (Pope & Feldman-Summers, 1992). These findings support the observation that most professionals who have recently received their degrees are likely to have limited training and experience in child abuse topics (Alpert & Paulson, 1990). A survey of APA-accredited clinical, school, and counseling psychology graduate programs found that only 11% offered courses in the area of child abuse, and the three types of programs did not differ in the amount of training students received related to child maltreatment (Howe et al., 1992). Given the magnitude of child maltreatment as a social problem, it is surprising that professional education across disciplines has not instituted such training. Because professionals are likely to face reporting decisions at any point in their career (Alpert & Paulson, 1990; Wilson, Thomas, & Schuette, 1983), it is also surprising that professional training has been most concentrated at the postdegree continuing education level (Kalichman & Brosig, 1993).

Training in child maltreatment issues can occur during graduate practica and internships, through postgraduate fellowships, during case conferences, in continuing education courses, and in workshops. Training can also take place within graduate education through specific courses or as a content area bridged across a curriculum. With respect to developing a specific course covering child maltreatment topics, Alpert and Paulson (1990) described a model graduate course in child sexual abuse. Topics included the scope and prevalence of sexual abuse, laws and mandated reporting, the initial and long-term effects of child maltreatment, developmental considerations, assessment and interviewing techniques, treatment, and prevention. In addition, Alpert and Paulson described similar content for a graduate consultation course. Examples of student assignments, topics and formats for class discussions, and techniques for supervision were also suggested. In addition, several books that provide excellent descriptions of abused children and families could be considered as texts or text supplements (e.g., Finkelhor, 1986; MacFarlane et al., 1986; Walker et al., 1988; Wurtele & Miller-Perrin, 1992; Wyatt & Powell, 1988).

A potential problem, however, when training in mandated reporting occurs in graduate studies is that program graduates often practice in states different from the one in which they were trained. Because states vary with respect to specific aspects of reporting laws, such as definitions of abuse and legal thresholds for reporting, statutes will not transfer across states. Thus, although general issues such as ethics of reporting, guidelines for filing a report, and detection of child abuse will generalize across states, it may be necessary for state licensing boards to be responsible for ensuring that professionals are knowledgeable regarding state reporting statutes and requirements.

Training experiences could be targeted to specific professional groups working in particular settings or to mandated reporters in general. Short-term and intensive training can focus specifically on mandated reporting of suspected child abuse, whereas in-depth approaches, such as courses, seminars, and practica, could be broadly related to child abuse and only cover reporting as one content area. Coverage of child abuse and reporting can occur in assessment practica, ethics, social policy, and child development courses. Graduate research methods courses could also cover relevant issues, including detailed procedures for informed consent with limited confidentiality for mandated reporting.[5] Across training contexts, coverage of mandated reporting would be expected to encompass detailed discussions of several general areas, including legal requirements to report, maltreatment detection techniques, decision-making processes, and procedures for reporting. Each of these content areas is discussed in the following text.

Legal Requirements for Mandated Reporting

Human service professionals are expected to be closely acquainted with the specific mandatory reporting laws and requirements of their state. Familiarity with reporting laws is best achieved by reviewing current state reporting statutes, including legal definitions of child abuse and neglect. Specific attention should be paid to who is required to report, what is required to be reported, and when reporting is required. Reporting statutes can be obtained by contacting state child protection agencies (listed in appendix B). There are also a number of free booklets and pamphlets available from state agencies that discuss mandated reporting. (See appendix C for a bibliography of selected materials.) Because reporting laws are still evolving, mechanisms can also be built into continuing education for informing professionals of up-to-date legislation and policy changes. Current information can be made available, once again, through state licensing boards.

Awareness of state statutes, however, is only a starting place for professional training with respect to reporting laws. Reporting requirements also need to be placed in the context of local social service structures. For example, definitions of abuse and neglect, as well as legal thresholds for reporting, could be viewed in the context of local criteria for screening reports. Involving local representatives of the child protection system can enhance understanding of mandated reporting within specific communities. Social service representatives can help discuss the interrelationship between legal requirements to report and the child protection process. Discussions and presentations could be tailored by child protection workers to fit the needs of specific groups of mandated reporters.

Reporting laws can also be placed in the context of professional standards for ethical conduct. Strategies can be developed to manage issues of confidentiality and trust within the constraints of mandated reporting. Training professionals to implement informed consent procedures that include discussions of limited confidentiality can lead to more integrative interpretations of mandatory reporting laws as they are related to professional confidentiality.

---

[5]Researchers frequently face situations that involve similar limits to confidentiality. A common situation is one in which researchers studying depression identify participants who have suicidal ideations or intentions to commit self-inflicted harm. Procedures that have been developed by investigators for managing these situations may be applied to conditions of mandated reporting.

Failure to report suspected child abuse carries the potential for both criminal and civil actions against mandated reporters, and it is important that professionals be aware of the differences between these two types of liability. Criminally, failure to report is a misdemeanor in most states, whereas civil suits usually involve professional negligence. In addition to receiving legal penalties, professionals can be sanctioned by licensing boards and ethics committees for not reporting. It is necessary for mandated reporters to know that they cannot be held liable for reporting suspicions of child abuse when reports are filed in good faith, even when the reports are not substantiated on investigation. Finally, professionals should be aware of legal requirements placed on the report receiving agency, such as the maximum amount of time allowed for response to a report and the degree to which law enforcement agencies can be involved in the investigation process. This information provides a realistic framework for reporters' expectations and allows professionals to be well informed and knowledgeable resources for families.

Child Maltreatment Detection

Recognizing child abuse, particularly when presented by subtle signs and nonspecific indicators, requires more than knowledge of mandatory reporting laws. Nonspecific indicators of child abuse can easily be missed when professionals are unfamiliar with the signs and symptoms of different types of maltreatment at different periods of child development. Professionals with little experience in detecting child maltreatment might not recognize particular patterns of emotional responses or behaviors as indicative of maltreatment. Less specific indicators of child maltreatment can also be confused with clinical symptoms resulting from nonabusive situations, such as parental and family conflicts. Professionals unfamiliar with the etiology of child abuse and neglect, and with the family constellations associated with child abuse, are not likely to suspect abuse when presented with subtle signs. Thus, report decision-making criteria are most effective when they are based on knowledge of empirically defined descriptors of child abuse and neglect. Knowledge alone, however, only results in checklists of symptoms that tend to be insufficient to accurately detect child maltreatment (Finkelhor, 1984).

Beyond knowledge of the more frequent indicators and characteristics of child maltreatment are the skills associated with detecting signs of abuse. Professionals not only need to know what to look for in identifying child maltreatment, they also require methods for examining their suspicions. For example, specific interviewing techniques can be developed for following up on hunches and suspicions within the context of professional relationships (Heiman, 1992). Drawings and interactive play are often used to facilitate young children's expressions of traumatic experiences (Wiehe,

1992). Addressing issues of autonomy and self-concept can help reduce concerns that may inhibit adolescents from discussing maltreatment experiences. It is also necessary that techniques for interviewing children, adults, and families be sensitive to variations in culture, gender, and developmental periods. For example, it is not uncommon for professionals to misinterpret normative child rearing practices of parents from unfamiliar cultural backgrounds as abusive (Gray & Cosgrove, 1985).

In addition to using specific interview techniques to elicit information from children and adults pertaining to indicators of child abuse, the general atmosphere of the interview can be constructed to facilitate disclosures of abusive conditions. Encouraging children and adults to talk about abuse is regarded as a critical step to child abuse intervention (Finkelhor, 1984). Reassuring and supporting children and adults that talking about abusive experiences will result in greater child protection can help create an environment within which disclosures occur.

Professionals tend to rely more on interpersonal interviews in cases of suspected child abuse than on specific assessment tools, primarily because of the lack of reliable and valid instruments (Friedrich, 1993; Levy, 1989; Mantell, 1988; Walker et al., 1988). The only standardized assessment instrument developed for administration to children is the anatomically correct doll interview for use in cases of sexual abuse. Although the use of dolls as an assessment technique has been controversial, some studies have suggested that standardized administrations demonstrate acceptable reliability and validity (Walker, 1988; White, Strom, Santilli, & Halpin, 1986). Although there are few other valid abuse assessment instruments administered directly to children, there are several useful models available for conceptualizing and organizing information gathered in interviews. For example, Walker et al. developed a scheme for organizing potential risk factors associated with physical and sexual abuse based on identifiable characteristics of abusers, victims, family members, and social–situational factors. Similarly, Sgroi, Porter, and Blick (1982) constructed a conceptual framework for validating child sexual abuse. Sgroi et al.'s model incorporates behavioral characteristics of victims and physical indicators of child sexual abuse, both of which are evaluated within the context of levels of child development. Models such as these provide a framework within which professionals may structure their observations and suspicions of child abuse.

In addition to interview techniques and conceptual models, there have been advances in the development of standardized instruments administered to adults. One promising assessment tool for sexual maltreatment, the Child Sexual Behavior Inventory (CSBI), has recently been developed (Friedrich, Grambsch, Broughton, Kuiper, & Beilke, 1991; Friedrich et al., 1992). The CSBI consists of 35 items assessing a wide range of child behaviors including sexual self-stimulation, sexual aggression, gender role behaviors, and personal boundary violations. Each of the behavioral indicators is rated on a 4-point scale by a parent or caregiver. The instrument is modeled after the Child Behavior Checklist (Achenbach & Edelbrock, 1983) and has demonstrated acceptable levels of reliability and validity. The CSBI may be of use in evaluating cases of child sexual abuse because it is based on empirically identified behaviors related to child sexual victimization. However, because the measure is completed by a caregiver it may have limited use in cases of intrafamilial sexual abuse and with parents who minimize child behavior problems.

With respect to assessing adults, Milner (1986, 1989, 1990, 1991; Milner, Gold, & Wimberley, 1986) has developed the Child Abuse Potential Inventory (CAP), a standardized and objective test for screening abusive, or potentially abusive, adults. The CAP consists of 160 items on an agree–disagree response format. Items compose a number of subscales, including several that serve as indicators of a propensity to commit child abuse, such as parental rigidity, unhappiness, distress, and family problems, as well as indexes of scale validity. Although the CAP has shown great promise, it was not developed as a definitive indicator of abusiveness and should be considered as only one piece of information in exploring suspicions and screening cases of child abuse.

The complexity of child abuse is difficult to grasp from readings and checklists of indicators alone. Therefore, training in child abuse detection needs to include experiential approaches. Case conferences, for example, can provide detailed descriptions and allow for interactive case discussions. Case conferences also afford the opportunity to critically examine difficult cases and illustrate the differential diagnostic value of specific indicators of abuse. Local experts from children's hospitals and departments of pediatrics, and child maltreatment specialists from a variety of professional backgrounds may be invited to case conferences. Videotapes depicting clinical interviews with victims, perpetrators, and families can also provide the opportunity for focused discussions and immediate feedback on the accuracy of varying interpretations of signs of maltreatment. Videotapes dynamically present signs of maltreatment and show the way that subtle signs of abuse and neglect can accumulate over time. The context within which indicators of maltreatment arise can also be made more salient through video presentations. The likelihood that experiential learning will transfer to later performance is increased when trainees are provided with the most realistic experiences possible. Training resources, including videotapes, are often available through child abuse organizations and interest groups. (See list in appendix D.)

Recognizing indicators of child maltreatment also requires a developmental framework for subtle signs of child abuse and neglect because behaviors and emotional reactions carry different meanings at different developmental periods (Kendall-Tackett et al., 1993). Sensitivity to developmental differences is essential when the source of the suspicion is a child or adolescent, as well as when a parent describes a child's behavior and his or her expectations of children. In this respect, developmental psychologists can offer expertise in consultation and collaboration in constructing methods and models for detecting child abuse.

Report Decision Making and Procedures for Reporting

Training professionals to recognize and manage child maltreatment cases, at least with respect to mandated reporting, requires an explication of the processes involved in report decision making (Handelsman, 1989). Report decision making will be enhanced when professional training is built on a decision-making model. Technologies developed in decision analysis can be of use in mandated reporting because decision analysis applies abstract theoretical principles to practical decision-making problems (Fischhoff, 1992). An analytical approach to reporting decisions focuses on identifying options, evaluating consequences associated with these options, weighing the alternatives according to their relative importance, assessing the probabilities of consequences, and combining these considerations to arrive at a decision (Fischhoff, 1992). Although specific training in decision analysis is necessary for its proper implementation, in a less formal manner these concepts can be used to develop report decision-making strategies.

In addition to receiving training in report decision-making processes, professionals could be assisted in developing guidelines and strategies for reporting. Step-by-step procedures, such as those presented in Figure 16, could be constructed for professionals and may be tailored specifically for professional settings within which suspected maltreatment occurs. For example, a psychologist working in an interdisciplinary agency might be required to follow specific internal procedures prior to reporting, such as filing a report with a designated administrator. Likewise, professionals working in residential care facilities will need to manage reports of suspected maltreatment within the context of treatment center policies (Rindfleisch & Bean, 1988). With respect to specific reporting procedures, training in child abuse reporting should address strategies for discussing limited confidentiality early in professional relationships, methods for keeping records of information disclosed in a report, methods for establishing relationships with child protection workers, and procedures for following up on reports.

MANDATED TRAINING IN CHILD MALTREATMENT AND MANDATED REPORTING

An emerging professional issue related to child maltreatment reporting is mandatory training for professionals in child abuse and neglect. In support of mandated training, the APA Ad Hoc Committee on Child Abuse Policy recommended that "state licensing boards consider requiring child abuse knowledge base for purposes of licensure and relicensure" (Walker et al., 1989, p. 11). The committee also recommended that the APA link course work or other training in child abuse to professional and graduate program eligibility for accreditation (Walker et al., 1989). These two initiatives would ensure that practicing psychologists, and perhaps all psychologists, would meet minimal standards of familiarity with and knowledge of child abuse and neglect, including mandated reporting requirements.

Training in child abuse issues has become mandatory in some states, including California, Iowa, and New York, as a requirement for professional licensure. Courses typically cover legal requirements to report, legal definitions of child abuse and neglect, identification of significant indicators of abused and neglected children, characteristics of abusive parents, and procedures for reporting. Requirements for training are, at least in part, a reaction to the magnitude of child maltreatment as a social crisis and the widespread difficulties professionals have faced when interpreting reporting laws. In addition, state licensing boards may be reacting to the increased frequency with which professionals are being held liable for failure to report.

Although some states have initiated mandated child abuse detection training for professionals, these requirements have not been fully supported by professionals. Many believe that mandated training could infringe on the rights of professionals and could be of questionable relevance when applied to all licensed psychologists. Another potential problem with mandatory training is the increased resistance met by most attempts to legislate professional activities. Resistance may be even greater in the case of mandated training in child maltreatment detection because it is so closely linked to mandated reporting; that is, training becomes a mandate connected to yet another mandate.

Criticisms of mandated child abuse detection training, however valid they may be, do not negate the need for greater professional competence in managing cases of child maltreatment. Human service professionals are likely to have contact with child abuse, if for no other reason than the high base rate of maltreatment found in populations that they serve. Professional and graduate training programs will most likely experience greater pressure in the future to include child maltreatment detection as a component of their curriculum. Credentialing and accreditation agencies will also need to develop standards of minimal competence with respect to child maltreatment if such training is to be required. Given our current knowledge and understanding of child abuse, however, further research is needed to empirically identify characteristics of child abuse before standards for training can be implemented.

CONCLUSION

Human service professionals work within fairly well defined roles such as therapist, health care provider, evaluator, and educator. Society has, however, defined an additional role for most human service professionals, namely that of mandated reporter. As a part of the child protection system, mandated reporters function to assist in identifying cases of child abuse. Human service professionals are often in positions that could lead them to discover abused children and abusive conditions as a result of contact with persons experiencing difficulties related to, or concurrent with, child maltreatment. This is the reason human service providers are specified as mandated reporters. However, human service professionals do not yet function optimally as mandated reporters because they often view reporting as being at odds with their professionally defined roles.

For professionals to serve the public best as therapists, evaluators, and educators, as well as fulfill their social responsibilities as mandated reporters, reporting must be integrated into existing professional roles. Reporting suspected child abuse can be managed within the context of most professional relationships as a specific case of referral for consultation. Human service professionals frequently refer persons to agencies for specialized care and consultation, and the child protection system specializes in child maltreatment intervention. However, before professionals can be expected to be open to treating social service agencies as referral outlets, a renewed confidence in the child protection system will be required. The current state of crisis that the child protection system is facing (U.S. Advisory Board on Child Abuse and Neglect, 1990) makes it doubtful that professionals will view social service agencies as a viable referral. Thus, although professionals can be educated and trained with respect to child abuse and reporting, a competent and reliable child protection system is a prerequisite to responsible reporting.

Because professionals do not have control over society's level of commitment to reform the child protection system, alternative approaches to melding mandated reporting into existing professional roles must be developed. One such alternative involves developing strategies for mandated reporters to assist families within the child protection system. As mandated reporters, professionals can serve as resources for families and children during investigations and interventions. Professionals could keep booklets and pamphlets from state and community social service agencies on hand for families. Professionals could also discuss with families their own previous child protection system experiences, sharing their expectations of the child protection process. This type of information can set realistic expectations of the roles and functions of child protection workers. In addition, professionals can make families aware of their rights within the system and of the specific courses of action that are available to them in the event they are dissatisfied with a caseworker. Whether functioning as evaluators, teachers, researchers, or therapists, professionals can deal directly with the distress and anxiety frequently associated with child protection system involvement. Thus, mandated reporting can involve much more than phoning in a report of suspected child maltreatment. It may include activities that can be integrated into well defined professional roles.

8

DIRECTIONS FOR FURTHER RESEARCH

Scientific societies and professional organizations are especially influential in the formation and review of child and family policy. As such, they are able to lead the development and diffusion of relevant knowledge. (U.S. Advisory Board on Child Abuse and Neglect, 1990, p. 52)

We recommend a range of research including surveys of psychologists' attitudes, behaviors, and knowledge about child abuse; societal responses; child abuse reporting laws and psychological interventions looking at various factors including gender, primary professional affiliation, theoretical orientation, activity, training level, work with children, divisional status, etc. The use of survey questions as well as analogue and critical incident studies should be encouraged. (Walker et al., 1989, p. 13)

Much of child abuse reporting literature consists of commentaries and critiques either supportive of mandated reporting or calling for restrictions on reporting requirements. Empirical studies, however, have recently emerged to provide an objective evaluation of mandated child abuse reporting. In addition to seeking answers to questions surrounding professional responses to mandatory reporting laws, empirical research has also helped define problem areas themselves. For example, studies have described the scope of unreported child abuse and identified factors that reliably influence professionals' reporting decisions.

Brosig and Kalichman (1992b) reviewed the empirical literature on child abuse reporting and evaluated the most commonly used research methods. Among the methodological limitations noted by Brosig and Kalichman were problems associated with sampling techniques, measurement instruments, and the limited internal and external validity of most research designs. Although Brosig and Kalichman critically analyzed the research methods and findings in the mandated reporting literature, they offered relatively few suggestions for improved methods and further investigation. The focus of the present chapter is to fill this void by pointing the producers of mandated reporting literature toward avenues for future research built on the strengths of past studies. Lessons learned from the limitations of previous research will also be highlighted in an effort to advance the development of future studies. Strengths and limitations of existing paradigms are first explored, followed by suggestions for future research.

DESCRIPTIVE SURVEY STUDIES

Descriptive surveys seek to identify the experiences, perceptions, and factors that influence reporting decisions among mandated reporters. Surveys of mandated reporters have been conducted primarily through anonymous mailings to targeted professional populations. Although surveys have been fairly distinctive with respect to research hypotheses tested, descriptive surveys share several problems: They are invariably limited by sampling constraints, lack operational definitions of child abuse, and have a narrow focus of questions.

Surveys have drawn samples from a wide range of sources of mandated reporters, including state licensing boards (e.g., Brosig & Kalichman, 1992a; Kalichman et al., 1989; Kalichman & Craig, 1991), professional associations (e.g., Finlayson & Koocher, 1991; Swoboda et al., 1978), divisions of the APA (Koziol & Petretic-Jackson, 1989), and professional directories (e.g., Attias & Goodwin, 1985; Zellman, 1990). Samples drawn from professional association mailing lists will represent members and affiliates of a particular group who will likely hold views or values that may not be representative of nonmembers. For example, Koziol and Petretic-Jackson (1989) surveyed members of APA Division 37, Child, Youth, and Family Services, most likely a group of professionals with experience in child maltreatment detection and in areas of child advocacy. In contrast, random samples of professionals accessed through state psychological associations and licensing board mailing lists are limited to the geographical constraints of the specific states sampled. National samples of professionals drawn from nonaffiliated sources, on the other hand, would appear to be the strongest sampling procedure. In a national survey of mandated reporters, Zellman sampled over 2,000 mandated reporters from 15 geographically dispersed states. This study achieved its goal by obtaining a high degree of national representation of mandated reporters with more diversity in professional backgrounds than any other sample in this literature. Unfortunately, the foundation for Zellman's study was the assumption of homogeneity among mandated reporters, a proposition that has not been supported by a number of previous studies that demonstrated differences among professions in reporting tendencies and perceptions of abuse (Brosig & Kalichman, 1992b; Jackson & Nuttall, 1993).

Inadequate response rates have caused problems in a number of surveys across specific populations of professionals sampled. Table 5 summarizes the different methodologies used and response rates obtained in surveys of mandated reporters. Surveys conducted through the mail have had response rates ranging from 31% (Kim, 1986) to 69% (Wilson et al., 1983). The broad range of response rates observed in this literature may be accounted for by a number of factors. First, some studies have used procedures intended to optimize response rates, for example, sending follow-up reminder cards, mailing second surveys to nonrespondents, and contacting nonrespondents by telephone. However, many studies that have obtained the highest response rates have not used follow-up procedures. Thus, although studies that use follow-up procedures tend to be at the higher end of the distribution of response rates, these studies are often matched by others that do not use such procedures. The expense associated with respondent prompts and contacts must therefore be weighed against their potential for increased response rates (Dillman, 1978).

High response rates without follow-up procedures have been attained by studies conducted by sample insiders, researchers who are members of the targeted professional population. Three studies that illustrate this point were conducted by researchers affiliated with university programs linked to the profession and based in the state sampled. One study conducted by the Morehead State University Leadership and Foundations Department (Wilson et al., 1983) obtained a 69% response from public school counselors in Kentucky. The second study was conducted by the Department of Educational Psychology at the University of Wisconsin (Wilson & Gettinger, 1989) and obtained a response rate of 49% from school psychologists in Wisconsin. Similarly, Kalichman, Craig, and Follingstad (1990) obtained a 68% response rate among licensed psychologists in their home state of South Carolina, as compared with the 59% response from licensed psychologists sampled in the same manner and in the same study but from the neighboring

TABLE 5
Procedures and Response Rate for Surveys of Professionals

Authors	Number of Surveys Sent	Target Groups	Follow Up	Response Rate
Swoboda et al. (1978)	236	psychologists, psychiatrists, and social workers from Nebraska professional associations	None	37%
James et al. (1978)	300	physicians sampled from directories	None	32%
Wilson et al. (1983)	349	school counselors selected from Kentucky state directory	None	69%
Attias & Goodwin (1985)	255	psychiatrists, psychologists, and counselors selected from a telephone directory	None	43%
Kim (1986)	387	physicians selected from professional listings and directories	None	31%
Pope et al. (1987)	1000	members of APA Division 29 (psychotherapy)	None	46%
Haas et al. (1988)	500	members of APA Division 29 (psychotherapy)	postcard enclosed with survey to indicate that survey was completed and to request results; nonrespondents to first survey were sent a second survey	59%
Pope & Bajt (1988)	100	senior psychologists with ethics backgrounds	None	60%
Willis & Wells (1988)	154	police officers	researchers distributed and collected surveys in person; but surveys completed in privacy	92%
Kalichman et al. (1989)	467	psychologists in South Carolina and Georgia	None	68% (SC) 53% (GA)

Authors	Number of Surveys Sent	Target Groups	Follow Up	Response Rate
Green & Hansen (1989)	258	500 members of American Association of Marital and Family Therapists initially contacted; surveys sent with no further follow-up	Two-stage sampling	40%
Wilson & Gettinger (1989)	280	Wisconsin school psychologists	None	47%
Zellman (1990)	2030	physicians, pediatricians, psychologists, social workers, school principals, and child care providers	reminder cards, second surveys, and phone calls to nonrespondents	59%
Kalichman & Craig (1991)	899	psychologists in Oklahoma and Minnesota	None	42% (OK) 37% (MN)
Finlayson & Koocher (1991)	644	pediatric psychologists	reminder and thank you cards; survey was brief to increase response rate with no follow-up	47%
Pope & Vetter (1992)	1319	American Psychological Association members		51%
Kalichman & Brosig (1992)	1200	psychologists in Colorado and Pennsylvania	None	44% (CO) 44% (PA)
Brosig & Kalichman (1992a)	1000	psychologists in Illinois and Washington	None	36% (IL) 42% (WA)

state of Georgia. Contributing to the South Carolina response rate may have been that one of the authors in the study, Follingstad, was the president of the South Carolina Psychological Association at the time of the study. Although the authors did not suggest that the study was conducted through or endorsed by the association, the familiarity of the researchers to potential respondents might have bolstered response rates. Thus, researcher credibility, whether gained through follow-up procedures or familiarity with participants, appears to play a role in maximizing response rates.

Response to mail surveys almost invariably reflects sampling biases (Kerlinger, 1973). Survey recipients who have minimal contact with children and little experience with child maltreatment detection might be less likely to participate in studies compared with professionals who have experienced difficulties related to mandated reporting. Possible systematic bias limits the external validity of these studies because professionals with a greater personal interest in mandated reporting and experience in child maltreatment will probably be more likely to respond to such surveys. Although surveys have resulted in similar patterns of results, with approximately one third of respondents having failed to report at least one case of suspected child abuse, it is possible that this rate of reporting does not accurately represent mandated reporters as a group. The observed consistency in reporting behaviors across studies may, therefore, actually represent an artifact of sampling biases rather than general professional behavior.

In contrast to mail surveys, studies conducted using methodologies that do not rely on postal return have obtained impressive response rates. For example, Willis and Wells (1988) achieved a 92% response rate in their survey of police officers, in which surveys were delivered and collected from respondents at their place of employment. Similar methods have been used successfully in surveys of community mental health workers (Kalichman et al., 1988, 1992), Head Start personnel (Nightingale & Walker, 1986), and professionals attending child abuse seminars (Finkelhor, 1984). However, the limitation that accompanies these nearly 100% response rates is questionable generalizability due to the targeting of specific settings. Professionals surveyed at one agency or professional conference cannot be assumed to be representative of a population of professionals. Thus, surveys conducted by means of postal return and on-site administration represent different types of possible sampling bias.

Specific questions and items included in surveys as measures of perceptions and behaviors are also methodologically limited because they only represent themes that have evolved in the literature rather than actual phenomena in practice. Qualitative assessments of the issues facing professionals who suspect child maltreatment were not conducted prior to generating lists of such issues to be included in surveys. Instead, researchers identified a finite set of factors believed to influence reporting and placed them along numerical response scales. Unfortunately, the selection of items is usually based on the personal experiences of researchers. For example, Kalichman and Brosig (1993) asked licensed psychologists to rate nine factors along numerical scales with respect to the importance of each in their reporting decisions. Factors included in the survey were upholding the law, protecting the child, quality of child protective services, apparent seriousness of abuse, and avoiding disruptions to therapy. The use of this finite set of factors prohibited the study from investigating whether the specific factors sampled were representative of the universe of influences in reporting decisions. Thus, although the selection of survey items in a study is not arbitrary, there has been little linkage between surveys and the experiences of mandated reporters.

Another internal validity problem found in descriptive surveys of mandated reporters is that the surveys usually fail to operationally define key terms relevant to reporting. For example, surveys asking professionals about their history of reporting suspected child abuse do not define reporting thresholds or other standards related to reporting. For example, Kalichman et al. (1989) asked survey respondents, all of whom had professional experience with child abuse detection and treatment, if they had ever reported. Based on responses to this single question, Kalichman et al. concluded that professionals indicating that they had never reported child abuse had at some point failed to report. Similarly, Kalichman and Craig (1991) measured reporting compliance by asking respondents, "Have you ever seen a case where you had suspected child abuse and decided not to report?" Unfortunately, neither of these surveys verified whether cases not reported involved conditions under which reporting may not have been necessary, such as those referred to professionals by the child protective system. Therefore, it is likely that rates of underreporting are inflated in survey studies. Similar problems are apparent with respect to operational definitions of physical abuse, sexual abuse, emotional maltreatment, and neglect. Undefined survey terms could lead researchers to false conclusions based on participants' interpretations of poorly defined questions.

CASE VIGNETTE AND ANALOGUE STUDIES

Researchers investigating factors influencing reporting decisions have typically used hypothetical case vignettes. Most studies develop several versions of a case description varied by manipulating specific case characteristics. The limited generalizability, or external validity, of vignette studies with respect to actual behavior is the most common criticism of this literature. Unfortunately, studies that present case scenarios are often limited in terms of internal validity as well. Alexander and Becker (1978) provide a complete discussion of the pitfalls and limitations associated with experimental vignette studies, and Brosig and Kalichman (1992b) cite several examples of these problems in the mandated reporting literature. For example, case scenarios used to simulate professional reporting decisions are often confounded because they simultaneously manipulate case characteristics. Without exception, studies manipulating the degree of abuse severity have simultaneously presented different degrees of evidence for the occurrence of abuse. Specifically, case scenarios have included bruises as an indicator of physical abuse, but have inadvertently increased the perceived severity of abuse (e.g., Kalichman & Craig, 1991). Studies using these methods have concluded that increased evidence for abuse results in increased tendencies to report (e.g., Finlayson & Koocher, 1991; Zellman, 1990). However, an alternative interpretation is that perceived severity of abuse accounted for differences in report decision making. If perceptions of severity are in fact determined by degrees of evidence, severely abused children with subtle signs of abuse will probably be overlooked in comparison with children who have bruises or who verbally disclose abuse.

Study participants are also frequently asked to respond to more than one case scenario with multiple manipulations across cases (e.g., Nightingale & Walker, 1986; Zellman, 1990, 1992). For example, Zellman (1990) presented participants with a series of different brief vignettes in which the order and versions were randomly determined. One of Zellman's physical abuse vignettes read:

> The Reeds, a well-dressed middle-class family who are new to your school, come to see you because neither parent can get their 6-year-old son Kevin to obey. Mr. Reed tells you that he uses a belt on Kevin just as his dad did to him but lately it isn't working. Mr. Reed admits that he hit Kevin yesterday and the belt left a mark on his neck. When you ask to see it, you observe several raised welts. (p. 328)

In the same study, Zellman used the following as a sexual abuse vignette:

> During his annual physical, Richard Lewis, an accountant, reveals that recently he has been drinking heavily. When you question him, he confides that several times recently when he has gotten drunk, he has lost control of himself and has fondled his 14-year-old daughter, Gina. (p. 328)

As can be seen, the two vignettes vary in more ways than just the manipulation of type of maltreatment. In fact, the two conditions present completely different circumstances related to the occurrence of child abuse. Although Zellman (1990) discussed systematic influences of manipulated factors, the simultaneous manipulation of case characteristics inextricably confounded the study results. In addition, vignettes were tailored to specific professionals and professional settings and then aggregated across professions. Thus, despite Zellman's extensive procedures for avoiding order effects, presenting participants with more than one version of a vignette that varied the context embedding the factors of interest resulted in multiple levels of simultaneous manipulations. It was not possible for Zellman to identify causal relationships among variables, and the results of the regression analyses were open to competing interpretations.

Although a common error in vignette studies, presenting participants with more than one case scenario followed by comparisons across vignettes assumes that all variables are kept constant with the exception of factors of interest (Alexander & Becker, 1978; Myers, 1979). In addition, although the order of vignettes can be randomized or counterbalanced to control for order effects between vignettes, the order of variables manipulated within vignettes cannot be systematically controlled because of the logical order of the narrative. Case scenarios are also disparate from real life reporting situations because professionals typically evaluate their suspicions with follow-up questions and cannot do so when responding to hypothetical cases.

As methodologically limited as they may be, vignette studies have provided the only evidence that professional decisions to report suspected child abuse are systematically influenced by case characteristics. These studies have shown that factors that influence reporting decisions are complex and interactive. Future studies could use videotaped vignettes, as opposed to case scenarios presented in questionnaire format, to provide closer ecological validity and complex manipulations of factors influencing reporting decisions. Such studies might ask professionals to view cases and indicate points at which they would be inclined to report. Research that goes beyond paper–pencil surveys will be more expensive in terms of both time and money, but the costs might be offset by the value of the results.

Whereas most vignette studies have manipulated specific characteristics of clinical case scenarios, recent studies have treated other dimensions of reporting situations as experimental vignettes. For example, Kalichman and Brosig (1992) and Brosig and Kalichman (1992a) used state reporting statutes as experimental vignettes, manipulating specific component phrases to evaluate the relative influence of specific changes in statutory wording. Brosig and Kalichman presented licensed psychologists with one of two laws following a case scenario. In this study, the Colorado reporting law was treated as an experimental vignette with one specific segment manipulated, a phrase from the Mississippi law. The two experimental vignettes are shown below with the manipulated factor in italics:

> *Colorado law*: Any psychologist who has reasonable cause to know or suspect that a child *has been subjected to abuse* or who has observed the child being subjected to circumstances or conditions which would reasonably result in abuse shall report.
>
> *Experimental law*: Any psychologist who has reasonable cause to know or suspect that a child *brought to him/her or coming before him/her for treatment, has been subjected to abuse* or who has observed the child being subjected to circumstances or conditions which would reasonably result in abuse shall report. (p. 488)

Thus, Brosig and Kalichman were able to experimentally test the effects of a specific statutory clause on reporting decisions. Similar procedures could be used to test the differential effects of other legal standards, including definitions of child abuse and neglect, limits of confidentiality, and narrow versus broad reporting criteria. In the course of such studies, professionals could be asked to respond to systematic manipulations of various standards in order to evaluate the relative influence of each on reporting. Legal standards could also be tested against each other within the context of specific case characteristics.

CRITICAL INCIDENT AND NATURALISTIC EVALUATION RESEARCH

The limited scope and lack of ecological validity of paper–pencil studies has prompted researchers to go beyond questionnaires in evaluating professional issues related to mandated child abuse reporting. One approach has been to naturalistically examine mandated reporting through retrospective clinical case reviews. Harper and Irvin (1985), for example, reviewed the reporting status of 107 cases involving children being treated on a psychosomatic unit at a children's hospital. The study was conducted through a qualitative analysis of case histories involving suspected child abuse in an effort to determine the effects of reporting on therapeutic relationships. Cases that were reported to the child protection system, as well as those not reported, were evaluated as to their positive and negative effects. Harper and Irvin found that the majority of cases reported in the context of ongoing therapy resulted in positive outcomes with respect to child welfare and continuing treatment. Of importance here is the fact that these findings were based on actual case reviews as opposed to survey responses.

Harper and Irvin's (1985) methods, however, were based on the investigators' subjective impressions of cases rather than an objective coding system. For example, one of the study results was reported as follows: "In only two of the 49 cases that involved mandated reporting did we feel that parents became less able to work on the child's behalf . . . similar impressions were obtained with regard to the child's welfare" (p. 553). Thus, qualitative evaluation of cases, although rich in details that characterize the complexity of suspected child abuse, are likely to be contaminated by investigator biases.

Watson and Levine (1989) followed up on Harper and Irvin's (1985) findings in a more methodologically sound evaluation of 65 psychotherapy cases from an outpatient child and adolescent clinic. Cases were evaluated and analyzed through the coding of information obtained in systematic chart reviews. The researchers, therefore, quantified the data for categorical level analysis rather than relying on subjective impressions. However, because only one researcher coded the data, it was not possible to determine the reliability of the coding system. Watson and Levine noted this limitation and attempted only to code "objective indices in the records" (p. 251), such as whether or not clients terminated treatment, as opposed to subjective judgements of treatment outcome. Watson and Levine tabulated and statistically analyzed several objective case characteristics, including the lapse of time in treatment when a report occurred, whether or not the report breached client confidentiality, and the outcome of reporting with respect to client maintenance of treatment. The major study findings supported Harper and Irvin's results, showing that most reports filed within the context of a therapeutic relationship may be minimally disruptive to the treatment process. Following up further on this line of research, Levine, Anderson, Terretti, Sharma, et al. (1991) and Levine, Anderson, Terretti, Steinberg, et al. (1991) conducted a qualitative analysis of therapist interviews regarding issues related to mandated reporting. These data, based on a phenomenological approach to the reporting process, confirmed many of Watson and Levine's, and Harper and Irvin's findings.

Case evaluations and personal accounts have provided data that more closely characterize the complexity of child abuse reporting. These studies, however, tend to be limited in generalizability because they sample cases from only one setting, which may use idiosyncratic policies and procedures relevant to reporting. In addition, although findings from qualitative analyses, such as those discussed by Harper and Irvin (1985) and Levine, Anderson, Terretti, Sharma, et al. (1991) and Levine, Anderson, Terretti, Steinberg, et al. (1991), are of great descriptive value, it is difficult to estimate the predictive relationships among factors associated with particular case outcomes. Unfortunately, in conducting these studies, researchers have evaluated cases independent of characteristics of reporters and have not investigated mandated reporters' inclinations toward reporting specific cases over others.

A different approach to naturalistically evaluating mandated reporting was conducted by Berlin et al. (1991). This study investigated changes in pedophiliac patients' self-reports of repeated sexual abuse incidents during the course of treatment, before and after the enactment of specific mandated reporting legislation. Berlin et al. found that their patients ceased telling therapists about repeated offenses when reporting statutes in Maryland were changed to require psychiatrists treating pedophiles to report instances of suspected child sexual abuse. Consistent with experimental vignette studies (Brosig & Kalichman, 1992a; Kalichman & Brosig, 1992), Berlin et al. described a direct effect of changes in mandatory reporting laws on clinical practice. However, Berlin et al. did not provide adequate controls to account for changes in clinic policy that might have occurred simultaneously with the new legislation. For example, changes in informed consent procedures and clinic policies regarding mandated reporting might have inhibited self-reports more than did actual legal requirements to report. It is therefore possible that different informed consent procedures could have resulted in different patterns of self-disclosure from those reported by Berlin et al.

(Kalichman, 1991). In addition, the sample of cases Berlin et al. evaluated was most likely sensitized to the criminal justice system and did not represent persons typically suspected of child sexual abuse. These results are also constrained because they were derived from a single clinic with questionable generalizability.

To date, Lamond (1989) has published the only empirical study of the effects of mandatory reporting legislation on professional reporting behavior in natural environments extending beyond a single professional setting. The study evaluated reports of sexual abuse filed in New South Wales, Australia, before and after the implementation of legislation that required school-teachers to report suspected sexual abuse. Reports on other types of mal-treatment and reports filed by other professionals were monitored over the study period and showed no changes. However, changes were observed with respect to sexual abuse reporting by schoolteachers. The study demonstrated the effects of public policy on professional reporting behavior. These data, therefore, represent actual reporting behavior and changes in reporting in a targeted professional population.

The aforementioned studies provide models for the development of research paradigms that more closely reflect the realities of suspected child abuse and mandated reporting. Professional accounts of reporting decisions in response to implemented changes in policy have converged with findings from surveys, questionnaires, and experimental vignettes. However, because ecologically valid research methods more closely represent the reporting process, innovative naturalistic designs should be developed in future re-search.

AVENUES FOR FUTURE RESEARCH ON MANDATED CHILD ABUSE REPORTING

The APA Ad Hoc Committee on Child Abuse Policy (Walker et al., 1989) made a number of recommendations for future research regarding child abuse. Among these suggestions was a call for surveys conducted with professionals regarding attitudes and knowledge related to child maltreat-ment and professionals' responses to mandated reporting. The committee also suggested interdisciplinary collaborative research to address child abuse from diverse professional perspectives. Many of the Ad Hoc Committee's recommendations appear to have influenced subsequent research initiatives, including special issues and special sections of journals (e.g., *Professional Psychology: Research and Practice, 21*(5), 1990; *Law and Human Behavior, 17*(1), 1993; and *Law and Policy, 14*(1, 2), 1993). In addition, the Mini-Convention on Child Abuse at the 1991 APA Convention in San Francisco contained a number of papers and panels addressing policy issues in response to the committee's recommendations. Although these efforts have demon-strated a positive movement toward child abuse policy research, including mandated reporting, further studies are needed. The following strategies and areas of study are suggested as a start toward stimulating ideas for future research. The identified problems, questions, and hypotheses could be molded into viable research projects that would provide valuable contributions to the literature on mandated child abuse reporting.

Future studies on issues related to mandatory reporting laws will need to develop and use ecologically valid methods. With few exceptions, investigations of reporting suspected child abuse have relied on self-report measures. Examples of ecologically valid methods of study could include case evaluations of reported and unreported suspected child abuse from diverse clinical and research settings. Future studies might also build on the clinical evaluation methods of Harper and Irvin (1985), Watson and Levine (1989), and Levine, Anderson, Terretti, Sharma, et al. (1991). For example, professionals could be interviewed regarding report decision-making processes. Interviews could be structured to specifically elicit information relevant to applied decision analysis, including perceived costs and benefits of reporting and not reporting, weighing of potential outcomes, and saliency of reporting criteria. Qualitative as well as quantitative measures could be integrated in attempts to gather a breadth of data that could not be collected through paper–pencil surveys alone.

Ecologically valid research, such as in-depth interviews with professionals, case analyses, and direct observation conducted in clinical settings, is also needed to evaluate specific policies and procedures for reporting suspected child abuse. Few models have been developed for managing reports of child maltreatment and there is no evidence to support any particular set of procedures. Studies are needed to evaluate the relative effectiveness of specific reporting policies implemented across diverse professional settings. For example, studies can be conducted to evaluate procedures for independent practice as compared with other procedures implemented in facilities that use multidisciplinary treatment teams consisting of multiple mandated reporters.

The effects of narrow versus broad definitions of abuse and specific versus nonspecific legal requirements for reporting require careful empirical study. Determining the relative effects of broad and narrow definitions of abuse on reporting is a necessary step toward informed legislative change. Although narrow definitions might result in underreporting and broad definitions might promote overreporting, no study has sought to verify the relationship between legal definitions of child abuse and reporting decisions. Such studies will clarify the ambiguities in legal definitions of abuse by identifying definitions that facilitate and inhibit accurate reporting. The relative impact of such terms as *reasonable cause to suspect, knowledge of abuse,* and *cause to believe* have also not yet been systematically studied.

Future studies on definitions and standards could use a number of different research strategies. First, existing legal standards could be investigated through controlled comparison studies. For example, professionals might be asked to respond to different definitions of child abuse and standards for reporting on the basis of experimental manipulations in which the definitions or standards are treated as experimental vignettes (Brosig & Kalichman, 1992a; Kalichman & Brosig, 1992). Such controlled analogue studies will evaluate the influence of specific features of the law and can be followed up with more ecologically valid procedures. The relative application of legal standards for reporting within various professional settings will also need to be evaluated.

Mandated reporters often hesitate to report suspected child abuse because they perceive the child protection system as inadequate. Research is needed to further evaluate professional perceptions of child protection workers and the way these perceptions affect reporting decisions. Human service professionals are primarily concerned with the welfare of persons they serve. Therefore, it stands to reason that professionals will hesitate to report cases to agencies that they believe inadequately manage reports. Researchers have not yet, however, investigated how closely professional perceptions of local child protection systems match up to actual agency performance. The extent to which professional perceptions are based on personal experience with the system as opposed to secondhand information from fellow professionals has also not been investigated.

Studies addressing professional perceptions of the child protection system will need to sample cases from more than one professional setting in more than one state. Diversity in sampling will prevent the evaluation of professional responses to the idiosyncracies of local systems and child protection resources. Professional perceptions of local child protective systems can also be tested against empirically identified characteristics of the system, such as complaints against agencies, worker caseloads, the availability of intervention resources, and lag times in responding to reports. Research of this type can, therefore, empirically examine the bases for professional perceptions of the child protection system and how these perceptions, both accurate and inaccurate, influence reporting decisions.

Descriptive research identifying signs of abuse and neglect within developmental periods will improve both abuse detection and reporting. Behavior problems, sexual acting out, emotional disturbances, and physical symptomatology are frequently observed among abused and neglected children (Browne & Finkelhor, 1986; Goldston et al., 1989; Walker et al., 1988). Although nonspecific symptoms related to abuse can raise suspicions of maltreatment, these signs frequently fall short of reporting thresholds. Failure to report knowledge of child abuse most likely results from concerns about confidentiality or child protection. In contrast, ambiguous and subtle indicators of child abuse do not even surpass reporting thresholds, making inhibiting factors less relevant. Thus, unidentified cases of child abuse can be reduced by developing sensitive criteria for professionals to use in child maltreatment detection.

In addition to research on behavioral signs of maltreatment, the nature of disclosures of maltreatment warrant further study. Although many professionals rely on verbal accounts of abuse in their reporting decisions (Brosig & Kalichman, 1992b; Finlayson & Koocher, 1991), disclosures of abuse from children may be infrequent (R. Pierce & L. Pierce, 1985; Reppucci & Haugaard, 1989) and are often discounted when recanted (Attias & Goodwin, 1985). Research on the base rates of verbal accounts of different types of abuse from children, perpetrators, and others could serve to improve professional responses to disclosures. Empirically defined indicators of child abuse should also fit within the context of parameters of child development. These descriptions could serve as solid ground for the construction of standardized reporting criteria.

Responses and reporting by professionals working outside of service delivery settings who could come in contact with cases of child abuse have not received adequate attention in the literature. There is a dearth of information concerning mandated child abuse reporting in non-service-delivery contexts, particularly research settings. To date, there have been no studies and little discussion of the frequency at which suspected child abuse is detected by researchers and the procedures that investigators use to manage cases of suspected child abuse. Issues faced by researchers who suspect that a participant has been maltreated or has been abusive may be substantially different from those in clinical service delivery settings. Studies are needed to evaluate the frequency of suspected child abuse detection in research contexts, how researchers manage such cases, and the degree to which researchers recognize their role as mandated reporters.

Beyond questions of when professionals should and actually do report, studies are needed to address procedural issues regarding how best to report. Although chapter 6 suggested guidelines for reporting suspected child abuse, there is no empirical evidence available to support any recommended procedures. Actual reporting and the content of reports may vary in the degree to which they evoke a child protective response from the child protection system. Information contained in a report, the manner in which a report is filed, and characteristics of the relationships between mandated reporters and social service workers might affect the processing of reports. Studies are needed to systematically evaluate the interactive process of reporting to determine optimal reporting procedures.

Research is needed to evaluate the impact of reporting and not reporting on the delivery of professional services. Although many human service professionals indicate that they do not report suspected child abuse because they are concerned that reporting will damage professional services, there is little empirical support for these beliefs. In fact, available evidence tends to support the opposite view (Levine, Anderson, Terretti, Steinberg, et al., 1991; Watson & Levine, 1989). Research is therefore needed to identify factors that lead to negative and positive outcomes of reporting. Research is also needed to evaluate procedures for managing limited confidentiality, informing parents or guardians of reports, and discussing reporting in the context of treatment relationships.

CONCLUSION

Research conducted on mandatory reporting laws constitutes small and focused segments of several literatures spanning social policy, ethics in professional practice, and child maltreatment intervention. The implications of mandated reporting can be addressed from a variety of perspectives in an effort to answer an array of questions. For example, researchers could investigate the value of standards for reporting based on professional responses to existing policies. Studies could also use naturalistic methods to investigate the functional application of standards across professions, professional settings, and circumstances of suspected abuse. Regardless of the direction taken, future studies that push toward direct implications for child protection policy should have the highest priority.

A necessary step toward advancing research in child abuse policy is the dissolution of structures that prohibit empirical study. Institutional obstacles often make it impossible to access information systems and study populations. The APA Ad Hoc Committee on Child Abuse Policy (Walker et al., 1989) noted some of these problems: "We encourage exploring barriers to research including human subject committees in universities, hospitals, and granting agencies as well as state statutory and regulatory schemes for protecting access to information about children and families" (p. 13). Barriers blocking investigators from accessing ecologically valid data sources force researchers to rely on more convenient and less compelling analogue methodologies.

Emphasizing ecologically valid methodologies in the study of mandated reporting demands that child protection agencies provide a structure conducive to accurate data collection. At present, however, such structures do not exist. The child protection system does not use uniform data management. Local agencies idiosyncratically define maltreatment, screen cases, and set criteria for investigation and substantiation, making studies across communities impossible. Studies conducted within a single agency face similar problems with regard to uniform record keeping, data tabulation, and management of duplicate reports. Ecologically valid studies conducted within professional settings, focusing on mandated reporters, will require similar accessibility. Efforts to expand beyond a single agency or clinic will also result in the most generalizable findings with the farthest reaching implications.

Also in need of research are the professional implications of mandated reporting of elderly and spouse abuse, and suspected maltreatment of persons with disabilities. Although only some states have enacted reporting legislation with respect to elderly and spouse abuse, it appears to be on the horizon for the rest. Most of the issues of confidentiality, reporting thresholds, and decision criteria that permeate child abuse reporting are likely to be raised with respect to these related problems. For example, definitions of elder abuse, management of disclosures of spouse abuse in the context of marital therapy, and recognition of maltreatment of persons with disabilities are all important areas for future research. As is the case with child maltreatment, an empirical literature can form the basis for social policies, and research can further our understanding of policy implications for professional practice.

9

FUTURE DIRECTIONS FOR LEGISLATION AND POLICY IN MANDATED CHILD ABUSE REPORTING

That the term of a penal statute creating a new offense must be suffi-ciently explicit to inform those who are subject to it what conduct on their part will render them liable to its penalties, is a well recognized requirement, consonant alike with ordering notions of fair play and the settled rules of law. A statute which either forbids or requires the doing of an act in terms so vague that men of common intelligence must differ as to its application violates the first essential of due process of law. (*Connally v. General Construction Company*, 1926)

High reporting thresholds reserve reporting for severe cases of abuse and cases most likely to benefit from state intervention. Reporting whenever suspicions occur, potentially erring on the side of overreporting, relies on low reporting thresholds. Reflective reporting (Weissman, 1991), on the other hand, involves exercising professional judgement in reporting sus-pected child abuse. These varied interpretations of reporting laws illustrate why current reporting statutes often fail to protect children, and how they contribute to jamming the child protection system.

Mandatory reporting statutes themselves have played a direct role in professionals' under- and overreporting of suspected child abuse. As previously discussed, reporting laws set ambiguous standards regarding when reporting is required and provide vague definitions of child maltreatment. Statutory wording is, to a certain degree, intentionally vague. Terms like *reason to believe, reasonable suspicion, reasonable cause to suspect mental injury,* and *harm* allow for judicial discretion in court decisions. Broad definitions of abuse and general reporting standards limit the potential for excluding abusive situations from reporting requirements. General terms, therefore, are inclusive and serve the purpose of capturing a maximum number of abuse cases. The problem, however, is that vague statutes are difficult to interpret and are likely to lead to noncompliance. As stated by Jones and Welch (1989), "It is widely recognized that to observe the law one must first understand what the law is, i.e. the law must be clear" (p. 44).

In contrast to vague statutory wording, mandatory reporting laws can also be narrow in their reporting requirements. Narrow statutes tend to be objective and defined in absolute terms. However, narrow statutes are also more likely to result in restricted reporting. As noted by Besharov (1978):

> The dilemma of choosing between general, and therefore somewhat vague, definitions and specific, and therefore potentially over-narrow, definitions will be with us for some time. Listing with precise specificity all those actions that constitute child abuse and neglect raises the possibility of inadvertently excluding dangerous situations that should be included. Generalized definitions risk over-broad applications that include behavior that should not be considered abusive or neglectful. (p. 474)

Thus, in terms of legal definitions of child abuse, as well as other dimensions of reporting standards, the relative costs and benefits associated with over-reporting versus underreporting remain the core issues.

Proposals for legislative change to improve the mandatory reporting system reflect three different levels of legislative action. First, it has been suggested that the mandatory reporting laws themselves are consistent with child protection policies and do not require reform. Instead of legislative change, advocates of this position recommend that the existing system be supported and reporting statutes be enforced. Those holding a second point of view differ by acknowledging problems with current child abuse reporting laws and by advocating clarification of legal definitions of maltreatment and reporting standards. This position accepts the current structure of mandated reporting, but proposes changes to increase the ability of the statutes to protect children. Finally, those touting a third position have been highly critical of existing reporting statutes and call for substantial reform of the reporting system. In this chapter, these three levels of proposed legislative change are reviewed.

MINIMAL REFORM: STRENGTHENING
AND SUPPORTING EXISTING SYSTEMS

It is difficult to find discussions of mandated reporting laws that offer an unqualified endorsement of them. Rather, reporting laws represent one facet of the child protection system. Despite the plethora of criticism directed at mandated reporting, some authors have rejected the notion of statutory reform (e.g., Small, 1992). One argument along these lines is that the mandated reporting system is necessary and the laws have been subjected to continual reform since their initial enactment. Lists of mandated reporters including an array of professionals and definitions of all types of maltreatment have been subsumed under the laws. In addition, systematic increases in reporting have occurred as the laws have emerged and expanded (Besharov, 1990; Lamond, 1989; USDHHS, 1988). From this perspective, mandatory reporting laws are currently sufficient to meet their child protection goals, and the laws are functioning to detect child abuse.

If it is assumed, however, that the laws themselves do not require reform, an explanation is needed as to why numerous mandated reporters act outside the law or misinterpret the meaning of the statutes. One possible reason is that professionals are ill equipped to detect and manage reporting in their professional practice. From this perspective, professional training to familiarize reporters with the laws and increase their understanding of reporting requirements is necessary for responsible reporting. However, mandated reporters rarely have any practical or didactic graduate educational experiences in child abuse and reporting. Although most professionals may be aware of reporting laws, legal standards are still being misinterpreted and misapplied. As previously discussed, training in child abuse detection and reporting has been widely advocated as a means of correcting current problems with reporting.

Training professionals in child abuse should be considered a viable avenue for improving professional practice. However, there is little evidence to suggest that professionals who lack such training are less inclined to report. For example, Finlayson and Koocher (1991) found that pediatric psychologists with specialized training in sexual abuse were no more likely to report than respondents without such training. Kalichman and Brosig (1993) did, however, identify a relationship between specific types of training experiences and reporting history. Among licensed psychologists sampled, Kalichman and Brosig found that those who had not reported suspected child abuse were more likely to obtain postgraduate training in child maltreatment through continuing education and workshops, as compared with participants who always reported. Although their data were not longitudinal, Kalichman and Brosig suggested that this relationship reflected the tendency for professionals to seek further training after experiences with unreported suspicions. Thus, there appears to be a need for information and skills training related to child abuse detection and reporting in graduate programs and internships (Pope & Feldman-Summers, 1992).

A second factor independent of mandatory reporting laws that might contribute to lower rates of reporting is the child protection system itself. Professionals who help families are required to report suspected child abuse to agencies perceived as being at a disadvantage for implementing adequate interventions. Consistent with professionals' perceptions, the child protection system is in crisis and will, at least in its current state, probably inhibit reporting (U.S. Advisory Board on Child Abuse and Neglect, 1990). Social commitment to child protective service reform would, therefore, build a stronger foundation for reporting. Enhanced trust between mandated reporters and the child protection system would also likely result in more effective reporting of suspected child abuse because the entire reporting process and its outcome will improve. These approaches to mandated reporting therefore hinge on better trained reporters and better resourced report-receiving agencies. In addition, changes in the child protection system will reinforce mandatory reporting laws by making reporting a more potent intervention.

There is no shortage of proposals to reform the child protection system, the most substantive and potentially influential of which has come from the U.S. Advisory Board on Child Abuse and Neglect (1990). In a comprehensive set of recommendations following the declaration of child maltreatment as a national emergency, the members of the board, who come from diverse professional backgrounds, called for social reform of state child protection systems. The board appealed to elected officials to provide leadership and for all citizens to provide a unified response to the child maltreatment crisis. With respect to the child protection system itself, the board identified three major problems requiring immediate attention: case overloads among child protection workers, the crisis in foster care, and the system's inability to focus on the needs of children. The board also provided recommendations with specific objectives within each of the three problem areas, providing a national agenda for reforming child protection systems. With regard to reporting, the board indicated that reforming the system should result in increased adherence to reporting standards.

ADAPTIVE REFORM: MODIFYING THE EXISTING STATUTES

Problems associated with mandated reporting are most commonly attributed to the mandatory reporting laws themselves, and it is therefore often suggested that the statutes be reformed. However, there is little consensus on the degree to which specific components of the law are to be revised and how such changes will most benefit child protection (Weisberg & Wald, 1984). Four components of reporting laws have drawn the most attention among reformists: definitions of child abuse, standards for required reporting, immunity for reporters, and abrogation of privileged communications. Following is a brief summary of each of these suggestions.

Definitions of Child Abuse and Neglect

As discussed in previous chapters, reporting laws define child maltreatment in two very different ways: either in broad/general or narrow/restrictive terms. Broad legal definitions tend to be vague and ambiguous, allowing professionals to set their own standard for what constitutes suspected child abuse. As stated by Otto and Melton (1990), "Exactly what the professional needs to see or believe in order to report abuse and thereby comply with the reporting statute is not made clear in most statutes" (p. 64). In contrast, narrow definitions run the probable risk of omitting dangerous situations from reporting requirements (Besharov, 1978). Thus, legal definitions of child abuse drive the potential for over- and underreporting, at least in part, depending on whether definitions are broad or narrow, respectively.

An examination of legal definitions of child abuse suggests that they are completely divorced from the past two decades of research on child abuse. For example, there are few behavioral descriptors of abusive acts or symptoms of victimization included in reporting statutes. It is troublesome that legal definitions do not embrace the identifiable parameters of signs and circumstances related to child abuse, but it is not surprising. The most ambiguously defined form of child maltreatment, psychological–emotional abuse, is defined in many current statutes as mental injury or psychological impairment, and therefore does not provide clear standards for reporting.

Definitions of different types of child abuse present different problems for mandated reporting. Sexual abuse is typically defined on the basis of abusive actions and behaviors. Regardless of the type of touching, fondling, or exploitation, these behaviors constitute child sexual abuse. Thus, because sexual abuse is defined by a clear set of circumstances and conditions, rather than signs and symptoms, child sexual abuse allegations made by either children or adults tend to be difficult to attribute to nonabusive situations. This is also true for neglect, in which failing to provide basic needs, exposing a child to potential harm, or leaving young children unattended invariably constitutes child neglect (Otto & Melton, 1990; Wald, 1975). This is not to say that sexual abuse and child neglect are easily detected; they are not. But when detected, sexual abuse and neglect are rarely confused with nonabusive circumstances.

Physical abuse and psychological–emotional maltreatment, on the other hand, tend to be less well defined, and both tend to be characterized by signs and symptoms presented by children. The specificity of definitions of physical abuse, in terms of manifest harm and injuries, facilitates nondiscriminatory applications of the law and increases the accountability of mandated reporters (Meriwether, 1986). There are, however, specific parental acts that are thought to be, on the basis of parental rights, outside of abuse definitions. For example, Besharov (1988) discusses corporal punishment, when reasonable and not excessive, as specifically not constituting abuse and therefore not reportable. Likewise, several states explicitly exclude corporal punishment from definitions of abuse (NCCAN, 1979). Thus, injuries and harm are the focal point of legal definitions of physical abuse, rather than parental behaviors, unless specifically defined as excessive.

A similar emphasis on signs and symptoms exists for definitions of psychological–emotional maltreatment. However, unlike physical abuse, injuries and harm sustained from psychological maltreatment are less clearly linked to specific parental acts. Although it is widely agreed that mental injury should be defined on the basis of specific behaviors exhibited by children, there is little empirical support for deriving such definitions (Corson & Davidson, 1987; Melton & Limber, 1989). Legal definitions of psychological maltreatment could therefore require inclusion of specific parental acts as conditions of abuse on the basis of their likelihood of resulting in psychological harm. Behaviors such as ridicule, humiliation, and emotional abandonment could be included as definitive indicators of psychological maltreatment (Garbarino et al., 1986).

Legislative changes in mandatory reporting laws should provide clear and objective definitions of child maltreatment, outlining specific parental behaviors and child symptoms if appropriate (Otto & Melton, 1990; Wald, 1975). Objective parameters for legal definitions can be developed from the empirical literature on child maltreatment. The practice of basing legal definitions of child abuse on the empirical literature has a long history. Definitions of physical abuse in the first reporting statutes relied heavily on Kempe et al.'s (1962) description of the battered child syndrome, including radiologic findings, bone fractures, and other identifiable injuries. Statutes later added sexual abuse, neglect, and psychological maltreatment, but these terms were defined in the absence of empirical work. For example, the Child Abuse Prevention and Treatment Act of 1974 predates by more than a decade the first comprehensive empirical works in sexual abuse and psychological maltreatment (e.g., Finkelhor, 1984, 1986; Garbarino et al., 1986). Additional amendments to child protection laws that address out-of-the-home abuse, including foster care, were also enacted prior to the appearance of substantive empirical literature in these areas (e.g., Besharov, 1987b; Russell & Clifford, 1987). Although it may not be unusual for legislation to precede research, and perhaps even prompt studies, mechanisms should be built into child abuse policy for periodic reviews of scientific literature and to establish revised standards as warranted by empirical findings.

Although definitions of child abuse and neglect can be refined and developed to provide specific and objective parameters for reporting, most legal definitions will likely retain catchall phrases, such as *endangered child*, maltreatment, *refusal to provide care when able to do so*, and *physical injury of nonaccidental nature*. One reason for including these terms is that they allow for professional discretion in reporting cases that have not yet reached the point of a child suffering harm. Vague definitions, therefore, can function in a preventive fashion by not requiring harm to have occurred before reporting is required (Bourne & Newberger, 1977). Broad and vague terminology in definitions of child abuse are also useful in judicial rulings (Giovannoni, 1989a). Restricting legal definitions of child abuse, while providing objective bases for reporting and increasing professional accountability, could hamper the ability of judges to make determinations on cases that do not neatly fit circumscribed definitions.

Given the multiple roles of legal definitions of child maltreatment and their implications (Giovannoni, 1989a), definitions may be reformed in terms of (a) redefining specific acts, omissions, signs, and symptoms of physical, sexual, and emotional abuse and neglect based on empirical research; (b) instituting periodic national reviews of legal definitions of abuse by panels of child maltreatment experts in order to provide a database for updating state definitions; and (c) retaining catchall phrases for the purpose of inclusiveness. Thus, legal definitions of child abuse should provide objective standards to guide professional and public behavior by clearly stating specific circumstances that constitute child abuse.

Determinations of When Reporting Is Required

Kempe et al. (1962), whose description of the battered child syndrome led to definitions of physical abuse, suggested that "the report that he [the physician] makes should be restricted to the objective findings which can be verified, and where possible, be supported by photographs and roentgenograms" (p. 23). However, the early statutes did not require any such precision in reporting, but instead refrained from defining the levels of certainty that abuse had occurred at which reporting would be required. Mandatory reporting laws in all states have followed the wording of the Model Child Protection Act in their requirements for reporting. The legal standard was such that laws

> do not require a reporter to know or be certain that a child has been abused or neglected. The degree of certainty most often expressed is "reason to believe" or "reasonable cause to believe or suspect," a standard based on the reasonable person's convictions. (NCCAN, 1979, p. 3)

Inclusion of *reasonable* as part of a legal standard allows for an objective element in required reporting because it is possible to determine whether or not reasonable professionals with similar levels of training and experience placed in a similar situation would suspect child abuse (Meriwether, 1986).

Laws providing that reports be based on rational grounds, rather than intuition, move toward a more objective standard but still may be too vague to enforce.

Along with vague definitions of child abuse, legal thresholds for reporting on the basis of reason to suspect have been questioned as unconstitutionally vague. Meriwether (1986), for example, pointed out that the "use of broad, and ambiguous language to define reportable abuse may subject the statute to constitutional challenge" (p. 151). As Meriwether predicted, the vagueness of Michigan's reporting statute formed the basis for the case of *People v. Cavaiani* (1988), discussed in chapter 1. Family therapist Cavaiani had been charged with failure to report suspected child abuse. His attorney challenged the Michigan reporting statute on the grounds that it was unconstitutional, based on First and Fifth Amendment rights to privacy and against self-incrimination, and based on its vagueness. The Michigan statute reads:

> A physician . . . psychologist . . . who has reasonable cause to suspect child abuse or neglect shall make immediately, by telephone or otherwise, an oral report, or cause an oral report to be made, of the suspected child abuse or neglect to the Department. (Michigan Department of Social Services, 1989, p. 2)

At the level of a circuit court, the statute was ruled unconstitutional, with the judge stating that the law was void due to its failure to provide a "precise standard for adhering to and enforcing the law" (Denton, 1987b). The state appealed the decision of the lower court and brought the case to the Michigan State Supreme Court. However, the challenge did not proceed because Cavaiani was found not guilty of failure to report and the higher court would only hear the case against the statute if Cavaiani was found guilty.

Aside from the ruling in *Cavaiani*, there is further evidence that mandatory reporting statutes are overly vague and that their vagueness interferes with compliance. First, among the approximately one third of mandated reporters responding to surveys who indicate that they have not reported suspected child abuse, the most common reason for not reporting is uncertainty as to when reporting is required (Brosig & Kalichman, 1992b). Second, despite high rates of not reporting, there are few arrests for failure to report. In fact, the Cavaiani case was among the first criminal cases of failure to report suspected child maltreatment to be tried (Robert Muckenheim, personal communication, July 15, 1992). Thus, as Meriwether (1986) suggested, the vague wording of mandatory reporting laws interferes with compliant behavior and inhibits law enforcement. Mandatory reporting laws, therefore, require statutory reform in order to clearly state when reporting is required.

Changes similar to those recommended for definitions of abuse could also be applied to legal thresholds for reporting. Statutes could explicitly define both *knowledge* and *reasonable suspicion*. Certain circumstances, such as disclosures of abuse, could be specifically defined as meeting the threshold for reporting suspected child abuse unless there are compelling reasons to do otherwise. First, a statute could state that all allegations and verbal disclosures of abuse require reporting. Unfortunately, no statute specifies reporting disclosures of abuse, although such a standard is justified by the low base rate of false allegations. Although false allegations occur (Wakefield & Underwager, 1991), they are rare, and it is impossible to recognize false allegations outside of an investigation. Second, any observations of injuries in the absence of known accidental cause, as well as observations of abusive or negligent behavior, could constitute required reporting. Other direct evidence of maltreatment could also be included as specifically meeting legal reporting thresholds, such as having seen sexually explicit films or photographs of children and being able to identify the children depicted or those who possess these materials; possessing knowledge of a child being denied nutrition or medical care; and possessing knowledge of young children being left unattended (Besharov, 1990). Finally, the term *reasonable suspicion* could also be retained as a catchall phrase to account for any maltreatment not indicated by definitive acts or signs and for those situations in which subtle indicators accumulate.

Another aspect of mandatory reporting laws that continues to face reform is the specific source of the information leading to suspicions of child abuse. When operating under laws that only require reporting of situations in which the information source is an alleged child/victim, professionals do not readily report situations that fall outside the legal requirement (Brosig & Kalichman, 1992a; Kalichman & Brosig, 1992). Most states, however, have updated their reporting laws since they were originally enacted to include the requirement that suspicions raised by an adult also be reported. States that have not yet made this change are being urged to do so. For example, the Pennsylvania Department of Public Welfare (1992) has specifically recommended that the state legislature

> amend Section 6311 of the [Child Protective Services Law] CPSL to require mandated reporters to report suspected abuse based on information received without requiring that the child come before the reporter. This change encourages more complete reporting of suspected child abuse and tends to broaden the safety net of services which may prevent serious or repeated abuse. (p. 19)

Thus, most states have recognized the limitations of narrow reporting requirements and only a handful of states have retained them.

Legislative reform to reduce statutory vagueness has been recommended in two areas: (a) provide mandated reporters with clear definitions of expectations for their behavior under the law, and (b) eliminate restrictions on the sources of information that would otherwise meet legal standards for reporting. Reducing the vagueness of reporting laws before it becomes necessary to undertake costly challenges to their constitutionality will result in greater adherence and accountability among mandated reporters.

Immunity for Mandated Reporters

There have been few recommendations to reform this component of reporting laws. It is widely agreed that mandated reporters should not be held liable for reports filed in good faith, and that such immunity is necessary for reporting requirements to be effective because it removes the threat of legal sanctions that might otherwise inhibit reporting (Meriwether, 1986; Schwartz, 1991, 1992). All state reporting laws include a statement of immunity, most of which specify that

> a person participating in good faith in making of a report, or photographs, or X-rays, or performance of a medically relevant test . . . or aiding and assisting in an investigation of a child abuse report . . . shall have immunity from any liability, civil or criminal, which might otherwise be incurred or imposed. The person shall have the same immunity with respect to participation in good faith in any judicial proceeding resulting from the report or relating to the subject matter of the report. (Iowa Department of Human Services, 1991, p. 30)

However, the immunity provided to mandated reporters, although reassuring, may not be necessary. In the absence of such a provision, it would still be necessary to prove a report to be malicious, or in bad faith, for a reporter to be held liable for reporting. Thus, with or without stated immunity, evidence for bad faith reporting opens the reporter up to liability. Besharov (1978) states that the provision is technically redundant and that the "presumption of good faith is a public relations provision, designed to soothe potential reporters" (p. 476). In this respect, however, immunity clauses in reporting laws do end up being highly valuable because without such an explicit statement numerous mandated reporters would be unlikely to report (Schwartz, 1991).

Besharov (1986b) suggested a second type of immunity for professionals who, in good faith, do not report. Assuming that mandated reporters are concerned with child welfare and have an interest in protecting children from harm, Besharov suggests that professionals only be held liable when not reporting occurs in bad faith. Besharov points out that this provision could decrease the number of unnecessary reports because the current standard penalizes the negligent failure to report but grants immunity for incorrect reports. As Besharov specifically stated, "Fearful of being sued for not reporting, some professionals play it safe and report whenever they think there is the slightest chance that they will subsequently be sued for not doing so" (p. 29). Contrary to Besharov's position, however, surveys have shown that concerns about the law and the potential for liability play a minimal role in professionals' reporting decisions (Brosig & Kalichman, 1992a). Besharov's ideas for granting immunity for not reporting have received little attention thus far, but might be discussed more as an option to reduce overreporting if the child protection system remains in crisis and unable to manage large volumes of reports.

Abrogation of Privileged Communications

A number of mandated reporters who treat perpetrators have opposed abrogating privileged communication under reporting statutes. Most complaints have centered around how the requirement is likely to interfere with self-referrals of offenders into therapy and the unlikely self-disclosure of offenses while in treatment. Offenders are more likely to step forward for treatment in an environment in which they are safe from criminal charges than they would be if there was a mandate to turn them over to authorities (Kelly, 1987; Smith & Meyer, 1984; R. Weinstock & D. Weinstock, 1989). Treatment professionals have argued that required reporting interferes with rehabilitation and in the long run endangers children (Berlin et al., 1991).

To correct this problem, critics of the requirement have called for guaranteeing confidentiality when treating offenders in order to encourage them to seek voluntary therapy. As a specific recommendation, Smith and Meyer (1984) stated:

> Medical privileges and psychotherapist–client privileges should not be lost each time an abuser "confesses" the abuse to a psychotherapist or physician. To encourage abusers to seek therapy and be open in therapy, they should be assured that their confession of child abuse to a therapist will not be used against them in a criminal case or in child custody proceedings. Destroying the privilege will seldom directly benefit a child, and when there is a possibility of a child custody hearing (e.g., in a divorce action), it makes it extremely difficult for an abuser to seek effective therapy and remain open in the course of therapy. (p. 363)

Smith and Meyer (1984) did, however, specify circumstances in which privileged communication dissolves. Specifically, only disclosures made directly by an abuser or an abuser's spouse would remain confidential, whereas information disclosed by any other source would fall outside of the privilege. Second, Smith and Meyer state that privileged communications would be subject to the condition that treatment is progressing successfully, meaning that when treatment breaks down the privilege is discontinued. Finally, under these provisions privileged communications would immediately dissolve when a child is threatened with harm. This recommendation is aimed at facilitating an environment that promotes open disclosure.

Although retaining privileged communications under special circumstances with perpetrators in treatment would open doors to self-referred therapy and allow for the necessary openness in treatment relationships, there are several reasons why privilege has not been granted under most current statutes. Although it is agreed that privileged communications would necessarily be dissolved when a child is endangered, this policy would prohibit early intervention and prevention. In addition, at least with respect to child sexual abusers, the efficacy of treatment for perpetrators is known to be low and the probability for repeated offense substantial (Furby, Weinrott, & Blackshaw, 1989). Therefore, potential costs associated with maintaining privileged communications are high. Retaining privileged communications with abusive adults emphasizes child maltreatment as a mental health problem and de-emphasizes abuse as criminal behavior. Thus, before maintaining privileged communications in the treatment of offenders it will be necessary to develop demonstrably effective treatment technologies.

SYSTEMIC REFORM: AN OVERHAUL OF EXISTING STRUCTURES

Amidst the many suggestions for tightening up and clarifying existing reporting laws, proposals to redesign the mandated reporting system have been few. For example, citizen action groups called Victims of Child Abuse Legislation (VOCAL) consider reporting statutes to be destructive and intrusive to families and advocate a complete revision of the child protection system, but these groups offer few specific suggestions for policy change (Besharov, 1990). Legislation that requires human service professionals to report suspected child abuse tends to bring functionally independent service sectors together, including the child protection system and the education, mental health, and medical professions. However, aside from the law itself, mandated reporters and report-receiving agencies are usually unconnected and at worst can be adversarial.

Human service professionals are required to report reasonable suspicions of child abuse and are therefore given some discretion in reporting. However, the law does not stipulate how much discretion should go into a report of suspected child abuse and whether or not such discretion should vary among mandated reporters. For example, should child clinical psychologists be held to the same discretionary standard as a commercial film processor or an X-ray technician? Should a psychiatrist with 20 years of experience in treating pedophiles be granted more discretion than a hospital intern? These questions are not addressed by existing reporting statutes. Zellman (1990) found that mandated reporters who exercise greater discretion are equally knowledgeable and as well trained in child maltreatment as professionals who consistently report every case of suspected abuse. However, reporters who demonstrate discretion were more likely to be confident in their reporting decisions and were more often considered a resource for reporting by their colleagues. Zellman also found that discretionary reporters were more likely to hold negative views of the child protection system. Discretionary reporters have also been found to take the seriousness of abuse and the potential effects of reporting on the family into account in their reporting decisions (Kalichman & Brosig, 1993). Thus, unreported suspected child abuse is likely to occur among well-trained professionals.

Based on Zellman's (1990) findings, Finkelhor and Zellman (1991) proposed flexible reporting options for mandated reporters with specialized training in child abuse. Finkelhor and Zellman recommended that professionals who meet specific standards of training be able to attain a special status within the child protection system. According to Finkelhor and Zellman, professionals with demonstrated competence in child abuse detection and intervention should be afforded the opportunity to register themselves with the child protection system and be given discretionary reporting options. For example, a professional with documented training and experience in treating child-abusive adults would not be required to report previous acts of abuse that surface in therapy assuming that there were no indications of immediate danger to a child and that therapy would be compromised otherwise. Discretion under Finkelhor and Zellman's plan would also be limited to circumstances in which there is no serious danger to a child and in which a criminal investigation is not warranted. Therefore, cases of serious physical abuse and all cases of sexual abuse would be subject to the usual standards for reporting. Finkelhor and Zellman outline recommendations for instituting their plan in local child protection agencies. The proposal would both capitalize on professional training and streamline the number of mandated child abuse reports.

Finkelhor and Zellman's (1991) innovative approach to exploiting professional discretion in mandated reporting warrants close consideration by child protection agencies as new solutions are sought for problems of overreporting and underreporting. Mandated reporters working with the child protection system can establish standards for registered levels of discretionary reporting. Such a system would also promote professional training and provide a status for those who pursue such training. Finkelhor and Zellman's proposal could be fashioned into a system that would maximize the use of limited child protection system resources without compromising intervention efforts.

CONCLUSION

Mandatory child abuse reporting laws are in need of reform. As they stand, the laws are outdated by the empirical knowledge base on child abuse and neglect; they set legal standards that do not translate to professional settings; and they are too vague to assist in child protection. In effect, virtually any situation in which a child is distressed could raise a reportable suspicion of child maltreatment and, at the same time, only the most severe and salient signs of abuse would necessarily fall under the reasonable suspicion standard. The vagueness of the statutes fosters over- and under-reporting and compromises the protection of children. Without a clear public policy to guide professional behavior in terms of required reporting, mandated reporters set their own reporting standards and, in effect, make public policy through their reporting decisions. Thus, the mandated reporting system cannot function in the best interest of children because professionals cannot know what or when to report except in those cases in which it is known that a child has been harmed.

Mandatory reporting laws can be revised in clearer terms without instituting strict reporting criteria or raising reporting thresholds. For example, a legal standard that defines reasonable suspicion as encompassing any verbal allegation in which the perpetrator or victim is identifiable clarifies professional requirements to report verbal disclosures regardless of such factors as the child's age, the source of the allegation, or whether the allegation occurs in the midst of a custody dispute. To keep standards from becoming overly narrow, catchall phrases can be retained in addition to specifying particular circumstances that require reporting. Under current statutes, however, factors such as the characteristics of the child, the professional's experiences, and the severity of the alleged abuse may interfere with the reasonable suspicions standard because the statutes vaguely define child abuse. Clear standards, therefore, would likely result in increased accurate reporting of child abuse.

Statutory reform, however extensive, will not replace the necessity to increase professional training and address the national crisis in the child protection system. When placed in perspective, mandated reporting is a slice of social policy targeted at child abuse. The issue of reporting has captured the attention of human service professionals because of concerns about their role as mandated reporters, the ethical practice of their profession, and the protection of children. For mandated reporting to play an effective role in child protection, public policy will need to address professional responsibilities in a language and context relevant to professional roles and settings.

REFERENCES

Achenbach, T. M., & Edelbrock, C. (1983). *Manual for the child behavior checklist and revised child behavior profile.* Burlington: University of Vermont.

Adams, J. A. (1991). Is it (or is it not) sexual abuse? The medical examiner's dilemma. *Child Youth and Family Services, 15,* 129–143.

Adams, J. A., Harper, K., & Knudson, S. (1992). A proposed system for the classification of anogenital findings in children with suspected sexual abuse. *Adolescent and Pediatric Gynecology, 5,* 73–75.

Adams, J. A., Phillips, P. N., & Ahmad, M. (1990). The usefulness of colposcopic photographs in the evaluation of suspected child sexual abuse. *Adolescent and Pediatric Gynecology, 3,* 75–82.

Alexander, C., & Becker, H. (1978). The use of vignettes in survey research. *Public Opinion Quarterly, 42,* 93–104.

Alpert, J. L., & Paulson, A. (1990). Graduate-level education and training in child sexual abuse. *Professional Psychology: Research and Practice, 21,* 366–371.

American Medical Association. (1964). Battered child legislation. *Journal of the American Medical Association, 188,* 136.

American Psychological Association. (1990). Ethical principles of psychologists (amended June 2, 1989). *American Psychologist, 45,* 390–395.

American Psychological Association. (1992). Ethical principles of psychologists and code of conduct. *American Psychologist, 47,* 1597–1611.

American Psychological Association, Committee for the Protection of Human Participants in Research. (1982). *Ethical principles in the conduct of research with human participants.* Washington, DC: Author.

Ammerman, R. T., Cassisi, J., Hersen, M., & Van Hasselt, V. (1986). Consequences of physical abuse and neglect in children. *Clinical Psychology Review, 6,* 291–310.

Anonymous. (1992). *Individual conscience and psychologists' responsibility.* Unpublished manuscript.

Ansell, C., & Ross, H. (1990). Reply to Pope and Bajt. *American Psychologist, 45,* 399.

Assembly Bill No. 1133, LA Civil Code §43.92 (1985).

Attias, R., & Goodwin, J. (1985). Knowledge and management strategies in incest cases: A survey of physicians, psychologists, and family counselors. *Child Abuse and Neglect, 9,* 527–533.

Baily, T. F., & Baily, W. H. (1986). *Operational definitions of child emotional maltreatment.* (Available from EM Project, Bureau of Social Sciences, Maine Department of Human Services, Station #11, Main Street, Augusta, ME 04333.)

Baird, K. A., & Rupert, P. A. (1987). Clinical management of confidentiality: A survey of psychologists in seven states. *Professional Psychology: Research and Practice, 18*, 347–352.

Beeman, D. G., & Scott, N. A. (1991). Therapists' attitudes toward psychotherapy informed consent with adolescents. *Professional Psychology: Research and Practice, 22*, 230–234.

Berlin, F., Malin, H., & Dean, S. (1991). Effects of statutes requiring psychiatrists to report suspected sexual abuse of children. *American Journal of Psychiatry, 148*, 449–453.

Bersoff, D. N. (1975). Professional ethics and legal responsibilities: On the horns of a dilemma. *Journal of School Psychology, 13*, 359–376.

Besharov, D. J. (1978). The legal aspects of reporting known and suspected child abuse and neglect. *Villanova Law Review, 23*, 458–520.

Besharov, D. J. (1986a, August). Child abuse and neglect: Liability for failing to report. *Trial*, pp. 67–72.

Besharov, D. J. (1986b). Unfounded allegations—A new child abuse problem. *The Public Interest, 83*, 18–31.

Besharov, D. J. (1987a, November). Policy guidelines for decision making in child abuse and neglect. *Children Today*, pp. 7–10.

Besharov, D. J. (1987b). Reporting out-of-home maltreatment: Penalties and protections. *Child Welfare, 66*, 399–408.

Besharov, D. J. (1988). *Child abuse and neglect reporting and investigation: Policy guidelines for decision making.* Washington, DC: American Bar Association.

Besharov, D. J. (1990). *Recognizing child abuse: A guide for the concerned.* New York: Free Press.

Bourne, R., & Newberger, E. (1977). "Family autonomy" or "coercive intervention"? Ambiguity and conflict in the proposed standards for child abuse and neglect. *Boston University Law Review, 57*, 670–706.

Brassard, M. R., & Gelardo, M. S. (1987). Psychological maltreatment: The unifying construct in child abuse and neglect. *School Psychology Review, 16*, 127–136.

Brosig, C. L. (1992). *Child abuse reporting decisions: The effects of statutory wording of reporting requirements.* Unpublished masters thesis, Loyola University of Chicago.

Brosig, C. L., & Kalichman, S. C. (1992a). Child abuse reporting decisions: Effects of statutory wording of reporting requirements. *Professional Psychology: Research and Practice, 23*, 486–492.

Brosig, C. L., & Kalichman, S. (1992b). Clinicians' reporting of suspected child abuse: A review of the empirical literature. *Clinical Psychology Review, 12*, 155–168.

Bross, D. C. (1983, April). Professional and agency liability for negligence in child protection. *Law, Medicine, and Health Care*, pp. 71–75.

Browne, A., & Finkelhor, D. (1986). Impact of child sexual abuse: A review of the research. *Psychological Bulletin, 99*, 66–77.

Buie, J. (1989, November). Clinicians don't always tell of suspected abuse. *APA Monitor*, p. 20.

Butz, R. A. (1985). Reporting child abuse and confidentiality in counseling. *Journal of Contemporary Social Work*, 66, 83–90.

Caldwell, S., English, D., Foote, A., Hodges, V., Nguyen, Q., Pecora, P. J., Pien, D., Stallings, Z., Tong, C., Vendiola, D., & Ybarra, V. (1992). *An approach to strength and risk assessment with multicultural guidelines.* (Available from Peter J. Pecora, School of Social Work, JH-30, University of Washington, 4101 15th Street NE, Seattle, WA 98195.)

California Crime Prevention Center. (1988). *Child abuse prevention handbook.* Sacramento, CA: Author.

California State Department of Social Services. (1991). *The California child abuse and neglect reporting law: Issues and answers for health practitioners.* (Available from California Department of Social Services, Office of Child Abuse Prevention, 744 P. Street, M. S. 9–100, Sacramento, CA 95814.)

Camblin, L. D., & Prout, H. T. (1983). School counselors and the reporting of child abuse: A survey of state laws and practices. *School Counselor, 30*, 358–367.

Child Abuse Prevention, Adoption, and Family Services Act of 1988, §§100–294 (1988, April).

Child Abuse Prevention and Treatment Act of 1974, 42 U.S.C.S. §§5101–5115 (1979, Cum. Supp. 1988).

Connally v. General Construction Company, 269 U.S. 385 (1926).

Conte, J. R. (1992). Has this child been sexually abused? Dilemmas for the mental health professional who seeks the answer. *Criminal Justice and Behavior, 19,* 54–73.

Conte, J., Sorenson, E., Fogarty, L., & Rosa, J. D. (1991). Evaluating children's reports of sexual abuse: Results from a survey of professionals. *American Journal of Orthopsychiatry, 61,* 428–437.

Cook, S. (1991, June). *Role conflict in child protection work: Authority of helper.* Paper presented at the Third Biennial Conference on Community Research and Action, Tempe, AZ.

Corson, J., & Davidson, H. A. (1987). Emotional abuse and the law. In M. R. Brassard, R. Germain, & S. N. Hart (Eds.), *Psychological maltreatment of children and youth* (pp. 185–202). Elmsford, NY: Pergamon Press.

Crime Prevention Center. (1988). *Child abuse handbook.* (Available from the Office of the Attorney General, P.O. Box 944255, Sacramento, CA 94244–2550.)

Crouch, J. L., & Milner, J. S. (1993). Effects of child neglect on children. *Criminal Justice and Behavior, 20,* 49–65.

Curran, W. (1977). Failure to diagnose battered child syndrome. *New England Journal of Medicine, 296,* 795–796.

Daro, D., & McCurdy, K. (1992). *Current trends in child abuse reporting and fatalities: The results of the 1991 annual fifty state survey.* (Available from the National

Committee for the Prevention of Child Abuse, 332 S. Michigan Ave., Suite 1600, Chicago, IL 60604.)

Davidson, H. (1988). Failure to report child abuse: Legal penalties and emerging issues. In A. Maney & S. Wells (Eds.), *Professional responsibilities in protecting children* (pp. 93–102). New York: Praeger.

Dawes, R. (1989). Experience and validity of clinical judgement: The illusory correlation. *Behavioral Sciences and the Law, 7,* 457–467.

Denton, L. (1987a, June). Child abuse reporting laws: Are they a barrier to helping troubled families? *APA Monitor,* p. 1.

Denton, L. (1987b, October). Michigan child report law ruled unconstitutional. *APA Monitor,* p. 23.

DePanfilis, D., Holder, W., Corey, M., & Oelson, E. (1986). *Child at risk field training manual.* Charlotte, NC: ACTION for Child Protection.

Dillman, D. (1978). *Mail and telephone surveys: The total design method.* New York: Wiley.

Dubowitz, H., Black, M., Starr, R., & Zuravin, S. (1993). A conceptual definition of child neglect. *Criminal Justice and Behavior, 20,* 8–26.

Eastman, A. M., & Moran, T. J. (1991). Multiple perspectives: Factors related to differential diagnosis of sexual abuse and divorce trauma in children under six. *Child and Youth Services, 15,* 159–175.

Ebert, B. W. (1992). Mandatory child abuse reporting in California. *Forensic Reports, 5,* 335–350.

Eckenrode, J., Munsch, J., Powers, J., & Doris, J. (1988). The nature and substantiation of official sexual abuse reports. *Child Abuse and Neglect, 12,* 311–319.

Eckenrode, J., Powers, J., Doris, J., Munsch, J., & Bolger, N. (1988). Substantiation of child abuse and neglect reports. *Journal of Consulting and Clinical Psychology, 56,* 9–16.

Ellerstein, N., & Canavan, J. (1980). Sexual abuse of boys. *American Journal of Diseases of Children, 134,* 255–257.

Engfer, A., & Schneewind, K. A. (1982). Causes and consequences of harsh parental punishment: An empirical investigation in a representative sample of 570 German families. *Child Abuse and Neglect, 6,* 129–139.

Faller, K. C. (1985). Unanticipated problems in the United States child protection system. *Child Abuse and Neglect, 9,* 63–69.

Faller, K. C. (1990). *Understanding child sexual maltreatment.* Newbury Park, CA: Sage.

Finkelhor, D. (1984). *Child sexual abuse: New theory and research.* New York: Free Press.

Finkelhor, D. (1985). Sexual abuse and physical abuse: Some critical differences. In E. H. Newberger & R. Bourne (Eds.), *Unhappy families* (pp. 21–30). Littleton, MA: PSG.

Finkelhor, D. (1986). *A sourcebook on child sexual abuse.* Newbury, CA: Sage.

Finkelhor, D. (1987). The sexual abuse of children: Current research reviewed. *Psychiatric Annals: The Journals of Continuing Psychiatric Education, 17*, 233–237, 241.

Finkelhor, D. (1990). Is child abuse over-reported?: The data rebut arguments against less intervention. *Public Welfare, 48*(1), 23–29.

Finkelhor, D., & Zellman, G. (1991). Flexible reporting options for skilled child abuse professionals. *Child Abuse and Neglect, 15*, 335–341.

Finlayson, L., & Koocher, G. (1991). Professional judgment in child abuse reporting in sexual abuse cases. *Professional Psychology: Research and Practice, 22*, 464–472.

Fischhoff, B. (1992). Giving advice: Decision theory perspectives on sexual assault. *American Psychologist, 47*, 577–588.

Friedrich, W. N. (1993). Sexual victimization and sexual behavior in children: A review of recent literature. *Child Abuse and Neglect, 17*, 59–66.

Friedrich, W. N., Grambsch, P., Broughton, D., Kuiper, J., & Beilke, R. L. (1991). Normative sexual behavior in children. *Pediatrics, 88*, 456–464.

Friedrich, W. N., Grambsch, P., Damon, L., Hewitt, S., Koverola, C., Lang, R. A., Wolfe, V., & Broughton, D. (1992). Child sexual behavior inventory: Normative and clinical comparisons. *Psychological Assessment, 4*, 303–311.

Fryer, G. E., Bross, D., Krugman, R., Denson, D., & Baird, D. (1990). Good news for CPS workers: An Iowa survey shows parents value services. *Public Welfare, 48*(1), 38–41.

Furby, L., Weinrott, M., & Blackshaw, L. (1989). Sex offender recidivism: A review. *Psychological Bulletin, 105*, 3–30.

Garb, H. N. (1989). Clinical judgment, clinical training, and professional experience. *Psychological Bulletin, 105*, 387–396.

Garbarino, J. (1987). What can the school do on behalf of the psychologically maltreated child and the community? *School Psychology Review, 16*, 181–187.

Garbarino, J., Guttman, E., & Seeley, J. (1986). *The psychologically battered child.* San Francisco: Jossey-Bass.

Gelardo, M. S., & Sanford, E. (1987). Child abuse and neglect: A review of the literature. *School Psychology Review, 16*, 137–155.

Gelinas, D. (1983). The persisting negative effects of incest. *Psychiatry, 46*, 312–332.

Giovannoni, J. (1989a). Definitional issues in child maltreatment. In D. Cicchetti & V. Carlson (Eds.), *Child maltreatment* (pp. 3–37). Cambridge, England: Cambridge University Press.

Giovannoni, J. (1989b). Substantiated and unsubstantiated reports of child maltreatment. *Children and Youth Services Review, 11*, 299–318.

Goldston, D. B., Turnquist, D. C., & Knutson, J. F. (1989). Presenting problems of sexually abused girls receiving psychiatric services. *Journal of Abnormal Psychology, 98*, 314–317.

Gomes-Schwartz, B., Horowitz, J., & Cardarelli, A. (1990). *Child sexual abuse: The initial effects.* Newbury Park, CA: Sage

Goodwin, J., Sahd, D., & Rada, R. T. (1982). False accusations and false denials of incest: Clinical myths and clinical realities. In J. Goodwin (Ed.), *Sexual abuse: Incest victims and their families* (pp. 17–26). Boston: John Wright.

Gray, A. (1987, August). North Carolina experience. In L. Pantano (Chair), *Duty to warn, protect, and report: Criminal and civil implications*. Symposium conducted at the 95th Annual Convention of the American Psychological Association, New York.

Gray, E., & Cosgrove, J. (1985). Ethnocentric perception of child-rearing practices in protective services. *Child Abuse and Neglect, 9,* 389–396.

Green, A. H. (1983). Child abuse: Dimension of psychological trauma in abused children. *Journal of the Academy of Child Psychiatry, 22,* 231–237.

Green, S. L., & Hansen, J. C. (1989). Ethical dilemmas faced by family therapists. *Journal of Marital and Family Therapy, 15,* 149–158.

Haas, L. J., Malouf, J. L., & Mayerson, N. H. (1986). Ethical dilemmas in psychological practice: Results of a national survey. *Professional Psychology: Research and Practice, 17,* 316–321.

Haas, L. J., Malouf, J. L., & Mayerson, N. H. (1988). Personal and professional characteristics as factors in psychologists' ethical decision making. *Professional Psychology: Research and Practice, 19,* 35–42.

Handelsman, M. M. (1989). Ethics training at mental health centers. *Community Mental Health Journal, 25,* 42–50.

Harper, G., & Irvin, E. (1985). Alliance formation with parents: Limit setting and the effect of mandated reporting. *American Journal of Orthopsychiatry, 55,* 550–560.

Haughton, P. B. (1977). Child abuse: Early diagnosis and management. In A. Rodriguez (Ed.), *Handbook on child abuse and neglect* (pp. 14–24). Flushing, NY: Medical Examination.

Hedberg, A. (1991, August). *Child abuse reporting—A personal and professional trauma and trial.* Discussion session, 99th Annual Convention of the American Psychological Association, San Francisco.

Heiman, M. L. (1992). Annotation: Putting the puzzle together: Validating allegations of child sexual abuse. *Journal of Child Psychology and Psychiatry, 33,* 311–329.

Helfer, R. E. (1975). Why most physicians don't get involved in child abuse cases and what to do about it. *Children Today, 4,* 28–32.

Herbert, C. P. (1987). Expert medical assessment in determining probability of alleged child sexual abuse. *Child Abuse and Neglect, 11,* 213–221.

Herman, J. (1981). *Father–daughter incest.* Cambridge, MA: Harvard University Press.

Herrenkohl, E. C., & Herrenkohl, R. C. (1979). A comparison of abused children and their nonabused siblings. *Journal of the American Academy of Child Psychiatry, 18,* 260–269.

Herzberger, S. D. (1988). Cultural obstacles of abuse by professionals. In A. Maney

& S. Wells (Eds.), *Professional responsibilities in protecting children: A public health approach to child sexual abuse* (pp. 33–53). New York: Praeger.

Heymann, G. (1988). Mandated child abuse reporting and the confidentiality privilege. In L. Everstine & D. Everstine (Eds.), *Psychotherapy and the law* (pp. 145–155). New York: Grune & Stratton.

Hoffman-Plotkin, D., & Twentyman, C. T. (1984). A multimodal assessment of behavioral and cognitive deficits in abused and neglected preschoolers. *Child Development, 55*, 794–802.

Holder, W., & Corey, M. (1986). *Child protective services risk management: A decision making handbook.* Charlotte, NC: ACTION for Child Protection.

Howe, A. C., Bonner, B., Parker, M., & Sausen, K. (1992, August). *Graduate training in child maltreatment in APA-approved psychology programs.* Paper presented at the 100th Annual Convention of the American Psychological Association, Washington, DC.

Hutchison, E. D. (1993). Mandatory reporting laws: Child protective case finding gone awry? *Social Work, 38*, 56–63.

Illinois Department of Children and Family Services. (1992). *Service delivery: Subchapter a—Procedures 300—Reports of child abuse and neglect.* (Available from Illinois Department of Children and Family Services, Station 75, State Administrative Offices, 406 East Monroe Street, Springfield, IL 62701.)

In re Gray, 85 Crs. 33130 (Durham County Superior Court, NC, 1985).

In re Hedberg, No. M043157-7 (Municipal Court, Consolidated Fresno Judicial Court, Calif. Nov. 1, 1990).

Iowa Department of Human Services. (1991). *Recognizing and reporting child abuse and neglect.* Des Moines: Author.

Jackson, H., & Nuttall, R. (1993). Clinician responses to sexual abuse allegations. *Child Abuse and Neglect, 17*, 127–143.

James, J., Womack, W., & Strauss, F. (1978). Physician reporting of sexual abuse of children. *Journal of the American Medical Association, 240*, 1145–1146.

Jones, D. P. H., & McGraw, J. M. (1987). Reliable and fictitious accounts of sexual abuse to children. *Journal of Interpersonal Violence, 2*, 27–45.

Jones, J., & Welch, B. (1989). Mandatory reporting of child abuse: Problems and proposals for solutions. In L. Walker, J. Alpert, E. Harris, & G. Koocher (Eds.), *Report to the APA Board of Directors from the Ad Hoc Committee on Child Abuse Policy* (pp. 44–46). Washington, DC: American Psychological Association.

Judge Baker Children's Center. (1990). *Privacy and confidentiality in mental health services.* Boston: Author.

Kalichman, S. C. (1990). Reporting laws, confidentiality, and clinical judgment: Reply to Ansell and Ross. *American Psychologist, 45*, 1273.

Kalichman, S. C. (1991). Laws on reporting sexual abuse of children. *American Journal of Psychiatry, 148*, 1618–1619.

Kalichman, S. C., & Brosig, C. L. (1992). The effects of child abuse reporting laws on psychologists' reporting behavior: A comparison of two state statutes. *American Journal of Orthopsychiatry, 62,* 284–296.

Kalichman, S. C., & Brosig, C. L. (1993). Practicing psychologists' interpretations of and compliance with child abuse reporting laws. *Law and Human Behavior, 17,* 83–93.

Kalichman, S. C., & Craig, M. E. (1991). Professional psychologists' decisions to report suspected child abuse: Clinician and situation influences. *Professional Psychology: Research and Practice, 22,* 84–89.

Kalichman, S. C., Craig, M. E., & Follingstad, D. (1988). Mental health professionals and suspected cases of child abuse: An investigation of factors influencing reporting. *Community Mental Health Journal, 24,* 43–51.

Kalichman, S. C., Craig, M. E., & Follingstad, D. (1989). Factors influencing the reporting of father–child sexual abuse: Study of licensed practicing psychologists. *Professional Psychology: Research and Practice, 20,* 84–89.

Kalichman, S. C., Craig, M. E., & Follingstad, D. (1990). Professionals' adherence to mandatory child abuse reporting laws: Effects of responsibility attribution, confidence ratings, and situational factors. *Child Abuse and Neglect, 14,* 69–77.

Kalichman, S. C., Craig, M. E., & Follingstad, D. (1992). Mental health professionals' treatment of child abuse: Why professionals may not report. In E. Viano (Ed.), *Critical issues in victimology* (pp. 130–139). New York: Springer.

Keith-Spiegel, P., & Koocher, G. P. (1985). *Ethics in psychology: Professional standards and cases.* New York: Random House.

Kelly, R. J. (1987). Limited confidentiality and the pedophile. *Hospital and Community Psychiatry, 38,* 1046–1048.

Kempe, C., Silverman, F., Steele, B., Droegemueller, W., & Silver, H. (1962). The battered-child syndrome. *Journal of the American Medical Association, 181,* 17–24.

Kendall-Tackett, K. A., Williams, L. M., & Finkelhor, D. (1993). Impact of sexual abuse on children: A review and synthesis of recent empirical studies. *Psychological Bulletin, 113,* 164–180.

Kentucky Department of Social Services. (1989). *Child abuse, neglect, and dependency: A guide for people who work with children in Kentucky.* (Available from the Department of Social Services, Cabinet for Human Resources, 275 E. Main Street 6W, Frankfort, KY 40621.)

Kerlinger, F. N. (1973). *Foundations of behavioral research.* New York: Holt, Reinhart, & Winston.

Kim, D. S. (1986). How physicians respond to child maltreatment cases. *Health and Social Work, 11,* 95–106.

Kinard, E. M. (1985). Ethical issues in research with abused children. *Child Abuse and Neglect, 9,* 301–311.

Kitchener, K. S. (1988). Dual-role relationships: What makes them so problematic. *Journal of Counseling and Development, 67,* 217–221.

Knapp, S. (1983). Counselor liability for failing to report child abuse. *Elementary School Guidance Counseling, 17,* 177–179.

Koocher, G. P. (1988). A thumbnail guide to "duty to warn" cases. *The Clinical Psychologist, 41,* 22–25.

Koocher, G. P., & Keith-Spiegel, P. (1990). *Children, ethics, and the law: Professional issues and cases.* Lincoln: University of Nebraska Press.

Koziol, R., & Petretic-Jackson, P. (1989). The role of psychologists in the evaluation of child sexual abuse: An examination of training, experiences, attitudes, behaviors, and intervention strategies. In L. Walker, J. Alpert, E. Harris, & G. Koocher (Eds.), *Report to the APA Board of Directors from the Ad Hoc Committee on Child Abuse Policy* (pp. 49–52). Washington, DC: American Psychological Association.

Krugman, R. D. (1990). Physical indicators of child sexual abuse. In A. Tasman & S. Goldfinger (Eds.), *Review of psychiatry,* (Vol. 10, pp. 336–343). Washington, DC: American Psychiatric Press.

Lamond, D. (1989). The impact of mandatory reporting legislation on reporting behavior. *Child Abuse and Neglect, 13,* 471–480.

Landeros v. Flood, 551 Calif. P.2d 389 (1976).

Leong, G. B., Eth, S., & Silva, J. A. (1992). The psychotherapist as witness for the prosecution: The criminalization of Tarasoff. *American Journal of Psychiatry, 149,* 1011–1015.

Levin, P. G. (1983). Teachers' perceptions, attitudes and reporting of child abuse/neglect. *Child Welfare, 62,* 14–20.

Levine, M., Anderson, E., Terretti, L., Sharma, A., Steinberg, K., & Wallach, L. (1991). Effects of reporting maltreatment on the psychotherapeutic relationship. In S. Kalichman (Chair), *Mandatory child abuse reporting: A research and policy update.* Symposium conducted at the 99th Annual Convention of the American Psychological Association, San Francisco.

Levine, M., Anderson, E., Terretti, L., Steinberg, K., Sharma, A., & Wallach, L. (1991). *Mandated reporting and the therapeutic alliance in the context of the child protection system.* (Available from the Baldy Center for Law and Social Policy, State University of New York, 511 O'Brian Hall, Buffalo, NY 14260.)

Levine, M., & Battistoni, L. (1991). The corroboration requirement in child sex abuse cases. *Behavioral Sciences and the Law, 9,* 3–20.

Levine, M., & Doherty, E. (1991). The Fifth Amendment and therapeutic requirements to admit abuse. *Criminal Justice and Behavior, 18,* 98–112.

Levine, M., & Levine, A. (1992). *Helping children: A social history.* New York: Oxford University Press.

Levy, R. J. (1989). Using "scientific" testimony to prove child sexual abuse. *Family Law Quarterly, 23,* 383–409.

Lewis, D. O., Shanok, S. S., Pincus, J. H., & Glaser, G. H. (1979). Violent juvenile delinquents: Psychiatric, neurological, psychological, and abuse factors. *Journal of the American Academy of Child Psychiatry, 18,* 307–319.

MacFarlane, F., Waterman, J., Conerly, S., Damon, L., Durfee, M., & Long, S. (Eds.). (1986). *Sexual abuse of the young child*. New York: Guilford Press.

Mannarino, A. P., & Cohen, J. (1986). A clinical–demographic study of sexually abused children. *Child Abuse and Neglect, 10*, 17–23.

Mantell, D. M. (1988). Clarifying erroneous child sexual abuse allegations. *American Journal of Orthopsychiatry, 58*, 618–621.

Maryland Social Services Administration. (1988). *Child maltreatment in Maryland*. (Available from Office of Child Welfare, 311 West Saratoga Street, Baltimore, MD 21201.)

Mazura, A. C. (1977). Negligence–malpractice-physicians' liability for failure to diagnose and report child abuse. *Wayne Law Review, 23*, 1187–1201.

McCoid, A. H. (1965). The battered child and other assaults upon the family: Part one. *Minnesota Law Review, 50*, 1–58.

Melton, G. B., & Corson, J. (1987). Psychological maltreatment and the schools: Problems of law and professional responsibility. *School Psychology Review, 16*, 188–194.

Melton, G. B., & Davidson, H. A. (1987). Child protection and society: When should the state intervene? *American Psychologist, 42*, 172–175.

Melton, G. B., & Limber, S. (1989). Psychologists' involvement in cases of child maltreatment. *American Psychologist, 44*, 1225–1233.

Meriwether, M. H. (1986). Child abuse reporting laws: Time for a change. *Family Law Quarterly, 20*, 141–171.

Michigan Department of Social Services. (1989). *Child protection law*. Lansing: Author.

Miller, R. D., & Weinstock, R. (1987). Conflict of interest between therapist–patient confidentiality and the duty to report sexual abuse of children. *Behavioral Sciences and the Law, 5*, 161–174.

Milner, J. S. (1986). *The Child Abuse Potential Inventory: Manual* (2nd ed.). Webster, NC: Psytec.

Milner, J. S. (1989). Additional cross-validation of the Child Abuse Potential Inventory. *Psychological Assessment: A Journal of Consulting and Clinical Psychology, 1*, 219–233.

Milner, J. S. (1990). *An interpretive manual for the Child Abuse Potential Inventory*. Webster, NC: Psytec.

Milner, J. S. (1991). Medical conditions and Child Abuse Potential Inventory specificity. *Psychological Assessment: A Journal of Consulting and Clinical Psychology, 3*, 208–212.

Milner, J. S., Gold, R. G., & Wimberley, R. C. (1986). Prediction and explanation of child abuse: Cross-validation of the Child Abuse Potential Inventory. *Journal of Consulting and Clinical Psychology, 54*, 865–866.

Muehleman, T., & Kimmons, C. (1981). Psychologists' views on child abuse reporting, confidentiality, life and the law: An exploratory study. *Professional Psychology, 12*, 631–638.

Muehleman, T., Pickens, B., & Robinson, F. (1985). Informing clients about the limits to confidentiality, risks, and their rights: Is self-disclosure inhibited? *Professional Psychology: Research and Practice, 16,* 385–397.

Myers, J. (1979). *Fundamentals of experimental design* (3rd ed.). Boston: Allyn & Bacon.

National Association of Social Workers. (1980). *Code of ethics.* Silver Spring, MD: Author.

National Center on Child Abuse and Neglect. (1979). *Child abuse and neglect: State reporting laws.* (Available from the Clearinghouse on Child Abuse and Neglect Information, P.O. Box 1182, Washington, DC 20013.)

National Center on Child Abuse and Neglect. (1989). *State statutes related to child abuse and neglect: 1988.* (Available from the Clearinghouse on Child Abuse and Neglect Information, P.O. Box 1182, Washington, DC 20013.)

Newberger, E. H. (1983). The helping hand strikes again: Unintended consequences of child abuse reporting. *Journal of Clinical Child Psychology, 12,* 307–311.

Newman, R. (1987). *The psychotherapist's duty to report child abuse and the legislature's duty to strike a better balance.* Unpublished manuscript.

Nightingale, N. N., & Walker, E. F. (1986). Identification and reporting of child maltreatment by Head Start personnel: Attitudes and experiences. *Child Abuse and Neglect, 10,* 191–199.

Oates, R. K., Forrest, D., & Peacock, A. (1985). Self-esteem and abused children. *Child Abuse and Neglect, 9,* 159–163.

O'Connor, K. (1989, July). Professional conflicts and issues in child abuse reporting and treatment. *The California Psychologist,* pp. 22–23.

Otto, R., & Melton, G. (1990). Trends in legislation and case law on child abuse and neglect. In R. Ammerman & M. Hersen (Eds.), *Children at risk: An evaluation of factors contributing to child abuse and neglect* (pp. 55–83). New York: Plenum Press.

Paradise, J. E., Rostain, A. L., & Nathanson, M. (1988). Substantiation of sexual abuse charges when parents dispute custody or visitation. *Pediatrics, 81,* 835–840.

Paulsen, M. G. (1967). Child abuse reporting laws: The shape of the legislation. *Columbia Law Review, 67,* 1–49.

Pecora, P. J. (1991). Investigating allegations of child maltreatment: The strengths and limitations of current risk assessment systems. *Child and Youth Services, 15,* 73–92.

Pennsylvania Department of Public Welfare. (1992). *Child abuse and neglect report.* Harrisburg: Author.

People v. Cavaiani, 172 Mich. App. 706, 432 N.W.2d. 409 (1988).

People v. Cavaiani, 432 Mich. 835, 434 N.W.2d. 411 (1989).

Pierce, R. L., & Pierce, L. H. (1985). Analysis of sexual abuse hotline reports. *Child Abuse and Neglect, 9,* 37–45.

Pope, K. S., & Bajt, T. (1988). When laws and values conflict: A dilemma for psychologists. *American Psychologist, 43,* 828–829.

Pope, K. S., & Feldman-Summers, S. (1992). National survey of psychologists' sexual and physical abuse history and their evaluation of training and competence in these areas. *Professional Psychology: Research and Practice, 23,* 353–361.

Pope, K. S., Tabachnick, B. G., & Keith-Spiegel, P. (1987). The beliefs and behaviors of psychologists as therapists. *American Psychologist, 42,* 993–1006.

Pope, K., & Vasquez, M. (1991). *Ethics in psychotherapy and counseling.* San Francisco: Jossey-Bass.

Pope, K. S., & Vetter, V. (1992). Ethical dilemmas encountered by members of the American Psychological Association: A national survey. *American Psychologist, 47,* 397–411.

Priest, R., & Wilcoxon, S. (1988). Confidentiality and the child sexual offender: Unique challenges and dilemmas. *Family Therapy, XV,* 107–113.

Pruitt, J. A., & Kappius, R. E. (1992). Routine inquiry into sexual victimization: A survey of therapists' practices. *Professional Psychology: Research and Practice, 23,* 474–479.

Racusin, R. J., & Felsman, J. K. (1986). Reporting child abuse: The ethical obligation to inform parents. *Journal of the American Academy of Child Psychiatry, 25,* 485–489.

Reinhart, M. A. (1987). Sexually abused boys. *Child Abuse and Neglect, 11,* 229–235.

Reppucci, N. D., & Haugaard, J. J. (1989). Prevention of child sexual abuse: Myth or reality. *American Psychologist, 44,* 1266–1275.

Rindfleisch, N., & Bean, G. (1988). Willingness to report abuse and neglect in residential facilities. *Child Abuse and Neglect, 12,* 509–520.

Roane, T. H. (1992). Male victims of sexual abuse: A case review within a child protective team. *Child Welfare, LXXI*(3), 231–239.

Rosenthal, J. A. (1988). Patterns of reported child abuse and neglect. *Child Abuse and Neglect, 12,* 263–271.

Russell, S. D., & Clifford, R. M. (1987). Child abuse and neglect in North Carolina day care programs. *Child Welfare, LXVI,* 149–163.

Rycraft, J. R. (1990). Redefining abuse and neglect: A narrower focus could affect children at risk. *Public Welfare, 49*(1), 14–21.

Saulsbury, F., & Campbell, R. (1985). Evaluation of child abuse reporting by physicians. *American Journal of Diseases of Children, 139,* 393–395.

Schwartz, A. (1991, March). Child abuse—Despite the law it's not reported. *Chicago Bar Association Record,* pp. 24–28.

Schwartz, A. (1992, April). *Child abuse in the schools.* Paper presented at the Loyola Conference on Child Abuse: Clinical, ethical, social, and legal dimensions, Chicago, IL.

Sebold, J. (1987). Indicators of child sexual abuse in males. *Social Casework: The Journal of Contemporary Social Work, XX*, 75–80.

Sgroi, S. (1982). *Handbook of clinical intervention in child sexual abuse.* Lexington, MA: Lexington Books.

Sgroi, S., Porter, F., & Blick, L. (1982). Validation of child sexual abuse. In S. Sgroi (Ed.), *Handbook of clinical intervention in child sexual abuse* (pp. 39–79). Lexington, MA: Lexington Books.

Sink, F. (1988). A hierarchical model for evaluation of child sexual abuse. *American Journal of Orthopsychiatry, 58*, 129–135.

Small, M. A. (1992). *Policy review of child abuse and neglect reporting statutes.* Paper presented at the 100th Annual Convention of the American Psychological Association, Washington, DC.

Smith S., & Meyer, R. (1984). Child abuse reporting laws and psychotherapy: A time for reconsideration. *International Journal of Law and Psychiatry, 7*, 351–366.

Smith, T. S., McGuire, J., Abbott, D., & Blau, B. (1991). Clinical ethical decision making: An investigation of the rationales used to justify doing less than one believes one should. *Professional Psychology: Research and Practice, 22*, 235–239.

Southard, M. J., & Gross, B. H. (1982). Making clinical decisions after Tarasoff. In B. Gross & L. Weinberger (Eds.), *New directions for mental health services: The mental health professional and the legal system* (pp. 93–101). San Francisco: Jossey-Bass.

Stadler, H. A. (1989). Balancing ethical responsibilities: Reporting child abuse and neglect. *The Counseling Psychologist, 17*, 102–110.

Straus, M., & Gelles, R. J. (1990). *Physical violence in American families: Risk factors and adaptations to violence.* New Brunswick, NJ: Transaction.

Swets, J. A. (1992). The science of choosing the right decision threshold in high-stakes diagnostics. *American Psychologist, 47*, 522–532.

Swoboda, J. S., Elwork, A., Sales, B. D., & Levine, D. (1978). Knowledge of and compliance with privileged communication and child abuse reporting laws. *Professional Psychology, 9*, 448–457.

Tarasoff v. Board of Regents of the University of California, 551 P.2d 334 (Calif. S. Ct. 1976).

Taylor, L., & Adelman, H. (1989). Reframing the confidentiality dilemma to work in children's best interests. *Professional Psychology: Research and Practice, 20*, 79–83.

Turner, A. (1982). What subjects in survey research believe about confidentiality. In J. E. Sieber (Ed.), *The ethics of social research: Surveys and experiments* (pp. 151–165). New York: Springer-Verlag.

U.S. Advisory Board on Child Abuse and Neglect. (1990). *Child abuse and neglect: Critical first steps in response to a national emergency.* (Available from the author, Switzer Building, Room 2070C, 200 Independence Avenue, SW, Washington, DC 20201.)

U.S. Department of Health and Human Services. (1988). *Study findings: Study of national incidence and prevalence of child abuse and neglect: 1988.* Bethesda, MD: Westat.

Van Eenwyk, J. R. (1990). When laws and values conflict: Comment on Pope and Bajt. *American Psychologist, 45,* 399–400.

Wakefield, H., & Underwager, R. (1988). *Accusations of child sexual abuse.* Springfield, IL: Charles C Thomas.

Wakefield, H., & Underwager, R. (1991). Sexual abuse allegations in divorce and custody disputes. *Behavioral Sciences and the Law, 9,* 451–468.

Wald, M. (1975). State intervention on behalf of "neglected" children: A search for realistic standards. *Stanford Law Review, 27,* 985–1040.

Walker, C. E., Bonner, B., & Kaufman, K. (1988). *The physically and sexually abused child: Evaluation and treatment.* Elmsford, NY: Pergamon Press.

Walker, L. E. (1988). *Handbook on sexual abuse of children.* New York: Springer.

Walker, L. E., Alpert, J., Harris, E., & Koocher, G. (1989). *Report to the APA Board of Directors from the Ad Hoc Committee on Child Abuse Policy.* Washington, DC: American Psychological Association.

Watkins, S. A. (1989). Confidentiality: An ethical and legal conundrum for family therapists. *The American Journal of Family Therapy, 17,* 291–302.

Watson, H., & Levine, M. (1989). Psychotherapy and mandated reporting of child abuse. *American Journal of Orthopsychiatry, 59,* 246–256.

Weinstock, R., & Weinstock, D. (1989). Clinical flexibility and confidentiality: Effects of reporting laws. *Psychiatric Quarterly, 60,* 195–214.

Weisberg, R., & Wald, M. (1984). Confidentiality laws and state efforts to protect abused or neglected children: The need for statutory reform. *Family Law Quarterly, 18,* 143–212.

Weissman, H. N. (1991). Forensic psychological examination of the child witness in cases of alleged sexual abuse. *American Journal of Orthopsychiatry, 61,* 48–58.

Wells, S. (1988). On the decision to report suspected abuse or neglect. In A. Maney & S. Wells (Eds.), *Professional responsibilities in protecting children* (pp. 191–202). New York: Praeger.

Wells, S., Downing, J., & Fluke, J. (1991). Responding to reports of child abuse and neglect. *Child and Youth Services, 15,* 63–72.

Wells, S., Stein, T., Fluke, J., & Downing, J. (1989). Screening in child protective services. *Social Work, 34,* 45–48.

White, S., Strom, G. A., Santilli, G. A., & Halpin, B. M. (1986). Interviewing young sexual abuse victims with anatomically correct dolls. *Child Abuse and Neglect, 10,* 519–529.

Wiehe, V. R. (1992). *Working with child abuse and neglect.* Itasca, IL: F. E. Peacock.

Wilcoxon, S. A. (1991). Clarifying expectations in therapy relationships: Suggestions for written guidelines. *Journal of Independent Social Work, 5,* 65–71.

Wilkins, M. A., McGuire, J., Abbott, D., & Blau, B. (1990). Willingness to apply understood ethical principles. *Journal of Clinical Psychology, 46,* 539–547.

Williams, H. S., Osborne, Y., & Rappaport, N. (1987). Child abuse reporting law: Professionals' knowledge and compliance. *The Southern Psychologist, 3*, 20–24.

Willis, C. L., & Wells, R. H. (1988). The police and child abuse: An analysis of police decisions to report illegal behavior. *Criminology, 26*, 695–715.

Wilson, C. A. & Gettinger, M. (1989). Determinants of child-abuse reporting among Wisconsin school psychologists. *Professional School Psychology, 4*, 91–102.

Wilson, J., Thomas, D., & Schuette, L. (1983). Survey of counselors on identifying and reporting cases of child abuse. *School Counselor, 30*, 299–305.

Wisconsin Department of Health and Social Services. (1985). *Investigation handbook for child protective service workers*. Madison, WI: Author.

Wurtele, S. K., & Miller-Perrin, C. L. (1992). *Preventing child sexual abuse: Sharing the responsibility*. Lincoln: University of Nebraska Press.

Wyatt, G. E., & Powell, G. J. (Eds.). (1988). *Lasting effects of child sexual abuse*. Newbury Park, CA: Sage.

Zellman, G. (1990). Report decision-making patterns among mandated child abuse reporters. *Child Abuse and Neglect, 14*, 325–336.

Zellman, G. (1992). The impact of case characteristics on child abuse reporting decisions. *Child Abuse and Neglect, 16*, 57–74.

Zellman, G., & Antler, S. (1990). Mandated reporters and CPS: A study in frustration. *Public Welfare, 48*, 30–37.

Zielinski, S. (1992, April). *Clinical perspectives in child abuse*. Paper presented at the Loyola Conference on Child Abuse: Clinical, ethical, social, and legal dimensions, Chicago, IL.

APPENDIX A

Glossary of Child Abuse
and Neglect Terminology

Many terms that are commonly used in reference to child maltreatment are likely to be unfamiliar to nonmedical and nonlegal professionals. The following glossary presents some of the terminology frequently found in medical and legal reports as well as physical descriptions of child abuse and neglect.

ABRASION A wound in which an area of the body surface is scraped of skin and/or mucous membrane.

ACUTE PANCREATITIS A severe inflammation of the pancreas. When present in children its most common cause is trauma.

ADJUDICATORY HEARING Held by juvenile and family courts to determine the occurrence of abuse or neglect and appropriate state interventions. States vary in terms, definitions, and scope of the court functions.

ARACHNOID A delicate membrane of the spinal cord and brain that may be damaged due to trauma.

ASPHYXIATION Breathing impaired to the extent of loss of consciousness with potential for brain damage or death. Cause can be varied, including strangulation, suffocation, smothering, and smoke inhalation.

ATROPHY Wasting of body tissues or organs.

AVITAMINOSIS (HYPOVITAMINOSIS) A condition that results from a deficiency of one or more essential vitamins.

BASILAR SKULL FRACTURE A fracture to the base of the brain case, near the nose and ears. Could involve loss of spinal fluid and risk of infection.

BONE SCAN A nuclear study to diagnose early or minimal fractures.

BONE SURVEY A total body X-ray to determine fractures in the absence of obvious symptoms. Old fractures can be detected with this procedure.

BURNS Wounds resulting from the application of excessive heat. Degree classifications: 1st degree, scorching or painful redness of skin; 2nd degree, formation of blisters; and 3rd degree, destruction of outer layers of skin.

CALCIFICATION Formation of bone. Amounts of calcium deposits can be detected by X-ray and used to identify healed fractures.

CALLUS New meshwork of bone formed during the healing process of a fracture.

CALVARIUM Dome-like portion of the skull.

CELLULITIS Inflammation of the loose tissue underneath the skin.

CEREBRAL EDEMA (CONTUSION OF THE BRAIN) Brain swelling that may be associated with bleeding into the tissues of the brain.

CHILD PROTECTIVE SERVICES The social service agency or division of a larger social agency in most states charged with receiving and investigating reports, and providing services for victims and victims' families in cases of child abuse and neglect.

COLPOSCOPY A binocular magnifying device, traditionally used in gynecology, often used in the physical examination of sexual abuse cases.

CONGENITAL Physical condition present at birth, regardless of etiological cause.

CONTUSION Wound producing injury to soft tissue without a break in the skin, causing bleeding into surrounding tissue.

COURT APPOINTED SPECIAL ADVOCATE Usually a volunteer who ensures that the needs and interests of a child in judicial process are being met.

CRANIUM The skull.

DIAPHYSIS The shaft of a long bone.

DISLOCATION The displacement of bone, usually at the joint. May or may not be accompanied by fractures.

DISPOSITION HEARING Held by juvenile or family court to determine the placement and services for cases that have proceeded through adjudication.

DRUG DEPENDANT NEWBORN An infant under 28 days of age exhibiting abnormal growth and/or neurological signs coupled with strong evidence that the mother was substance abusive during pregnancy.

DURA MATER A tough fibrous membrane that covers the brain and spinal cord.

ECCHYMOSIS The passage of blood from ruptured blood vessels into subcutaneous tissue, marked by purple discoloration of the skin.

EDEMA Swelling caused by an excessive amount of fluid in body tissue; follows a bump or bruise.

EPIDURAL HEMATOMA Blood that is above the dura (cover of the brain or spinal cord).

EPIPHYSIS Growth center near the end of a long bone, usually wider than the shaft and separated from the shaft by a growth plate.

EXTRAVASATED BLOOD Discharge or escape of blood into tissue.

FAILURE TO THRIVE SYNDROME (FTT) The child's, height, weight, and motor development are significantly below the average growth rate expected for their chronological age. FTT may result from severe emotional and physical neglect of a child, however, about 30% of cases involve an organic condition. When caused by parental neglect, the symptoms will often reverse with proper nurturing.

FAMILY PRESERVATION–REUNIFICATION The belief, established in law and policy, that children and families should be maintained together if the safety of children can be ensured.

FONTANEL The soft areas, or spots, on an infant's skull where bones have not yet grown together.

FRACTURE A broken bone. There are numerous types of breaks, some of which are indicative of abuse.

BUCKET HANDLE TEARS Total fractures of the wider part of a long bone, between the end and the shaft, such that it is loose and floating.

CHIP FRACTURE A small piece of bone is flaked from the major part of the bone.

COMMINUTED FRACTURE Bone crushed into many pieces.

COMPOUND FRACTURE Fragments of bone cut through soft tissue, causing a wound.

CORNER FRACTURE The corner of the wider part of a long bone is torn off during wrenching or twisting injuries.

SIMPLE FRACTURE Bone breaks without wounding the surrounding tissue.

SPIRAL FRACTURE Twisting causes the fracture to encircle the bone like a spiral.

TORUS FRACTURE A folding, bulging, or buckling fracture.

GOOD FAITH Standard that applies to determinations for reporting. In general, good faith applies if any reasonable person, given the same information, would draw a conclusion that a child may have been abused or neglected.

GUARDIAN AD LITEM An attorney or lay person who serves as a child's representative in juvenile or family court. Considers the best interest of the child in an advocacy manner.

HEMATOMA A swelling caused by a collection of blood in an enclosed space (e.g., under the skin or skull).

HEMORRHAGE The escape of blood from the vessels; bleeding.

HYPHENA Hemorrhage within the front chamber of the eye, often appearing as a bloodshot eye. The cause may be a blow to the head or violent shaking.

IMMUNITY Protects reporters from civil law suits and criminal prosecution resulting from filing a report of suspected child abuse in good faith.

IMPETIGO A contagious and rapidly spreading skin condition that occurs principally in infants and young children. Characterized by red blisters that develop rapidly into pustules, commonly around the mouth and nose. May be an indicator of neglect or inadequate living conditions.

JUVENILE AND FAMILY COURTS Established to resolve conflicts and intervene in the lives of families in a manner that promotes the best interest of the children and the families.

LACERATION A cut or wound of the skin in which the edges are jagged or separated and may require stitches.

MALNUTRITION Failure to receive adequate nourishment. Can result from a lack of food or specific vitamins. Can be a sign of neglect, poverty, or an organic condition.

MARASMUS A wasting away of fat and muscle, associated with inadequate nourishment.

MEDICAL NEGLECT Failure to provide medical care in preventing or treating illness. Can occur as a result of not seeking assistance in cases of emergency or from not following prescribed treatments.

METAPHYSIS Wider part of a long bone between the end and the shaft. It contains the growth zone of the bone.

OCCIPITAL Referring to the back of the head.

OSSIFICATION Formation of bone.

OUT-OF-HOME CARE Child care, foster care, or residential care provided by individuals and institutions to children who are placed outside of their families, usually under the jurisdiction of juvenile or family court.

PETECHIA A small spot on a body surface caused by a discrete hemorrhage.

PETITION Document filed with a court to initiate a civil child protection proceeding. Contains all of the detailed allegations of abuse, but not the facts to support abuse.

PIA MATER A fine vascular membrane that envelopes the brain and spinal cord under the arachnoid membrane and dura mater.

PREMATURE A neonate who is less than 2500 g at birth, unrelated to gestational age.

PREPONDERANCE OF EVIDENCE The burden of proof for civil cases in most states, including child maltreatment proceedings. The standard means that the evidence presented by the attorney for the child protection agency is more credible than the evidence presented by the defendant party.

PROPOSED CONFIRMED Reports in which the preponderance of evidence substantiates abuse and identifies the perpetrator.

PROTECTION ORDER Issued by a judge to control or restrain the behavior of an allegedly abusive adult or any other person who may harm the child or interfere with the disposition.

PURPURA A condition, caused by hemorrhages into tissues, characterized by purplish discolorations running together over any part of the skin or mucus membranes.

RAREFACTION Loss of density, as in a bone that has lost calcium.

RETINAL HEMORRHAGE Bleeding that can be seen on the retina, detected by viewing the eye through an opthamoscope.

REVIEW HEARING Held by juvenile or family court to review dispositions and determine the need to maintain placements. All states require such a reevaluation process for cases, but the time frame for reviews varies. Federal law requires (for federal funding) a review of cases 18 months after disposition and continued reevaluation at regular intervals to determine final resolutions of cases.

RICKETS Condition of disturbed bone development due to Vitamin D deficiency.

SCURVY Condition caused by vitamin C deficiency, characterized by weakness, anemia, and spongy gums, and other symptoms.

SUBARACHNOID BLEEDING Bleeding that occurs between the pia and arachnoid membranes covering the brain and spinal cord.

SUBDURAL HEMATOMA A collection of blood beneath the dura (outermost covering of the brain). The hematoma may result from a blow to the head or from shaking.

TERMINATION OF PARENTAL RIGHTS HEARING Legal proceeding to free a child from parents' legal custody, allowing the adoption by others. The determination made by the court, using a legal standard of clear and convincing evidence, is that the parents will not be able to provide adequate care for the child in the future. This burden of proof is higher than a preponderance of evidence.

TRAUMA An internal or external injury or wound brought about by an outside force; usually used to describe an injury due to violence.

WHIPLASH-SHAKEN INFANT SYNDROME Injury to an infant or child resulting from shaking, often as a misguided form of discipline. Common symptoms include head bleeding and detached retinas. Repeated occurrences can result in developmental disabilities.

APPENDIX B

Directory of State Child Protection Agencies

This listing of state offices of child protective services is provided as a resource for information regarding specific mandatory reporting statutes and includes phone numbers of local reporting agencies. The list is current as of the publication date, but all information is subject to change on a state-by-state basis.

Alabama Division of Family and Children's Services Office of Child Protective Services, 1031 Ann Street, Montgomery, AL 36107 (205)261-1220

Alaska Division of Family and Youth Services PO Box 110630, Juneau, AK 99811-0630 (907)465-3191

Arizona Department of Child Protective Services 4020 North 20th Street, Phoenix, AZ 85016 (602)266-0282 or (602)265-0612

Arkansas Child Protective Services PO Box 1437 Slot 830, Little Rock, AR 72203 (501)682-1001; in state (800)482-5964

California Office for Child Abuse Prevention Department of Social Services, 714–744 P Street, Room 950, Sacramento, CA 95814 (916)445-7546

Colorado Department of Social Services Central Registry for Child Protection 1575 Sherman Street, 2nd Floor, Denver, CO 80203-1714 (303)866-3003

Connecticut Division of Children and Protective Services 170 Sigourney Street, Hartford, CT 06105 (203)566-2387; hotline (203)344-2599 or (800)842-2288

Delaware Division of Child Protective Services 805 River Road, Dover, DE 19901 (302)739-4802; hotline (800)292-9582

District of Columbia Family Services Administration, Child and Family Services Division 609 8th Street, NE, Washington, DC 20002 (202)727-0995

Florida Child Protective Service System 1317 Winewood Boulevard, Tallahassee, FL 32399-0700 (904)487-4332; hotline (800)96-ABUSE

Georgia Division of Family and Children Services 878 Peachtree Street, NW Atlanta, GA 30309 (404)894-5506

Guam Child Protective Services PO Box 2816, Agana, GU 96910 (671)475-2617 or 475-2653

Hawaii Child Welfare and Protective Services 810 Richards Street, Suite 400, Honolulu, HI 96813-4728 (808)586-5690

Idaho Department of Health and Welfare, Field Operations Bureau of Social Services and Child Protection 450 West State, Third Floor, Boise, ID 83720-5450 (208)334-5700

Illinois Department of Children and Family Services 406 East Monroe Street, Springfield, IL 62701 (217)785-4010; out of state (217)785-4020; hotline (800)25-ABUSE

Indiana Division of Child Welfare—Social Services 402 West Washington Street, #W314, Indianapolis, IN 46204 (317)232-4956

Iowa Central Child Abuse Registry Hoover State Office Building, Fifth Floor, Des Moines, IA 50319-0114 (515)281-5581 or (515)281-3240; hotline (800)362-2178

Kansas Child Protection and Family Services Section Smith-Wesson Building, 300 S.W. Oakly Street, Topeka, KS 66606 (913)295-4705; hotline (800)922-5330

Kentucky Child and Youth Services Branch 275 East Main Street, 6W, Frankfort, KY 40621 (502)564-2136; hotline (800)752-6200

Louisiana Division of Children, Youth, and Family Services 333 Laurel Street, Baton Rouge, LA 70802 (504)342-4011

Maine Child Protective Services State House—Station 11, State Street, Augusta, ME 04333 (207)289-2983; hotline (800)452-1999

Maryland Child Protective Services Office of Family and Children's Services, 311 West Saratoga Street, Baltimore, MD 21201 (410)333-0221

Massachusetts Department of Social Services, Protective Services 24 Farnsworth Street, Boston, MA 02210-1211 (617)727-0900; hotline (800)792-5200

Michigan Office of Children and Youth Services, Protective Services Division 235 Grand Avenue, Suite 511, Lansing, MI 48909 (517)373-3572

Minnesota Department of Human Services, Community and Human Services 160 East Kellog Boulevard, St. Paul, MN 55101 (612)298-5655

Mississippi Bureau of Family and Children's Services, Protection Department 939 North President Street, Jackson, MS 39205 (601)354-6644; hotline (800)222-8000

Missouri Department of Social Services, Division of Family Services PO Box 88, Broadway Building, Jefferson City, MO 65103 (314)751-3448; hotline (800)392-3738

Montana Child Protective Services PO Box 8005, Helena, MT 59604 (406)444-5900

Nebraska Human Services 301 Centennial Mall South, PO Box 95026, Lincoln, NE 68509 (402)471-3121; hotline (800)652-1999

Nevada Division of Children and Family Services 410 E. Johnson Street, Carson City, NV 89710 (702)687-4760

New Hampshire Division of Children and Youth Services 6 Hazen Drive, Concord, NH 03301-6522 (603)271-4455; hotline (800)852-3345 ext. 4455

New Jersey Division of Youth and Family Services 50 East State Street—CN717, Trenton, NJ 08625 (609)530-8770; hotline (800)792-8610

New Mexico Department of Health and Human Services 2001 Vivigin Way, Santa Fe, NM 87504 (505)827-7450; hotline (800)432-6217

New York State Central Register of Child Abuse and Maltreatment 40 North Pearl Street, 11th Floor, Albany, NY 12243 (518)474-9516; hotline (800)342-3720, mandated reports (800)635-1522

North Carolina Division of Social Services—Child Protective Services 325 North Salisbury Street, Raleigh, NC 27611 (919)733-2580; hotline (800)662-7030

North Dakota Child Protective Services—Child Abuse and Neglect Program State Capitol, Bismarck, ND 58505 (701)224-4806

Ohio Child Protective Services 65 East State Street, 5th Floor, Columbus, OH 43215 (614)466-9824

Oklahoma Division of Children and Youth Services—Child Abuse/Neglect Section 5905 Classen Boulevard, Oklahoma City, OK 73118 (405)840-4976; hotline (800)522-3511

Oregon Child Protective Services 500 Summer Street, NE, Salem, OR 97310 (503)378-4722

Pennsylvania Office of Children, Youth, and Families PO Box 2675, Harrisburg, PA 17105-2675 (717)787-3984; hotline (800)932-0313

Puerto Rico Services to Families With Children PO Box 11398, Fernandez Juncos Station, Santurez, PR 00910 (809)724-1333

Rhode Island Division of Child Protective Services 610 Mt. Pleasant

Avenue, Building 9, Providence, RI 02908 (401)457-4943; hotline (800)RI-CHILD

South Carolina Department of Social Services PO Box 1520, Columbia, SC 29202-1520 (803)734-6179

South Dakota Department of Social Services 700 Governors Drive, Pierre, SD 57501 (605)773-3227

Tennessee Department of Human Services, Child Protection 1000 2nd Avenue, North, Nashville, TN 37202 (615)244-9706

Texas Protective Services for Families and Children PO Box 149030, Austin, TX 78714-9030 (512)450-3011; hotline (800)252-5400

Utah Child Protective Services 2835 South Main Street, Salt Lake City, UT 84165 (801)468-5400

Vermont Department of Social and Rehabilitative Services 103 S. Main Street, Waterbury, VT 05671 (802)241-2131

Virgin Islands Department of Human Services, Division of Social Services PO Box 550, Charlotte Amalie, St. Thomas, VI 00801 (809)774-9030

Virginia Bureau of Child Protective Services Blair Building, 8007 Discovery Drive, Richmond, VA 23229 (804)662-9084; hotline (800)552-7096

Washington Department of Children and Family Services Box 1366, Olympia, WA 98504 (206)753-0613

West Virginia Division of Social Services, Child Protective Services Office of Social Services, Building 6, Room 850, Charleston, WV 25305 (304)558-7980; hotline (800)352-6513

Wisconsin Bureau of Children, Youth, and Families 1 West Wilson Street, Madison, WI 53707 (608)267-7732

Wyoming Division of Public Assistance and Social Services Hathaway Building, 2300 Capital Avenue, Third Floor, Cheyenne, WY 82002 (307)777-6285

APPENDIX C

Bibliography of Free Booklets
Concerning Child Abuse and Reporting

These titles were collected through several avenues, including requests for information mailed to all state child protection agencies and national organizations dealing with child abuse and neglect. Most of these booklets contain information specific to a state, such as reporting laws or child protection procedures, as well as more general information that should be useful to professionals across states. Brochures and brief pamphlets are not listed.

ARKANSAS

Child abuse and neglect: Annual statistical report. Arkansas Division of Children and Family Services, PO Box 1437, Little Rock, AR 72203.

> Statistics for each type of maltreatment reported and substantiated, broken down by state regions, as well as other case characteristics. (35 pp.)

Child abuse and neglect: The Arkansas law and child protective services. (See address above.)

> A brief explanation of state laws and social services.

Secrets you shouldn't keep: The teen survival booklet. (See address above.)

> Targets adolescents and discusses many issues including drugs, date rape, as well as maltreatment; lists mandated reporters and their responsibility to report. (48 pp.)

CALIFORNIA

Child abuse prevention handbook. California Crime Prevention Center, Office of the Attorney General, PO Box 944255, Sacramento, CA 94244-2550.

> Provides state definitions of abuse and neglect and an extensive discussion of practical aspects of reporting, and professional roles and responsibilities. Includes several appendixes that detail aspects of the California child protection system. (98 pp.)

The California abuse and neglect reporting law: Issues and answers for health practitioners. California Department of Social Services, Office of Child Abuse Prevention, 744 P Street, M.S. 9-100, Sacramento, CA 95814.

> Raises specific concerns common among mandated reporters, including treatment issues and frequently asked questions. Detection and assessment issues are discussed as well as specific aspects of the reporting laws. Samples of forms used for reporting, policies for confidentiality, and community resources are included in appendixes. (28 pp.)

FLORIDA

Florida protective services system: Annual statistical report. Florida Protective Services System, 1317 Winewood Boulevard, Tallahassee, FL 32399-0700.

> Highlights statistical trends for all types of reported maltreatment broken down by districts and investigative findings. Reports are also broken down by specific indicators of abuse that are included in state definitions of abuse. (168 pp.)
> Monthly reports are also available.

HAWAII

A guide for mandated reporters. Child Protective Services, PO Box 339, Honolulu, HI 96809.

> Provides a brief description of state child protective services and mandatory reporting laws. A brief description of possible abuse indicators is also included. Phone numbers for reporting are provided. (14 pp.)
> Copy of state legislation regarding mandated reporting is also available.

ILLINOIS

Child abuse and neglect statistics: Annual report. Illinois Department of Children, Youth, and Families, 406 East Monroe, Springfield, IL 62701-1498.

> Tables, charts, and text detailing the rates of reporting and substantiation for various regions of the state, broken down by demographic characteristics. Includes definitions of abuse and neglect. (29 pp.)
> Also available, copy of *Abused and Neglected Child Reporting Act*.

IOWA

Recognizing and reporting child abuse and neglect. Iowa Central Child Abuse Registry, Hoover State Office Building, Fifth Floor, Des Moines, IA 50319.

> Presents descriptions of abusive families and practical information for identifying cases of child maltreatment. The state child protection system is also explained. Iowa reporting statutes are included as well as detailed explanations of the law. (34 pp.)

KANSAS

For mandated reporters: A guide about child abuse and neglect. Kansas Child Abuse Prevention Council, 715 West 10th Street, Topeka, KS 66612.

> Provides a detailed description of Kansas state definitions of all types of abuse as well as possible indicators for each type. Discussions of myths of sexual abuse and distinctions between abuse and accidents are also provided. The Kansas state reporting laws are also provided and discussed in detail. (18 pp.)

KENTUCKY

Child abuse, neglect, and dependency: A guide for people who work with children in Kentucky. Department of Social Services, Cabinet for Human Resources, 275 E. Main Street 6W, Frankfort, KY, 40621.

> Contains the state reporting statute, as well as all relevant definitions. Reporting and child protection procedures are also discussed in detail. Listing of county departments of social services is included. (20 pp.)

Also available, *Reporting child abuse and neglect: An educators guide.*

LOUISIANA

Understanding child protection in Louisiana. Louisiana Division of Children, Youth, and Family Services, PO Box 3318, Baton Rouge, LA 70821.

> Describes the purposes of child protection and the conditions that warrant child protection intervention. The discussion includes an explanation of the mandatory reporting laws as well as some guidelines for reporting and what might be expected after a report is filed. (10 pp.)

MARYLAND

Child maltreatment in Maryland: Annual report. Office of Child Welfare, Child Protective Services, 311 West Saratoga Street, Baltimore, MD 21201.

> Includes Maryland reporting statutes and their history, an explanation of child protection procedures, and annual rates of reported and substantiated abuse. (21 pp.)

MASSACHUSETTS

Packet of materials for reporting child maltreatment. Massachusetts Department of Social Services, Protective Services, 24 Farnsworth Street, Boston, MA 02210.

> Rather than a booklet, the Massachusetts Department of Social Services has collected a series of handouts that present an array of detailed and useful information. Included are various fact sheets, descriptions of abused children and abusive families, the state reporting law, statistical data on state patterns of abuse, and suggested readings.

Also available, statistical reports including *Substance abuse and family vio-*

lence, Child maltreatment statistics (annual report), and *Child maltreatment in Massachusetts demographic and reporting characteristics.*

MINNESOTA

What can I do to prevent harm to children. Minnesota Department of Human Services, Child Protective Services, 444 Lafayette Road, St. Paul, MN 55155-3830.

> Designed for professionals, this booklet describes Minnesota statutes in detail, including definitions and explanations of terms used in the reporting statutes. (33 pp.)

MISSOURI

Missouri laws relating to child abuse and neglect. Missouri Department of Social Services, Division of Family Services, PO Box 88, Broadway Building, Jefferson City, MO 65103.

> Presents all state statutes that apply to situations of child abuse and neglect, including mandated reporting. State laws and definitions are reprinted from statutes without further explanation. (32 pp.)

NEBRASKA

Status of the Nebraska Commission for the Protection of Children. Department of Social Services, PO Box 9506, Lincoln, NE 68509.

> Presents an update of state initiatives and committee reports related to child maltreatment and child protection. Lists members of various state task forces that could be useful as a directory of experts in areas such as screening, juvenile court, support services, etc. (50 pp.)

NEW JERSEY

Child abuse and neglect in New Jersey: Annual report. New Jersey Division of Youth and Family Services, 50 East State Street, CN717, Trenton, NJ 08625.

> Provides extensive and detailed statistics on reported and substantiated child abuse and neglect broken down by various demographic, geographic, and other characteristics. Includes state definitions of abuse and neglect. (28 pp.)

Also available, *Survival guide for parents* and *Protecting children and families in New Jersey.*

NEW MEXICO

Stop child abuse and neglect: Prevention and reporting kit. New Mexico Department of Health and Human Services, 2001 Vivigin Way, Santa Fe, NM 87504.

> Discusses characteristics of sexual, physical, and emotional abuse and neglect, including myths and facts related to each type of maltreatment.

The booklet defines relevant terms and presents physical and behavioral indicators for each. State laws regarding mandated reporting and procedures for reporting are included, as well as suggestions for preventing child maltreatment. Also included is a list of agencies for reporting suspected child maltreatment in New Mexico. (17 pp.)

NEW YORK

A guide to New York's child protection system. New York State Department of Social Services, 40 North Pearl Street, Albany, NY 12243-0001.

Provides a detailed description of the state child protection system and legal definitions of abuse and neglect. State reporting laws are also presented in detail. Appendixes include a directory of local child protection agencies and examples of state reporting forms. (61 pp.)

Mandated reporter manual. (See address above.)

Targeted to a range of professionals, reporting statutes and definitions of abuse are provided and explained. Details of immunity, confidentiality of reports, and penalties for failure to report are included. Information is provided concerning what to expect from a report and the role of the child protection system. Appendixes include lists of indicators of abuse, examples of state reporting forms, and a directory of local child protection agencies. (53 pp.)

Suspected child abuse: Identification and management in hospitals and clinics. (See address above.)

Primarily a resource for mandated reporters, particularly those working in hospitals and other clinical settings. State reporting laws and procedures are provided and discussed in detail. Appendixes include New York statutes related to child sexual abuse, checklists of indicators of abuse and neglect (directed at physicians), examples of state reporting forms, and a directory of local child protection agencies. (49 pp.)

OHIO

Child abuse and neglect. Ohio Department of Human Services, 65 East State Street, 5th Floor, Columbus, OH 43215.

A very readable and informative guide to detecting and reporting child maltreatment. Includes information for parents concerning prevention. Although not targeted at mandated reporters, the booklet contains information for professionals who have contact with children. Focuses on signs of child abuse and neglect, characteristics of abusive adults and abused children, and functions of the Ohio child protection system. (58 pp.)

OKLAHOMA

Child abuse and neglect statistics. Oklahoma Department of Human Services, 5905 Classen Boulevard, Oklahoma City, OK, 73118.

Provides a series of descriptive statistics for annual reports of child abuse and neglect, broken down by case characteristics, substantiation and counties. Statistics are depicted in figures and tables with explanations. Includes state definitions of abuse and neglect. (30 pp.)

Also available, *Child abuse and neglect fatalities in Oklahoma: A five-year study—1987–1991.*

PENNSYLVANIA

Child abuse report. Pennsylvania Department of Public Welfare, Office of Children, Youth and Families, PO Box 2675, Harrisburg, PA 17105-2675.

Details the rates of reported and substantiated maltreatment. Includes definitions of abuse, statistics broken down by demographic characteristics and geographic region, information concerning the child protection system, and local child protection agencies. Also includes a section on recommended amendments to child protection statutes. (24 pp.)

Also available, *The child protective services law.*

SOUTH CAROLINA

Assistance for educators in recognizing child abuse and neglect. South Carolina Department of Social Services, PO Box 1520, Columbia, SC 29202-1520.

Primarily focuses on definitions of abuse, detailed descriptions of child abuse and neglect, and case examples. Instructions for reporting are included. (16 pp.) Similar booklets are available for clergy, child care workers, and medical professionals.

TENNESSEE

He told me not to tell. Child Protective Services, 1000 2nd Avenue, North, Nashville, TN 37202.

Targeted to parents, a guide for talking with children about sexual abuse. The subtle signs that may indicate sexual abuse are discussed. Information is geared toward helping parents prevent, detect, report, and understand child sexual abuse. (25 pp.)

WASHINGTON

Child abuse: Guidelines for intervention by physicians & other health care providers. Department of Social and Health Services, Bureau of Children's Services, Box 1366, Olympia, WA 98504.

Discusses indicators of all types of child maltreatment, including behavioral and physical signs. Provides points for interviewing a child suspected of being abused and outlines procedures for reporting. (24 pp.)

Also available, *Educator's guide to child protective services.*

WISCONSIN

Wisconsin child abuse and neglect report. Department of Health and Social Services, Bureau of Children, Youth, and Families, 1 West Wilson Street, Madison, WI 53707.

> Defines abuse and neglect according to state laws and provides the state statutes. Includes detailed figures and charts of annual reporting and substantiation rates. Also provides addresses and phone numbers of local child protection agencies. (37 pp.)

PUBLICATIONS AVAILABLE FROM NATIONAL CHILD ABUSE AND NEGLECT ORGANIZATIONS

Physical child abuse, by Paula Jaudes and Leslie Mitchel. Available from the National Committee for the Prevention of Child Abuse, 332 South Michigan Avenue, Suite 1600, Chicago, IL 60604.

> Defines abuse and discusses factors leading to abusive situations. Indicators of abuse are outlined and suggestions for intervention and prevention are provided. Several cases are described to illustrate various aspects of physical abuse. (28 pp.)

Maltreatment of adolescents, by James Garbarino and Anne C. Garbarino. Available from the National Committee for the Prevention of Child Abuse, 332 South Michigan Avenue, Suite 1600, Chicago, IL 60604.

> Provides a detailed description of adolescent victims and the effects of maltreatment within the context of adolescent development. Specific attention is paid to the psychological effects on adolescents. Several treatment strategies are offered and suggestions for social changes are offered. (27 pp.)

A look at child sexual abuse, by Jon R. Conte. Available from the National Committee for the Prevention of Child Abuse, 332 South Michigan Avenue, Suite 1600, Chicago, IL 60604.

> Defines child sexual abuse and describes the characteristics of victims and perpetrators. Discusses the frequency and scope of child maltreatment and includes detailed discussions of treatment and prevention strategies. (45 pp.)

Emotional maltreatment of children, by James Garbarino and Anne C. Garbarino. Available from the National Committee for the Prevention of Child Abuse, 332 South Michigan Avenue, Suite 1600, Chicago, IL 60604.

> Discusses many complex issues related to defining emotional maltreatment, including detailed descriptions of cases involving emotionally abused children and abusive parents. (30 pp.)

Child abuse and neglect: A shared community concern. U.S. Department of

Health and Human Services, National Center on Child Abuse and Neglect, Clearinghouse on Child Abuse and Neglect, PO Box 1182, Washington, DC 20013.

> Presents a discussion of child maltreatment as a social problem and provides definitions of abuse and neglect. Discusses recognizing and reporting abuse, presents and discusses cases of reported abuse, lists state child protection agencies and national organizations concerning child abuse. (31 pp.)

Study findings: Study of the national incidence and prevalence of child abuse and neglect: 1988. U.S. Department of Health and Human Services, National Center on Child Abuse and Neglect, Clearinghouse on Child Abuse and Neglect, PO Box 1182, Washington, DC 20013

> Presents data for reported and nonreported rates of different types of child maltreatment. Provides national statistics and a detailed discussion of the methodology used to collect the data. (144 pp.)

Current trends in child abuse reporting and fatalities: The results of the 1991 annual fifty state survey. Available from the National Committee for the Prevention of Child Abuse, 332 South Michigan Avenue, Suite 1600, Chicago, IL, 60604.

> Provides reporting and fatality data as well as rates of all types of child maltreatment for each state. Trends and patterns of change in rates are also discussed. The report is updated annually. (24 pp.)

Child abuse and neglect: Critical first steps in response to a national emergency. U.S. Advisory Board on Child Abuse and Neglect, Switzer Building, Room 2070C, 200 Independence Avenue, SW, Washington, DC 20201.

> Official report of the U.S. Advisory Board on Child Abuse and Neglect. Outlines the state of the U.S. child protection system and details specific policy recommendations for system reform. The Advisory Board was interdisciplinary and its findings are relevant for all professionals involved with children and families. (168 pp.)

OTHER SOURCES

Report to the APA Board of Directors, from the Ad Hoc Committee on Child Abuse Policy. American Psychological Association, 750 First Street, NE, Washington, DC 20002.

> Discusses numerous problems faced by mandated reporters, particularly by psychologists. Includes a discussion of potential resolutions offered by child abuse experts and a transcript of an open forum held at the 1989 APA Annual Convention in New Orleans.

Impact of child maltreatment reporting laws [special issue]. (1992). The Child, Youth, and Family Services Quarterly: Newsletter of Division 37 of the American Psychological Association, 15(1). Available from Seth C. Kalichman, Community Health Behavior Program, Medical College of Wisconsin, 8701 Watertown Plank Road, Milwaukee, WI 53226.

Covers a wide range of issues involved in mandated reporting of suspected child abuse. Includes brief articles by Murray Levine, David Finkelhor, Douglas Besharov, Patricia Petretic-Jackson and Raymond Koziol, and Cheryl Brosig.

Assertiveness for neglecting mothers: An innovative treatment approach. Texas Department of Human Services, John H. Williams Human Services Center, PO Box 149030, 701 West 51st, Austin, TX 78751.

A training manual for group treatment of mothers who are at risk of neglecting children. Outlines the issues to be addressed in the program and provides a framework for a specific eight session intervention program. The description is highly detailed and prepared for use, including client assignments and session handouts.

APPENDIX D

Directory of Information Resources Regarding Child Maltreatment and Child Protection

Action for Child Protection, 4724 Park Road, Unit C, Charlotte, NC 28209 (704)529-1080.

Adam Walsh Child Resource Center, 7812 Westminster Boulevard, Westminster, CA 92683-4034 (714)898-4802; 319 Clematis Street, Suite 409, West Palm Beach, FL 33401-1579 (407)820-9000; 249 Highland Ave, Rochester, NY 14620-3036 (716)461-1000; 1400 Pickens Street, Suite 102, Columbia, SC 29201-3465 (803)254-2326.

American Bar Association, National Legal Resource Center on Children and the Law, 1800 M Street, NW, Suite 200, Washington, DC 20036 (202)331-2250.

American Humane Association, American Association for Protecting Children, 9725 East Hampton Avenue, Denver, CO 80231 (800)227-5242.

American Professional Society on Abuse and Children (APSAC), 332 South Michigan Avenue, Suite 1600, Chicago, IL 60604 (312)554-0166.

American Public Welfare Association, 810 First Street, NE, Suite 500, Washington, DC 20002 (202)682-0100.

Baldy Center for Law & Social Policy, Division of Children and Law, 511 O'Brian Hall, University at Buffalo, Buffalo, NY 14260 (716)645-2102.

C. Henry Kempe National Center for Prevention and Treatment of Child Abuse and Neglect, 1205 Oneida Street, Denver, CO 80220 (303)321-3963.

Childhelp USA, 6463 Independence Avenue, Woodland Hills, CA 91367-2617 (213)347-7280; national hotline for counseling and information (800)4-A-CHILD.

Child Welfare League of America, 440 First Street, NW, Suite 310, Washington, DC 20001-2085 (202)638-2952.

Committee for Children, 172 20th Avenue, Seattle, WA 98122 (206)322-5050.

Family Violence and Sexual Assault Institute, 1310 Clinic Drive, Tyler, TX 75701 (903)595-6600.

Films for the Humanities and Sciences, PO Box 2053, Princeton, NJ 08543-2053 (800)257-5126. (Several educational videotapes concerning child physical and sexual abuse are available for rental or purchase.)

Military Family Resource Center, Ballston Center Tower Three, Ninth Floor, 4015 Wilson Boulevard, Suite 903, Arlington, VA 22203 (703)696-4555.

National Center for Missing and Exploited Children, 2101 Wilson Blvd., Suite 550, Arlington, VA 22201-3052 (703)235-3900, (800)843-5678.

National Center for Prosecution of Child Abuse, 1033 N. Fairfax Street, Suite 200, Alexandria, VA 22314 (703)739-0321.

National Child Abuse Coalition, 733 15th Street, NW, Suite 938, Washington, DC 20005 (202)347-3666.

National Committee for the Prevention of Child Abuse, 332 South Michigan Avenue, Suite 1600, Chicago, IL 60604-4357 (312)663-3520.

National Crime Prevention Council, 733 15th Street, NW, Room 540, Washington, DC 20005 (202)393-7141.

National Network of Runaway and Youth Services, 1400 I Street, NW, Washington, DC 20005 (202)682-4114.

National Resource Center on Child Sexual Abuse, National Children's Advocacy Center, 106 Lincoln Street, Huntsville, AL 35801 (205)533-KIDS, (800)KIDS-006.

Parents Anonymous, National Office, 520 S. LaFayette Park Place, Suite 316, Los Angeles, CA 90057 (213)388-6685, (800)421-0353.

Parents United International, 232 E. Gish Road, First Floor, San Jose, CA 95112 (408)453-7611 ext. 124.

U.S. National Center on Child Abuse and Neglect, PO Box 1182, Washington, DC 20013 (703)385-7565, (800)394-3366.

Washington Risk Assessment Project, Department of Social and Health Services, Children's Services Research Project, 1602 NE 150th, N/17-2, Seattle, WA 98195 (206)448-4929.

INDEX

ABOUT THE AUTHOR

Seth C. Kalichman is an assistant professor in the Department of Psychiatry and Mental Health Sciences at the Medical College of Wisconsin. Dr. Kalichman has published several empirical studies, review articles, and book chapters concerning professional decisions to report cases of suspected child abuse. With the assistance of his colleagues and students, Dr. Kalichman introduced the use of experimentally controlled case vignettes to investigate factors influencing professionals' decisions to report suspected abuse. His research on child abuse reporting has been published in *Professional Psychology: Research and Practice*, *Child Abuse and Neglect*, *American Journal of Orthopsychiatry*, *Law and Human Behavior*, and *Law and Policy*. He has served on the American Psychological Association's Working Group on Legal Issues Related to Child Abuse and Neglect and has been an expert court witness in cases of professionals held liable for failure to report suspected child abuse.

Dr. Kalichman received his AA from Broward Community College, his BA in psychology from the University of South Florida in 1983, and his PhD in Clinical–Community Psychology from the University of South Carolina in 1990. After completing his clinical internship at the University of Mississippi Medical Center, Dr. Kalichman spent two years as an assistant professor of psychology at Loyola University of Chicago. Dr. Kalichman's research and clinical interests span several areas, including psychological interventions and public policy related to child abuse, psychological characteristics of sexually violent adults, and psychosocial interventions for AIDS prevention and treatment. His work in these diverse arenas stems from his commitment to applying psychological principles in order to solve serious social problems.